INTRODUCTION TO
Family Processes

FOURTH EDITION

INTRODUCTION TO
Family Processes

FOURTH EDITION

Randal D. Day
Brigham Young University

LAWRENCE ERLBAUM ASSOCIATES, PUBLISHERS
2003   Mahwah, New Jersey   London

Lawrence Erlbaum Associates, Inc., Publishers
10 Industrial Avenue
Mahwah, NJ 07430

Cover artwork and internal illustrations by Warren Gebert
Cover design by Kathryn Houghtaling Lacey

Library of Congress Cataloging-in-Publication Data

Day, Randal D., 1948-
    Introduction to family processes / Randal D. Day.--4th Ed.
        p. cm.
    Rev. ed. of: Family science / Wesley R. Burr, Randal D. Day, Kathleen S. Bahr, c1993.
    Includes bibliographical references and index.
    ISBN 0-8058-4038-9 (pbk. : alk. paper)
        1. Family. 2. Family--Research. I. Burr, Wesley R., 1936- Family science. II. Title.

    HQ518 .D39 2003
    306.85--dc21

                                                            2002026387

Books published by Lawrence Erlbaum Associates are printed on
acid-free paper, and their bindings are chosen for strength and durability.

Printed intheUnited States of America
10 9 8 7 6 5 4 3 2

This book is dedicated to my family:

My parents and siblings
who taught me about love and work.

My dear wife who teaches me the art of compassion.

My children and grandchildren
who bring light and joy into my life.

—RDD

CONTENTS IN BRIEF

CONTENTS

Contents

Contents

Contents

Contents

Contents

Contents

Contents

Contents

Contents

Contents

Contents

Contents

PREFACE

When we study something as complicated as families, *the perspective with which we begin influences what we think, what we see, and what we do*. For example, if we begin with a psychological perspective we focus on the role of psychic processes. If we begin with a historical, sociological, or economic perspective, we use different terms, ask different questions, emphasize different things, and think in different ways. Therefore, it is important to know which perspective is used in a book about families.

The perspective used in this book focuses on inner family life. Some researchers and teachers refer to this as a family dynamics approach or a family processes approach. When we study familial processes rather than psychological, sociological, historical, or economic processes, we try to understand the interior of the family and think first and primarily about what families are like and what is happening when they are enabling and disabling, healthy and unhealthy, successful and unsuccessful.

An important aspect of this approach is that we need to understand the nature of family life. This text was written with the assumption that families exist. That is not meant to be a flippant comment. It has long been suggested that we study the family in its own right. That is, families can exist as entities and do have the potential to be a force independent of the actors within the family. That does not mean it is a thing in the same way a shirt is a thing. However, families can exist in the same way that a team exists. Its members may choose to subscribe to the group and when they participate in family life a family is born.

Additionally, it assumes that families are goal seeking. Generally, families do the best they can to achieve certain goals they have chosen. In other words, they maximize their efforts and their resources to succeed. This approach would, therefore, also assume that families rarely set out to do poorly. Family members (and therefore families generally) make mistakes. However, most families try to do the best they can at using available resources as a strategy to succeed at whatever they think of as important.

To understand this unique world of the family we examine a different set of concepts, such as generational alliances, differentiation of self, emotional triangles, developmental tasks, analog messages, boundaries, emotional distance, family paradigms, and experiential aspects of mothering.

Preface

It is also important to understand that the study of family processes is a relatively new field in academia. It began in the middle decades of the 20th century when four groups of scholars began to concentrate on family processes. The four groups were family therapists, scholars in child development and family relations departments, a group of family oriented feminists, and a group of home economists. Each of these groups began to develop ideas that had not previously been developed in older disciplines such as sociology or history. Each group made important contributions to how we think about families. But when they began to develop ideas about family life, they were fairly independent and autonomous and they had little contact with each other. In the last few years, however, scholars have been attempting to integrate the main ideas in these different schools of thought and they have called the integrated perspective family science or family studies. This book is an attempt to integrate these ideas, and it is one of the few undergraduate texts that uses the family science perspective and integrates ideas that have been developed in each of those four areas of scholarship.

The field of family science is so new that many of the ideas in it are tentative and evolving. This means we should view the ideas in this book as emerging knowledge that is still being refined and tested. I believe the ideas in this book add important ideas to what has already been discovered in older fields, and I hope they will be useful to educators, counselors, policy makers, and family members. It was an exciting, educational, and exhilarating experience to gather and integrate the ideas, and it is hoped readers will share that enthusiasm.

A strong and enduring theme of this book is that (to paraphrase a line made famous by Dickens in his epic novel *Tale of Two Cities*) **the family realm is the best of human life and it is the worst of human life.** The best parts of family life are experienced as we find deep joy and greatest pleasure from our interaction with those whom we love and who love us the most. Family life is also a crucible that refines and tests and helps us grow and mature in ways that are noble and great and wonderful. If we are wise in the way we manage this precious part of our lives, family life can provide satisfactions, fulfillments, love, security, a sense of belonging, and other beauties and riches that are difficult to attain outside the family realm.

The undesirable parts of the family realm reflect the worst side of human relationships. More murder s are committed in families than any place else. Physical abuse is all too common. The privacy that allows intimacy and the deepest of love also allows sexual and emotional abuse. Family life is the source of some of the deepest frustrations, intense misery, immeasurable exploitation, and serious abuse that humans ever experience.

As I (re)wrote this text, it was my hope that ideas assembled here would assist readers in finding ways to increase the positive aspects of family life, avoid the undesirable parts that can be avoided, and more effectively manage the challenges and obstacles that cannot be avoided.

Some of the positive things that can come from healthy family life are intimacy that is not stifling, bonds without bondage, meaning and purpose, growth and progress, maturation and beauty, and enough security and stability that we have a sense of being in a wholesome home. On the negative side, our goals are to avoid violence, exploitation, dominance, abuses, tyranny, negligence, and other forms of excess that bring pain, hurt, disappointment, and inhumanity.

This is, in fact, the fourth rewrite of a book originally entitled *Family Science*. This project has been under construction for about 15 years and continues to be a work in progress. The thoughts and ideas contained here have changed many times over those years and I owe a deep debt of gratitude to those who have taken part. In particular, Wes Burr and Kathleen Bahr were original co-authors. They do not appear as authors in this version of the text, choosing, instead, to retire (in Wes' case) or to move on to other professional obligations. However, the mark of both of these contributors remains an essential feature of this work.

The original goal and dream for this book was that it would help families and those who help families better attain these positive parts of the family realm and avoid the undesirable parts. Thus, this book is written to and for those who live (or will live) in families and also for those who want to work professionally or as a volunteer to help families. Each of us can help in many ways. We can help our own families and our friends, and we can help in our professions and avocations.

Many contributions of our families, colleagues, students, and friends have played a key role in the intellectual journey that this book represents. There are two groups of colleagues who have given helpful direction and support. First are those upon whose shoulders we stand. This includes the many scholars whose work we use in this book and colleagues such as Reuben Hill, Beatrice Paolucci, Gerhard Neubeck, and Murray Straus, who provided invaluable mentorship and guidance.

The second group consists of those who have directly impacted this volume with ideas, support, encouragement, reactions, and suggestions. They include Howard Bahr, Ivan Beutler, Kathleen Bahr, Wesley Burr, David Imig, Barbara Settles, Bron Ingoldsby, Diane Fish, Alan Acock, Kathleen Gilbert, Deborah Gentry, Dave Dollahite, Carlfred Broderick, Tom Draper, Don Herrin, Tom Holman, James White, Rick Miller, and David Klein.

—*R. Day*

PART 1

Introduction to Family Processes

CHAPTER ONE

Adapting to Family Life
in Our Times

CHAPTER ONE

Main Points:

1. The study of family life is a relatively new but promising academic discipline.

2. When we study family life, personal experience is important but can color our objectivity. In addition, the study of family life is more complicated that we usually think.

3. By thinking about a variety of families and their experiences, we can begin to understand how complicated family life is.

4. It is impossible to not bring our personal biases into the study of most social sciences, especially the study of family life.

5. There are several reasons why family scientists believe the study of family life is important.

6. Family processes are the strategies that families use to reach family goals.

7. The definitions we use in studying family life focus our attention on what we study and how we study families.

8. We can understand families only when we discover their core ideologies and beliefs.

9. It is important to understand that the nature and structure of family life seem to be changing.

Adapting to Family Life in Our Times

INTRODUCTION

Family life is exciting and interesting. Many of us want to know how to make our own families stronger and how to assist other families as they struggle with life's difficulties. Often the lives of families are at the center of national news, political campaigns, movies, and heated congressional debates. We care about how families raise their children, spend money, decide where to live, and how they contribute to the economy. While much of the discussion about family life focuses on who people choose to marry, how many children they decide to have, and whether or not they divorce or stay married (or get remarried), the purpose of this text is to examine the interior of family life. A basic premise of this text is that we can do a better job of understanding families when we know more about the inner life of families.

Studying family life is unique. The examination of family life is a legitimate field of study. Many universities across the nation have programs dedicated to helping students better understand the complexities of family life. The information about family life in this text can assist a student as she or he chooses to form and build a family of procreation. A family of procreation includes us as adults, our spouse/partner, and children (by birth or adoption). Additionally, information about family life can help us begin to better understand the families in which we were raised. The underlying idea is that when we better understand some aspects of family interaction, we have the potential to increase the quality of those relationships.

Also, this information can serve as a foundation for learning how to work with families. Students who major in family science, social work, or sociology often find employment in community-based agencies that specialize in assisting families in difficulty. Some students attend graduate school. A few will choose a career teaching about family life in a university setting and others will seek out family counseling programs that train individuals to aid families who need more personalized assistance. Still others will find a variety of opportunities to become advocates for family related issues in their own communities. For example, most communities in the United States have a local branch of Habitat for Humanity. This excellent organization helps families build suitable homes. One of the important jobs in Habitat for Humanity is a committee that prepares families to do a better job of money and general family management.

Compared to more established academic disciplines such as math or biology, family science is relatively new. Most university departments and programs that offer courses in family life have come into existence since the 1960s. Further, most were originally found in "home economics" programs in which students were initially trained to teach home economics in high school settings. In the 1960s, the federal government increased funding to develop social programs designed to alleviate family problems such as poverty, family violence, and unwed pregnancy.

Since that time, many universities have developed programs that train students to work in community action-based agencies that attempt to respond to a wide range of family difficulties. Additionally, during the last 40 years, there has been an explosive growth of university- and government-sponsored research that focuses on family life. Typically, that body of research has centered on family life from a sociological point of view. For example, most of the original research about families examined such demographical questions as: How many families get divorced? What kinds of life events are correlated with divorce? How many remarry? How much violence is there in family life? How much money do families spend? Moreover, what happens to families when they experience income levels below the poverty line?

Only recently have researchers begun to ask questions about the intricacies of private family life. This type of research is much more difficult to complete; most families resist the type of scrutiny necessary to understand the events of daily life. Consequently, our understanding of family life is limited.

This text is an attempt to gather what we do know about what goes on "behind closed doors" in families. We will not discuss larger sociological issues such as divorce rates, remarriage rates, how many families are in poverty, or listing the names of agencies that work with families. Instead, the intent of this text is to introduce the reader to *family processes*. Family processes are the strategies and daily sequences of behavior used by family members to achieve goals. We will spend some time discussing who families are, but the bulk of this text is concerned with what families do. That is, how does their communication style help or hinder their efforts to achieve what they believe to be important? Similarly, how do they make decisions, allocate resources, design and execute rituals, and cope with stress and crises?

Studying family life is not the same as living family life. Unlike other academic pursuits (e.g., chemistry), nearly everyone experiences family life firsthand. While life experience can be helpful in understanding larger principles of family life, our personal perspectives can sometimes get in the way of objectivity.

For example, most of us know very little about the chemistry of life, even though we use chemicals and may have a superficial understanding of simple chemical

ACTIVITY 1.1 - FIND A CURRENT ARTICLE ABOUT FAMILY LIFE

1. Find a current article in the newspaper or magazine about the family. Paste the article in the space provided below.

2.   Summarize the message of this article.

3.   Are there any underlying assumptions you can discover the author(s) make in this article about families? For example, is the article pro-family, pro-alternative family, anti-family, worried about families, or educating families? Identify those assumptions.

interactions. With regard to the events of daily life, we live each day in an onslaught of daily events that constitute "history." Nevertheless, few of us take the time to study the trends, larger issues, and complexities of history.

Similarly, while most of us have been immersed in family life, we sometimes have the unrealistic idea that we know more about family life than we really do. A friend once said that teaching students about family was difficult because of this ready familiarity with the topic. He provided a useful metaphor in his explanation. He proposed that although a person might visit the bank regularly for years, depositing money, writing checks, balancing checkbooks, and monitoring savings, that did not qualify him or her to work in the bank. In other words, there is more to the study of the family than one would first imagine.

The study of family life must avoid generalizations and clichés.   To begin our voyage into inner family life, I would like you to read the following vignettes from the everyday lives of families. Some of these excerpts are about extraordinary events and the rest are about everyday family life. Within each chapter, there is a place to record your thoughts. The purpose of these *Journal of Thoughts* entries is to encourage you to think past the clichés of family existence and begin thinking more analytically and specifically about what happens in families on a daily basis as they try to solve problems, make decisions, allocate resources, and make sense out of a complicated world.

The following story reflects a special kind of family devastation. In the spring of 1998, deadly tornadoes ripped through Texas. Below is a segment from one of many stories of families whose lives were altered by these deadly acts of nature.

People often say that living through a calamity changes you in a deep and permanent way. But how? What's it really like to be a woman whose home is blown away, or who, clutching a child, walks away from the wreckage of an airplane?

Everything she owned was gone. Kimberley Brown and her husband, A.C., stood in the yard of their Lancaster, Texas, house and watched the dark clouds rolling in. An eerie looking rainbow—it glowed aqua and green—formed in the east. "It instantly felt that something very bad was about to happen," Kimberly recalls. She ran into the house, where her three children were sleeping. First, she went to her 8-year-old daughter Alexis' room and jostled her awake. Next, she got 4-year-old Elliott out of bed. By this time, the house had begun to shake and a roar filled the air. In a heartbeat, the roof was lifted and rain poured in. By the time Kimberly reached her third child—6-year-old A. C. III—toys, blankets, and stuffed animals were whirling everywhere. (Everyone survived and the next segment tells what they saw when they emerged from their hiding place.)

. . . When Kimberly emerged from what had been the laundry room, she says that the outside walls were no more than just a scattering of bricks and mortar. Later she would learn that the tornado had killed three people and destroyed 300 homes. She

would also discover that almost every memento, picture, and possession her family owned had been blown away or ruined. Some of the losses were especially painful: a wedding ring handed down from her grandmother, her wedding album, and all of her children's baby pictures. (D'Antonia, M., 1998)

The next two examples not only illustrate a few of the social problems facing children in families today, but also are stories of courage and hope.

By its very nature, Van Hughes' life had always followed an orderly pattern. A Navy chief master-at-arms with 18 years' service, Hughes would put in a five-day week at the Naval Training Station in San Diego, then drive 300-plus miles home to

Adapting to Family Life in Our Times

Mesa, Arizona, to spend weekends with his wife, Shirley. And with their two grown sons married and out of the house, the couple had looked forward to a tranquil retirement. They would travel, certainly, and perhaps buy that log cabin in the woods they had always talked about.

That was four years ago. Now it's Tuesday afternoon, and their one-story stucco home . . . is a study of suburban chaos. With several dogs and cats underfoot, 5-year-old Donicio is playing . . . on the living room computer. Soon his brothers and sisters—nine of them—arrive home from school in waves, grabbing newly bought juice and snacks in the kitchen.

. . . Instead of leading the leisurely life of a pensioner, [Hughes is]working as a security guard. . . . After all, he and Shirley have a new family to feed—a huge one. . . . In a shocking case, authorities learned in April, 1995, that 10 siblings were living in squalor, sharing a two-bedroom apartment in Phoenix with their birth mother, an aunt, and five cousins. Their four biological fathers were long gone, and their mother, later treated for alcoholism, often left them for days at a time.

. . . "Why don't we do something about it?" said Hughes. First they took in Donicio, Juan, Jose, now 9, Stephanie, 8, and Veronica, 6. Two years ago, a caseworker suggested they formally adopt not only those five, but their brothers and sisters who were scattered in various foster homes. "My mind told me, 'I'm 50 years old. What would I want 10 kids for at this age?" Van recalls. "But my heart told me it was the right thing to do." (Jerome & Haederle, 1999)

The cardboard barrel has been sitting empty in Marsha Flowers' backyard for more than a month now, but the Jamaican teenager hangs onto it as though it were a sacred totem. And in a way, it is. Five years after her mother emigrated to the United States, leaving Marsha and two sisters to fend for themselves in a Kingston slum, the barrel is one of the few tangible signs of her mother's love—and of her own frustrated desires. The barrel arrived from New York before Christmas, filled with food, photographs, clothes, and the tantalizing prospect of escape. Marsha, now 15, with ebony skin and a brilliant smile, is so fixated on "going foreign" that she has disengaged from nearly every aspect of daily life—except for the twice-annual barrels and their cargo of dreams. "My mother keeps promising me that I will soon be joining her," Marsha says, as much to herself as to anybody who will listen.

Marsha is lonely, but far from alone. So many Caribbean children are being left behind by emigrating parents—tens of thousands in Jamaica alone—that they have acquired their own name: "barrel children." This phenomenon can be found in almost any country with heavy emigration, from Mexico to China. . . . Nearly 30 percent of all Jamaicans now live in the United States, and the newest arrivals are often women trying to provide for the children they have left behind. But as months turn into years, and as dreams of riches and reunions fade, reality is sinking in: this new wave of emigration has wreaked havoc on a generation of Jamaican children. "It is not that the Caribbean mothers are wicked and cruel," says Claudette Crawford-Brown, a sociologist at the University of the West Indies. "They are simply forced to make a choice between satisfying their children's material needs or their emotional needs." (Larmer, 1996)

The next two examples deal with family crises that are even more extreme. They are about family members who experienced the shooting of students at the Columbine High School in spring 1999. In both of these examples, one can imagine the troubled and devastating time these families had. Sometimes the crises that families face are overwhelming.

. . . Families that kept their dead children's rooms locked up since April 20 have finally begun to open the doors: Dee Fleming goes inside her daughter Kelly's room with Kelly's friends, listens to stories about her daughter, and invites the girls to take home special keepsakes. The Mausers had always slept with their Daniel's door closed, but since summer they've kept it open. Patricia Depooter takes comfort in going into her son's room, gazing at his clothes and shoes as he left them that April morning, and even taking an occasional whiff of her favorite perfume. (Anonymous, 1999)

The suicide by the woman, Carla June Hochhalter, occurred about six months after her 17-year-old daughter, Anne Marie, was critically wounded and partly paralyzed in the April 20 shootings by two student gunmen.

This morning, Ms. Hochhalter, 48, asked to see a handgun at the Alpha Pawn Shop in Englewood. As a clerk handled paperwork, Ms. Hochhalter loaded the gun with bullets she had brought with her. She fired one bullet into a wall and a second one into her head, an Englewood police spokeswoman said. (Anonymous, 1999)

To Katherine Arnoldi, who had a daughter when she was just 17, the life of every single teenage mother is a potential Cinderella story: A young girl, rendered nearly invisible by her reduced status, works patiently and hard. Finally, her virtues are recognized and rewarded. Yet her salvation is not (in Arnoldi's version) some persnickety prince. This Cinderella goes to college.

"College changed my life," says Arnoldi, who, at 46, is a teacher of English literature at City University in New York, an artist and writer, and the author of the recently published autobiographical comic book "The Amazing True Story of a Teenage Single Mom." "When I had a kid," says Arnoldi, "it was like a river developed between me and everybody else. It was immediate—like a big whoosh—and suddenly everyone was over there where all the opportunities are. I was on an island, alone, and had to

figure out how to cross that gulf with all of them shouting, "Now look what you've done. Now you're going to want money from us. Don't even think of coming over here." (Smith, 1999)

Each of the stories above tells us about how people react to the decisions and crises of family life. Do you know how you react? What resources do you have to call upon? Among your resources might be other family members, your religion, your inner strength, how you make decisions, and your skill of solving difficult problems quickly. A primary theme of this text is that there is hope. Even if your family has or will experience difficult times or the usual stresses of daily living, we can make our family experience one that helps us cope and even survive.

In addition, some readers of this text will find themselves working with families that experience tough decisions and difficult life events. How will you react to their problems and how will you be able to assist them as they struggle for stability and try to meet their goals? We hope that the principles and ideas found here can be of assistance.

Biases in the study of family life. On a plane to Washington, DC recently, a young married couple was having a conversation. As they talked, it appeared that they were struggling with many relationship issues. After some time, the young man turned and asked a passenger if he was married. The man replied that he had been married for thirty years to the same person. The young man was incredulous. The older man showed him some pictures of his family, which seemed to convince the young man. His next question was haunting: "In today's world," he puzzled, "everyone gets divorced, very few of my friends want to get married, and they are not too thrilled about the idea of having kids. How is it that you are still married? How did you do

that?" The passenger said something about commitment and working hard, and that his relationship with his wife had not always been smooth. He wasn't sure his answer had helped much.

An important aspect of the above story is that each of us who writes about family science issues brings to his or her writing a personal history. Therefore, the first type of bias that we bring to the writing of this text comes from the experiences we have had being married and raising children. These events have greatly influenced our ideas about marriage, relationships, and family life. In addition, the places where we grew up, the experiences in our *families of origin*, and even our personal religious beliefs influence how we approach the writing of this text, just as your experiences influence how you read, interpret, and use the information found here.

Second, each author (at least in the social sciences) brings to the creation of a text an education-based bias; authors write from the biases of their training. Theories, research ideas, and the type of training they bring to the project influence them. While each of us tries to be as objective as possible, our experience, beliefs, and training often shine through.

To be specific, you should know from the onset that we believe family life is an essential, enduring, and crucial aspect of the human experience. You could say that we are biased in that regard. We assume that readers of this book want to know how to make family life better, not how to do away with family life.

Most people realize that family life is a two-edged sword; it can be a source of love, compassion, and fulfillment, but also can be a tumult of destruction, oppression, and violence. Either condition is possible; however, we believe it is the responsibility of each family member to learn how to make family life better for all involved. Therefore, another goal of this text is to convince you that by understanding the processes that occur in daily family life, you can change the quality of family life. In other words, one of our primary assumptions is that family members can make a difference in the quality of their family life.

The next sections present several ideas that should assist you as you begin the study of family life. First is a discussion of how family life is changing. Several basic changes are occurring in family life that are important to rethinking what families and their functions are. We will ask you to evaluate whether family life is disintegrating or merely changing with the times. Again, this is an area where one's strong beliefs shine through. Some family scholars view family life as the optimal forum for raising children and seeking personal happiness. Others view family life as mostly destructive and antiquated; they campaign for alternative life styles to emerge and replace family life.

Next, you are to consider what constitutes a family. This is a complicated discussion in which many family scholars reveal their personal biases about family life.

Finally, we will explore *family processes*. Even though our idea of what constitutes a family may be changing, and even though family life may or may not be the same as it was in times past, a key idea of this book is that families must meet the chal-

JOURNAL OF THOUGHTS 1.1: THE STORIES OF REAL FAMILIES

In the space provided below, write down any reactions you have after reading the stories of the families in your text. You may also want to comment on such topics as:

How important is everyday family life to the well-being of family members?

Why is it (or not) so important?

What do you think are the most important aspects?

What are the most important attributes of family life that help families succeed and survive?

SPOTLIGHT ON RESEARCH 1.1: THE FAMILY AND CHILD WELL-BEING
NETWORK

In 1993, the National Institute of Child Health and Development (NICHD)
created a network of top scholars to examine issues surrounding the well-being
of children. Under the auspices of the network, NICHD brought together an
all-star cast of researchers from a variety of disciplines and interests. The primary disciplines represented in this team of scholars were demography, economics, family science, medicine, child development, sociology, psychology, and
public policy. The network spent fours years investigating a number of key
issues including poverty, father involvement, changes in the welfare system, family processes, discipline practices used by parents, the effects of disability in children, and general family well-being. A key mission of the network was to examine trends in family and child well-being that influence and mold the ways that
children grow and interact with communities around them. One of the key
products of the network was a book that examined key ideas that need to be
studied about children and families. One of network members, Dr. Arland
Thornton, helped organize a "think-tank" seminar held in 1998 in Washington,
DC. Invited scholars were commissioned to write papers about a variety of topics representing a "what-we-know-and-what-we-don't-know" format. The
resulting book is called *The Well-Being of Children and Families* by Arland
Thornton (Ed.), 2001, University of Michigan Press: Ann Arbor, MI.
   At the end of the book, Thornton suggests that there are 18 recommendations
family scientists should pay attention to when thinking about the complexities
of family life. Below are six of those recommendations that relate to our text:

1. When we think of family life we should think in broad multi-dimensional
    terms. In other words, family life is not simply the study of a few people
    who live in a household. The economy, general health issues, public policy,
    and a host of other important topics influence family members.
2. Researchers and those who write about family life need to pay greater
    attention to the meaning of marriage and its interrelationships with the lives
    of individuals and families. In other words, who we live with may not be as
    important as the meaning we place on family life.
3. The family science community needs to pay greater attention to the role of
    father in families. Fathering has been, until recently, a forgotten topic in the
    study of family life.
4. Family scientists need to conduct more research about the inner life of fam-
    ilies. We call this kind of research family process based research.

5. We need to spend much more time studying the effects of sibling relationships as it relates to how children do later on in life.
6. We need to study the communities in which families live. The local neighborhoods have a great impact on family life.

lenges before them. They use strategies to solve problems, make decisions, and allocate resources. The study of family processes is the study of those strategies families use to maximize the goals the family sets out to achieve.

OUR VIEW OF DAILY FAMILY LIFE IS CHANGING

A key to understanding our attitudes about family life is to realize that many Americans have uncertain, vague, and even troubled ideas about the value of family life. On the one hand, most of us would agree that family life could be essential, fulfilling, and even wonderful. At the same time there is so much violence and distress in today's families that some suggest we should rethink the value of family life.

The debate about what constitutes a family illustrates how our thinking about family life has changed in recent times. In a survey taken in 1996, 66% of those surveyed indicated that they thought sexual relations between two adults of the same sex were "wrong" or "almost always wrong." (Davis & Smith, 1996). In addition, when young people were asked about their future lives, an overwhelming number of them clearly indicated that they believed marriage to be essential and important, and they intended on getting married and having children.

Another side to changing ideas about family life is revealed in a national study that was completed during two periods, 1957 and again in 1976. Respondents were asked about a hypothetical situation in which a person chooses never to marry. In mid-century, more than half of the respondents asserted that they would think of the person as selfish, immoral, deficient, and even "sick." By 1976, however, attitudes were changing and most respondents were neutral—only one third thought the individuals who chose not to marry were deficient in some way. Although this study has not been repeated in recent years, one would guess that remaining single would not be seen negatively, but would be described as an individual and acceptable choice.

Another side of modern family life was explored recently in a program about life aboard a U.S. Navy aircraft carrier. During one segment, the interviewer asked a young carrier pilot how he valued family life. He responded that it was the most important aspect of his life. He was then asked how much time he spent with his wife and child. It was clear that his job prevented him from spending more than a few weeks a year at home with them. The focus then shifted to an interview with his wife. She seemed somewhat bitter about Navy life and was adamant that her husband was gone more than 85% of the time and that she alone was raising their child.

The separation of marriage, sex, and childbearing/childrearing. In times past, many living in North American cultures (in fact in many cultures around the world) believed that sex with a person of the opposite sex, marriage, childbearing, and childrearing were a package deal. That is, an ethical, moral, religious ideal prevalent in Western society for hundreds of years has been that one had sex only with one's husband or wife and that having and rearing children was an extension of the marriage relationship.

Over the last 50 years, there has been a cultural shift. In the early years of this century, U.S. culture was more family centered. Now it is usually described as more individualistic and person centered. Prior to the 1900s families were much more patriarchal and collective in nature. Because family members relied on each other for survival, there was a sense of collectivity that pushed people to remain associated with the land, farm, and other family members. That association also demanded obedience, followers, and someone to be in autocratic control. The idea of families operating on any kind of democratic ideal was impractical and ineffective. Instead, the father (or father figure) was in charge and he was to be obeyed.

By the 1940s, things began to change dramatically. Before 1940, all but a small percentage of children were born into some form of family in which a marital union had occurred. During the last 50 years, our culture has engaged in a radical experiment where the focus is on the well-being of the individual instead of the family group. We are experimenting with the idea that we should empower and enhance the well-being of the individual directly rather than through the support of family-centered efforts. One result of this shift to individualism as a cultural mandate is that sex, close relationships, and childrearing are moving from family-centered activities to become individually centered activities. It is proposed by exponents of this approach that sex not be tied to marriage or even to close relationships, that sex not be tied to childbearing (i.e., that birth control methods prevent sex from leading to pregnancy), and that the birth of a child not necessarily be tied to a single monogamous relationship. More than one out of four children in the United States are born to parents who are not married. Among children born to African American mothers 70% are non-marital births (Waite & Gallagher, 2000). It is expected that in 2001, nearly 500,000 unmarried women will bear a child. Some predict that the cost to the taxpayers for these children is millions of dollars per year (Harris, 1997).

Many factors contribute to this cultural change in our thinking about marriage, parenting, and family life. Among the most visible reasons are changes in national economics, religious orientation, and changed perceptions of women's role in society. Those ideas can be examined when we consider fundamental changes in family life in a variety of cultural and work-defined arrangements.

For example, in an agricultural society, women and children are valuable resources to the family. The more children one has to share the work, the more productive the operation of the farm, orchard, estate, or ranch. In times past, it was much more important for individuals to bond and band together for protection, common task completion, and general self-preservation.

In sharp contrast, U.S. society after World War II has seen the rise of individual enterprise by men and women. There are few jobs left in any commercial sector that women cannot perform as well as men; physical strength is no longer a prerequisite of job performance in most cases. Additionally, there has been a significant change in attitudes about whether or not a woman should do the same types of jobs histori-cally performed only by men. For example, it has become common practice for women to serve in the military—once a bastion of the male-dominated workplace.

Many believe that a caretaker can rear children just as well as the child's par-ents. At no time in recorded history until now have parents been as willing to relin-quish the rearing of children to non-family members. This change in child-rearing practice could only have been made possible as we moved away from rural agricultural living. Today, only about 2 % of the U.S. population lives in a residential situation in which agricultural production is the primary source of income. This move away from agricultural-based income has had a significant influence on our attitude toward child bearing and rearing. In a fast-moving, individually based, entrepreneurial society, many consider children as a liability. In many Western countries, governments have resorted to offering large cash and goods incentives to parents who have children. In some countries and certain segments of U.S. culture, the fertility rates have fallen "below replacement." That is, there are not enough children being born to replace the adults when they die.

In summary, the culture of family is changing. About 40% of all children experience the dissolution of their parents' marriages. Most of those who come from families with divorced parents will have to adjust to a stepparent joining their families. Additionally, as many as 10–15 % of those who live in remarried families will witness a second divorce. Of the murders that occurred in 1992 in which the offender was known, nearly 10% of the deaths involved the murder of a spouse (U.S. Bureau of Justice Statistics, 1994).

There were about 5 million children born to unwed mothers in the United States between 1990 and 2000. That is a city twice the size of Seattle, Washington, of children born to mothers who are usually undereducated and live well below the poverty level. The birth father usually is not a part of the child's life, and the children's educational prospects are limited. The results of these types of cultural attitudes and behaviors toward children, families, and community life create concern for the well-being of the children of the future.

Therefore, studying daily family life has a greater purpose than to teach indi-viduals how to enjoy each other's company and be more fulfilled in close personal relationships. A major assumption in this book is that understanding daily life is a cru-cial issue that affects every sector of our society, including the well-being of our com-munities, in general.

WHAT IS FAMILY?

Defining *family* is not an easy task. In the late 1970s, then-President Jimmy Carter organized what came to be known as the White House Conference of Families. Unfortunately, little of the original agenda was discussed. One of the first questions that conference attendees considered was what constitutes a family. This important question needed to be answered. The various participants had specific agenda items to bring to the discussion that depended upon defining families in a certain way. An acrimonious battle ensued: The more conservative participants did not want the conference to use the language *families* but, instead, wanted the designation *family* to prevail. Of course, the agenda of the more conservative participants was that by using the term *family* it would help the conference focus on the widely held view (by their estimation a more widely held view of the general population) that family issues were about men and women marrying and having children. They further suggested that the focus of family life for the conference be limited to situations in which the mother was taking care of children at home.

The more liberal view was that restricting the conference to a discussion about one type of family configuration (i.e., man-woman-child, with the mother staying at home with her children) would necessarily exclude a discussion of family life that should encompass many individuals, many of whom were involved in family life but did not fit that narrow definition. Unfortunately for the conference, the battle over this one issue ended the conference without discussion of virtually anything else of significance to family life.

The position of many fundamentalist Christian churches is much like that of the Roman Catholic Church, in which marriage is seen as one of the essential sacraments of religious worship. Most take a conservative stand on what marriage should be like and many discourage or even prohibit divorce. Certainly most are opposed to same-sex marriage.

The discouragement of divorce became the province of some state legislatures in the late 1990s, with the emergence of the "covenant marriage" concept. Louisiana enacted an optional "covenant" form of marriage license in June 1997. According to this law, those who wish to enter into a covenant marriage must agree to premarital counseling. Additionally, the petitioners must sign an agreement that if they wish to divorce in the future, they must have specific grounds. This last item is in response to the *no-fault divorce* laws passed by every state in the United States during the 1970s and 1980s. In a no-fault divorce situation, partners can divorce without having to prove that the other spouse was at fault (e.g., committed adultery, became a convicted felon, etc.). Arizona and Arkansas enacted similar statutes.

However, the legal battles about what marriage is and who can participate rage on. In 1996, after a lengthy court battle, proponents of homosexual rights won a resounding victory in Colorado as the U.S. Supreme Court issued their ruling in the *Romer v. Evans* case. In *Romer*, the U.S. Supreme Court threw out Colorado's recently passed constitutional amendment that barred legislation protecting homosexuals from discrimination. This ruling was preceded in 1996 by a ruling in the Hawaiian lower court system in which the presiding judge ruled that the State of Hawaii had failed to prove that prohibiting same-sex marriage "furthered a compelling state interest." That is, the judge was not convinced that the state had produced evidence to show that preventing same-sex marriage was so important to the state's interest that same-sex partners could

---

JOURNAL OF THOUGHTS 1.2: WHAT DO YOU BELIEVE ABOUT FAMILIES?

Respond to the following questions about family life. Then ask two or three other people what they think. The purpose of this assignment it to help you realize that each of us brings to the study of the family different ideas, beliefs, and experiences that shape how we study and think about family life.

1. How important do you believe family life is to the well-being of children? In other words, is family "essential" to the well-being of children? Could they "turn out" just as good a well-functioning citizen if they were raised in some other way than in a family?

2. Is there some optimal family type that makes family life significantly better for family members than some other styles of family life? For example, can the tasks of family life (like raising children, satisfying individual needs, etc.) get accomplished just as well in a single-parent home as a two-parent home? How about two parents of the same sex?

be denied equal protection of the laws allowing marriage. In particular, he decided that even if the two same-sex parents were to raise a child, there was no body of substantial evidence showing that the child (or children) would be affected in a way that would be of interest to the state.

Public policy scholar William Galston proposes another point of view. In the *Essential Communitarian Reader* (Etzioni, 1998), Galston suggests that:

Evidence indicates that from the standpoint of the psychological development and educational achievement of children as well as their economic well being, the intact two-parent family is generally preferable to the available alternatives. It follows that a prime purpose of sound family policy is to strengthen such families by promoting their formation, assisting their efforts to cope with economic and social stress, and retarding their breakdown whenever possible. This "prime" purpose is not the only purpose: Family policy must also seek to ameliorate the consequences of family breakdown for children while recognizing that some negative effects cannot be undone. (Galston, 1998, p. 149)

He asserts that it would be absurd to suggest that all single-parent families are "dysfunctional" or that it is reasonable to hope that all families would have two parents. Instead, the suggestion is that two parents is the optimal family pattern.

How family life is defined in this text. As discussed above, there are many forms and styles that families can adopt. For example, when a remarriage is involved we usually refer to this configuration as a stepfamily. There are also single-parent families and even polygamous family types. In fact, polygamy (one man marries two or more women) has been practiced by more human societies than any other form of marriage. Most pre-industrial societies and Muslim societies allow this type of family arrangement.

Society's definitions of family life have changed over time in response to many cultural, religious, and economic transformations. Within each general historical period, there have been a variety of idealized marital concepts. Because it would be impossible to capture all of those idealized notions about family in one definition, it seems to reasonable to follow the lead of two prominent family scholars, Ira Reiss and Gary Lee (1988, p. 24). In their book *Family Systems in America*, Reiss and Lee suggest that one should define family in terms of its functions and not its structure. That is, instead of trying to capture all of the possibilities of who could be found in a family, it is more useful to ask what family groups do. They suggest four central functions of family life: providing sexual intimacy, reproduction, economic cooperation, and the socialization of children. According to most anthropologists, families found in most cultures and subcultures of the world perform these functions. Therefore, within this text a family is a group of individuals in which there is a generational connection present (i.e. a parent-child relationship is found). Additionally, family members provide close intimate contact (this is usually characterized by deeply held commitment, trust, respect, and a sense of long-term obligation.) Sexual intimacy is assumed to be an element of the relationship between the parents. The family group seeks to achieve goals by acquiring, allocating, and distributing resources (i.e., time, money, space, close personal contact).

It is also assumed that the level of *family-ness* of each family varies. This means that individuals may choose to participate and contribute to the core sense of family life with varying degrees of enthusiasm. In some cases, the federation of individuals is loosely connected and the beliefs, ideologies, goals, and values of the individuals do not overlap as much. In other cases, there is a stronger sense of the family group in which the individuals within the family share, subscribe, endorse, and contribute to central family ideals, ideologies, beliefs, and goals.

WHY IS THE STUDY OF FAMILY LIFE IMPORTANT?

The following is a list of reasons why many family scholars believe that the study of the family is important and useful in solving many of the problems facing our society:

Families are a fundamental unit of society. This idea reflects a belief that people everywhere in virtually every society have selected family life as the preferred way of living. Long ago humans discovered they could do better if they formed small family groups. Society seems to begin when individuals claim a family group. We have all seen pictures and movies of animals that begin their lives and must be quite independent from the beginning. A recent television special showed a baby wildebeest up and running from a lion within a few hours of birth. Contrast that image to the helplessness of an infant. A newborn baby relies on its mother for several months and depends on sustained family life for several years. Therefore, the family unit is fundamental to society because it protects and helps children survive to adulthood.

The best way to rear children is in families. Family researchers and family observers believe that the most effective forum for raising children is in families. A child's mother and father are more likely to take special and attentive interest in the well-being of their children. That is not to say that they always do a good job. Rather, overall, the job they do is usually better than a disinterested third party would supply. Parents are more likely to make better decisions about their children than would someone else.

Better family life means stronger community well-being. Amitai Etzioni (1993) has created an intellectual movement in which he suggests that strength in family life creates community strength. He suggests that when children perform better in school, are arrested less, are more responsible to civic law, and experience less violence

JOURNAL OF THOUGHTS 1.3: IS THE AMERICAN FAMILY CHANGING OR DYING?

Some family science research and teachers suggest that the family is merely changing as it adapts to modern cultural changes. Others declare that it is essential to retain fundamental family styles (i.e., marriage to different sex partners, limit divorce, ensure the birth of children within a marriage context, etc.). What is your view? Include in your response the reasons why you believe in the position you have taken.

Now give your response to the following questions that should guide your thinking and help you form a more educated opinion on this issue. Use the space below to record your ideas:

Questions that need to be considered:

1. Is family life today "better" than before?

2. Is marriage as we once knew it dead or dying?

3. Is family life "essential?"

4. Why do we (as a culture) care about the institution of marriage?

5. Why should you, the reader, care about these topics?

JOURNAL OF THOUGHTS 1.4: DO YOU THINK A PERSON WHO CHOOSES TO NOT MARRY IS SELFISH OR IN SOME WAY HAS A PROBLEM?

First, ask yourself and honestly respond to the above question. Next, ask at least three other people to respond to the question. If your respondents think that to not marry is a sign of some problem in the person's life, ask what that problem might be. Conversely, if they respond that marriage is purely an individual decision and represents no "defect" on the part of the unmarried person, ask them to elaborate their thoughts about marriage as choice rather than an obligation.

Record your finding below:

Continue your responses here. As you comment, be sure to include an analysis of what the people said that you interviewed. For example, ask yourself why they said the things they did. Did they respond that way because of a cultural expectation, moral tradition, self-interest, or something else? Try to understand the deeper meaning of what they are saying and report that here.

in homes, each of us in a community of families benefits. That is, the social and economic standard for all increases and each individual is better able to reach his or her desired life goals.

FAMILY PROCESSES

In our study of the family, it is critical to understand *family processes*. *Family processes* are the strategies used by family members to maximize family goals. For example, a family goal (derived from a core belief or ideology) may be that through education family members will have the greatest chance of doing well in life. Family processes are those strategies used to reach that goal, which could include tactics like saving money, insisting on certain family habits, and arranging time use so that family members are more likely to succeed in education. The communication we use, how we solve problems, and how we set and maintain boundaries are all examples of family processes.

It is a basic premise of this text that family goals are founded on core *ideologies*. That is, families are composed of individuals who have expectations, goals, ideals, and desires. The family represents the intersection where the expectations, goals, ideals, and desires of family members overlap. Therefore, sometimes "families" have some beliefs and ideas that are strongly held by the group. Of course, not everyone in a family unit totally subscribes to all beliefs and ideologies held by the other family members. However, the core ideas shared by family members become the core of family life.

The study of family life is also about families in which there is a loose federation of individuals who share very little. In such cases, the expectations, desires, goals, and ideals of the individuals may have more power to direct how family resources are distributed and allocated. In some families, the connection among families members may be so unconnected that the only things they share is a common place to sleep.

The above idea suggests that there are at least two distinct ways of examining family life. The first way is to examine the family as a definitional unit in which the actual structure of the membership is the focus. In that case, we would study family membership (who is there and who is not) and changes in membership (divorce, birth of a child, remarriage, etc.). On the other hand, another legitimate focus of study is the examination of the shared beliefs held by family members, regardless of who they are, and the strategies families use to achieve goals.

This book is about trying to discover what those beliefs and ideologies might be, how families organize around those ideologies, and finally, how those ideologies are acted out in everyday life. Ultimately we want to know what strategies families use to reach the goals they have and if there are ways to assist them so that they could more successfully reach those goals. Of course, we are also interested in those families in which the ideologies are not as well formed and the needs and wants of the individuals are more prominent.

It is also important to realize that the study of daily family life is relatively new. While students and sociological researchers have studied the family as an institution for many years, only a few scholars have turned their attention to inner family life. For more than a hundred years, social scientists have been intrigued with the study of the mind of the individual; we call that discipline psychology. This text focuses on the aspect of life that falls somewhere in between the study of the individual and the study of groups in society. Said differently, an important feature of this book is its focus on what happens "behind closed doors." Moreover, again, it is assumed that by studying the intricacies of daily life, we can have some chance of assisting individuals as they try to make daily family life better for those involved.

Not only have most social scientists studied families from the larger, macro view and looked at the family as an institution, but also most family scholars investigate the extraordinary. That is, they are interested in family crises such as divorce, death of a child or spouse, the effects of catastrophic poverty, or violence in families. While the study of these problematic areas of family life are important and have alerted us to the many challenges facing today's children and parents, there is another side of family life. That side is characterized by the ordinary, everyday events of life. In this book, we will spend most of our time talking about the ordinary choices and everyday decisions families make. Less time will be spent on the exotic, radical, and less routine. There is a growing awareness that the ordinary acts of daily living have a special power. Often the routine acts of daily life shape who we are and how our lives "turn out." Occasionally, a dramatic event will severely alter a family forever. Nevertheless, for most people, our lives are filled with the routine acts of daily living that combine together to form and shape who we really are.

CONCLUSION

The Protean family. In Greek mythology, a lesser-known but important god of the sea was known as Proteus. Proteus' claim to fame was that he could change his shape into various forms at will. The derivative word protean describes someone or something that has this same ability. The family seems to fall into this category. Families themselves take on many forms; they are changeable, polymorphous, and versatile. Additionally, the definitions of family life are also protean. Those who think about family life and have decided which type of small group is a family and which is not choose from among the many definitions available and select the one that best suits their purposes and ideological orientation.

For example, businesses or governmental agencies define family in ways that serve a particular purpose and are usually specific and precise. Billions of dollars are meted out each year in transfer payments to "family members." For example, insurance

ACTIVITY 1.2 - YOUR VIEW OF FAMILY LIFE

After reading the first chapter (and possibly having a discussion about it with someone), comment on the following in the space provided below.

1.   What do you think is the biggest problem facing families today?

2.   What do you believe is the primary solution to the problems you have listed?

3. What are the three primary problems you think your family does or will face in the future?

Adapting to Family Life in Our Times

companies will only cover the medical expenses of family members that fall within their restricted definition of *family member*. Some authors (cf. Cherlin, 1999, p. 19) suggest that such definitions fall into our notion of a *public family*.

Those wishing to broaden the definition of the family seek to make private family life (as opposed to public family life) an individual choice in which a variety of styles, configurations, and combinations are acceptable. Those who approach the study of family life from more traditional business or governmental points of view may seek to limit and constrict the definition of the family for economic reasons. In addition, those who view the family as a sacred religious institution may suggest a particular configuration and even gender role assignment within the family based on doctrine and beliefs that support their point of view.

It is not the purpose of this text to suggest to a wide and diverse audience which of the many definitions of family life one "ought" to adopt. Instead, it is a goal of this chapter that the reader should carefully consider this issue, be able to articulate a position about your personal definition of what constitutes family life, and be able to show how that definition flows from a central ideological or even practical notion.

In designing your definition of a family, you may wish to consider the beliefs of your parents, community members, friends, and other family members. From these you may be able to find and identify your personal family definition. The last task in this set of thought exercises is to consider what would be the optimal family, in your opinion. Too often, we design our definitions and make moral decisions while attempting to be overly inclusive and, in our attempt to be fair, we try to consider every version of a complicated matrix of possibilities. Instead, this exercise asks you to define family from the perspective of ideas, ideals, beliefs, and ideologies that you hold. In other words, what does family life mean to you and to those you contact, and what is your personal ideal about family life?

Chapter 1

1. What types of family difficulties might one study in the field of family science? *strategies + everyday processes. divorce/remarry rates, violence*

2. What does the term "protean" family refer to? *Changeable, polymorphous, + versatile.*

3. Is it possible to study the family without bringing a bias to that endeavor? *no.*

4. Explain what we mean by the idea that in U.S. culture there has been a move away from the idea that sex and childrearing are strongly linked to marriage? What evidence can you present to substantiate that claim? *People have sex + kids w/o marriage. married couples do not always have kids.*

5. What do we mean when we say that family life is unique? *Every family is different + perspective of family.*

6. Define what we mean by "family processes." Give several examples of different family processes. *strategies used by fam. members to maximize fam. goals.*

7. What percent of American children will experience divorce in their families of origin? *40%*

8. What do we mean when we say that we are defining family in terms of "function instead of structure?" *How they interact instead of is there a mom + a dad.*

KEY TERMS

Family of procreation
Family of orientation
Family processes
Protean family
Changing nature of the family
Families as a fundamental unit of society
The definition of family life
Family science is a new discipline

CHAPTER
TWO

Theorizing About Family
Life

Chapter Two

Main Points:

1. There are several theoretical approaches that assist us in our study of family life. Among them are rational/exchange, developmental/family life cycle, symbolic interaction, conflict, and systems theory.

2. Individuals join together to form a family and a family is an entity.

3. Family entities have goals and they try to maximize positive outcomes that reflect those goals.

4. As an entity or group of individuals tied together by a common set of goals and beliefs, families have systemic properties. This is sometimes called "wholeness" and refers to the idea that a system is a complexity of elements standing in interaction as an underlying pattern or structure.

5. Family groups or systems attempt to maintain stability over time. This is called homeostasis. Family systems also must adapt and change over time and this is called morphogenesis.

6. It is difficult to speak of causality when referring to system processes. Instead, one tries to identify patterns of interaction.

Theorizing About Family Life

INTRODUCTION

The study of family life is a complicated affair. Those who professionally study family behavior quickly realize that the intricacies of daily family living are far more difficult to understand than one would first imagine. We also realize that to better understand family life it is essential to appreciate the traditions of learning shaped by many scholars in recent decades. Some great minds have struggled with questions like: why do some families endure and others dissolve; why do some families excel at collecting and using resources wisely and others do rather poorly; and why do some families have chronic and destructive violence as a feature of their daily life and others are relatively violence free. To begin to understand these and many other complicated family processes, family scholars often initiate their journey of learning by considering several theoretical frameworks that have guided family research since the beginning of the family science discipline.

To many readers, the word theory produces a chill. However, it is critical to remember that an understanding of theoretical ideas is essential when we embark on any voyage of scientific discovery. Theoretical ideas have inspired discoveries in astronomy, biology, economics, and medicine. Whether one wants to discover new knowledge or to apply the ideas we already know, our efforts are much more effective if they are driven by theories.

When scholars or application specialists try to answer the question "What is going on here?" they are always building on the accumulated findings of others. In everyday life, people refer to this phenomenon when they say there is "no need to reinvent the wheel." One of the most important tasks of scholars and thinkers in family science is the work of collecting and organizing ideas into theories. From these core, fundamental ideas and principles of family life, comes a wealth of notions that can assist us in explaining why people do what they do. These constructs also can assist when we decide to change behaviors in our life that do not help meet the goals we have in mind.

In sum, theories are combinations of hunches, collected facts (or ideas we think are facts), and the accepted wisdom about aspects of a situation. They provide a common language for discussion about a topic and provide suggestions for research and application directions. Most of the theoretical ideas presented later will sound familiar and you may discover that many of them are rather common sense notions. However, these collected ideas represent our best thinking about the ways families and individuals in families set out to solve life's problems, build stronger relationships, and make daily decisions.

The theories we use in social science are representations or models for something tangible and real. Therefore, it is important to remember that theoretical ideas change and develop over time and are never meant to represent "truth" per se. Instead, theories are perspectives that help us understand reality and are merely constructs that we use as tools to approximate our understanding of the "real" world.

Suppose a researcher wanted to know if spirituality was an important aspect of family life. Where would she or he begin the search for explaining that idea? Just finding out how many times a family said grace at dinner might be a start. However, often we want to know more. We want explanations about how that ritualistic behavior came into being, why it continues, and what effect it may have on family life.

The theoretical ideas presented later have changed over time: scholars refine their thinking, reject some parts of the theory (or the entire theory itself), and sift through the myriad of available ideas to discover just the right collection of ideas that match the way they think about a situation. And, pragmatically speaking, we often search for ideas that work. Most family scientists want to see individuals and family units succeed and thrive, so we attempt to search for theoretical ideas that will assist us in explaining difficult and complex family issues. Just as maps must be revised to reflect changes in the physical environment, so are theories constantly being changed or discarded in search of simple but effective ways of helping families. A principle from math captures this idea: It is called Occam's Razor. This principle states that the best way to solve a problem is to use the fewest steps or fewest assumptions possible. Therefore, while these ideas may seem commonsensical, they have been shown to be the simplest yet most powerful explanations that help us understand complicated family life.

Another important feature of studying theories is the common language provided by our theoretical explanations. Theories provide a language or groups of common concepts that make it easier for those who study family life to communicate. So, when I write about the maximization principle in a later chapter of your text, both you and I will share a common understanding of what I mean by that and also what other family scholars have written about this idea.

As you read about the following theories, there will be several terms presented in each one. Your task is to understand how others have used those terms and think of examples in your personal life that illuminate those ideas. By learning and remembering these terms and ideas, you will better understand the information presented in the remainder of this text and in other family science courses and texts if you choose to study this discipline further

It is also important to realize that most of the theoretical ideas and terms presented next did not originate in the young discipline of family science. Instead, these ideas have, for the most part, a long and rich history in other disciplines such as sociology, economics, and psychology. Only recently (cf Beutler, Burr, Bahr, & Herrin, 1989) have family scientists begun to discuss the "family realm" as being somewhat unique and different from other social groups (such as the study of the workplace).

THEORIES USED IN FAMILY SCIENCE

Within the following pages of this chapter, several theories used in family sciences are presented. There are two important limitations you should know about the following synopsis of these theoretical ideas. First, each of the theories mentioned has a prominent history in the social sciences. Our glimpse of these complicated ideas only captures a small portion of the volumes written about each.

Second, these are not the only theories used by family scholars. There are many theories that have been suggested to explain family life. The overview below represents a quick look at the theories most frequently used and ones that appear in other chapters of this book. If you continue studying family science, you may wish to take a course that examines these and other theoretical ideas in depth. Additionally, the suggested readings at the end of this chapter provide a starting place for extended study about theoretical orientations in the discipline of family science.

Reductionism: A basic question. One of the more important questions in studying families (or any other social process) is how we approach the complexity of social life. An ongoing debate in social science centers on this topic. On the one hand, some believe that it is inappropriate and ineffective to "reduce" life to small fragments or parts of behavior. For example, a reductionistic oriented researcher would try to identify the tiny pieces of daily behavior that make up life. He/she would attempt to show that the parts matter and are connected. Additionally, he/she would suggest ways of intervening in a problem by targeting one or more of the parts for change.

Those who subscribe to a *holistic* view of human behavior believe that it is better to study the complexity of human existence by looking only at the whole person within a whole environment and in a context. They would resist examining the parts of human behavior and, instead, would only try to tell the larger picture.

A reductionistic perspective takes the view that one can successfully focus on the small parts of a family and figure out what that family will do in a variety of situations (Sprey, 2000). The small parts are usually the people within the family. So, the approach for many years in family studies has been to focus on each person in the family and note what roles they play (i.e., father, provider, caretaker, defender, etc.). For example, if one wanted to measure marital satisfaction, each partner was asked a few questions about how he/she thought the marriage was going. Sometimes the responses from both partners were statistically merged and guesses were made about how "happy" the marriage was. This created some problems for theorists and researchers. Many began to realize that marriages and families were more dynamic than merely the sum of the two scores.

Chapter 2

In other words, one point of view is that it may be very difficult if not impossible to measure the wholeness of a family by gathering information about each of its members and then somehow combining their answers to get an overall picture of the family. It seems there are only a few theoretical choices with regard to the study of the family.

First, we could continue on with the historical approach in which a researcher asks a family member (and usually it is only one member) some questions about his/her experience in that family. Using this approach, we assume that one person's view of the larger activities and beliefs of a group of people is sufficient. We would assume that this one person (and usually it is the mother's view) is accurate enough and so we use that view and treat it as reality. Let's use the example of measuring father involvement (Marsiglio, Amato, Day, & Lamb, 2000). Many researchers want to know if father involvement really matters in the lives of children. While the research in this area of study is relatively new, the findings have a wide variety of implications for public policy, custody issues, and what we think about children's well-being.

Most of the research about father involvement, however, has been done by asking mothers what fathers do in families. Does that seem odd to you? Many researchers think that approach *is* odd and have begun trying to get information from fathers. However, they typically do not like to answer surveys, they are hard to find, and, in general, are a difficult group with which to do research. A reductionistic approach has been to gather a few pieces of data from mothers about fathers with regard to a few activities he might do in family life. Then researchers would make some guesses about what that means for family life. To many researchers, that approach has seemed less than adequate.

JOURNAL OF THOUGHTS 2.1: WHAT IS A THEORY?

1. In the space provided, use the information from your text to "think" about what a theory is.

2. How would you use a theory?

3.   How do theories come about?

4.   What good are they?

SPOTLIGHT ON RESEARCH 2.1: POSTMODERNISM IN THE FAMILY AS VIEWED BY WILLIAM DOHERTY

An important reference book in family science is the *Handbook of Marriage and the Family, Second Edition* (1999), Sussman, M, Steinmetz, S, & Peterson, G. (Eds.). In Chapter Eight of this comprehensive overview of the research on family life, researcher and theoretician William Doherty reviews the emergence of postmodernism as an important theoretical orientation in the study of family science.

According to Doherty, the period of modernity is generally thought of as the time since the Middle Ages when individuals gained freedoms, industrialization occurred, and people began to adopt more rational approaches to the human condition rather than superstitious orientations. Further, aesthetic modernism moved people away from Victorian constraints and toward the enhancement of the prerogative of the individual. This enhanced view of individualism has driven much of social science research as a deeply held ideological assumption. Social scientists created the field of family science in an attempt to use rational, scientific methods (as opposed to religious, moralistic, or what they considered to be superstitious approaches) to understanding the context, meaning, and impact of family life on the individual and on society.

Postmodernism (as reported by Doherty) has been described as the "Big Bang" in family theory beginning in the 1970s. In the postmodern view, there is a general rejection of the rationality of the Enlightenment, a turning away from modern art, and literature, and a:

1. Rejection of the ideal of value of progress, per se.
2. Critical view of grand theories that try to capture human experience by using a few organizing constructs.
3. De-emphasis on the focus of the individual as the primary object of research.
4. Re-emphasis on the idea that culture (through language, tradition, and institution) can oppress and limit human growth.

The postmodern ideas have influenced researchers and theorists. For example, many family theorists are impatient with definitions of the family that adhere to established traditions and mores in our culture. They, instead, want the family to be defined in broader and more inclusive terms. Second, many family researchers have moved away from thinking that family life can be meaningfully studied using scientific, statistical, or other rational based approaches. Many prefer narrative approaches based on the stories families tell. This is sometimes labeled a post-positivist point of view. That is, it is a rejection of positivism that assumes that causes for human behavior can be identified and categorized. Instead, some postmodern researchers rely on qualitative research that rejects the idea that people's behavior and intentions can be reduced to statistical summaries.

Third, there is a strong movement toward explaining the life of families using everyday language instead of the language of science. This orientation is sensitive to issues of gender, equality in family life, and oppression of peoples everywhere but especially when it occurs within family life.

JOURNAL OF THOUGHTS 2.2: WHAT ABOUT THE REDUCTIONISTIC APPROACH?

1. In this segment, write about reductionistic perspectives in your own words.

2. Do you believe that human interaction can be dissected into small fragments? Why? Why not?

Theorizing About Family Life

Another approach that is gaining some popularity is to move away from a purely reductionistic view, gather information from several people in the family and then, using sophisticated statistics, see if there is a shared belief about what has happened in that particular family. For example, if we wanted to know more about father involvement we would ask mothers, fathers, and even children for their perceptions about what he does and what it means to them. The idea is that by combining the views of several people we might get closer to understanding the processes that happen in family life. This type of research is costly and still only provides an approximation about inner family life.

Still another approach rejects the idea that we could research inner family life by asking simple questions like "How many times did you spank your child last week?" Instead, qualitative researchers approach the study of family life by gathering narrative stories, observing the families in their homes, and then extracting from what they see and hear any patterns or themes that re-emerge.

The approach in this text. My approach is to listen to both voices. In this text, I have taken information from many different kinds of research studies; some of them are extremely reductionistic in nature and others are excellent example of narrative-qualitative studies. My belief is that each of the approaches we use has limitations, successes, and problems. Each is another way to try and tell the story about what happens behind closed doors in private family life. For now, it is the best we can do. The study of the family is still in its infancy and our collected information about inner family life is limited. Another bias of mine is that the more we move toward studying families rather than only studying the individuals in families, the better off we will be. In this text, I will repeatedly suggest to you that the study of family life is about the whole family rather than just one reductionistic part of the family.

FAMILIES SYSTEM THEORY

One metaphor that is often used to understand family life is to think of families as an interactive system. Systems are often defined a group of interacting parts (Broderick, 1993; Klein & White, 1995). This idea simply means that when describing any entity (a football team, a habitat in the forest, or a complex factory) it is assumed that all of the parts are connected and interrelated. In the case of family science, families are not a closed system like an airplane. A modern jet passenger plane is a self-contained relatively closed system. All of the parts (e.g., the compass, engines, and rudders) are parts of a complex group of parts collected together in one place and labeled an airplane. The airplane does receive fuel and food from outside sources and from time to time gets messages from other systems outside plane (e.g., other airplanes and the control tower). But for the most part, an airplane is a relatively closed system of parts and it has a rather singular mission.

On the other hand, families are probably more complicated than a jet passen-

ger plane. First, it is not a closed system. While some family systems scholars consider the people in the family to be the "parts," others write about the family system as being even more complicated than simply a collection of people. For these family scientists, the unit of analysis is the interaction found within the inner life of the family. That is, many family science researchers examine how patterns of interaction are formed, what effect those exchanges of feeling and information hold, and how family interaction can be changed. Therefore, within this systems framework, therapists and researchers assume that the family is the unit of observation and not the individual. This means that these researchers view a particular family as an entity and that the family members are connected together. This connection is defined in terms of the repeating patterns of interaction that are observed. The metaphor that used to describe these repeating rules of interaction and the patterns that seem to emerge is the term system.

Theorizing About Family Life

When theorists invented system theory, they were, for the most part, interested in closed systems consisting of machine parts (such as radar, rocket ships, and robots). While families, family members, and the interactions found within a family system are not nearly as predictable as pieces of metal and wire, there are some attributes of family life that are system-like.

Therefore, in this text, several systems ideas are used and applied to our understanding of family life. The first idea that is important to note is the assumption that systems theory makes about underlying "structures."

Underlying structures.   A primary theme of family science research is the idea that the role of the therapist or researcher is to discover underlying, hidden "structures." There are many social science researchers who have adopted this theme over the years. For example, this idea is at the heart of the writings of Sigmund Freud. In the Freudian approach to understanding the human psyche, the notion is that the skilled observer can detect hidden patterns or undiscovered, unresolved conflicts deep within the subconscious of the individual. And, that by finding, identifying, and revealing those hidden conflicts, one can attain a higher level of mental health.

This type of idea also extends to theories that describe the cognitive abilities of children and adults. Jean Piaget, for example, suggested that there were hidden, internal schemata or mental structures that direct our ability to solve problems and make sense out of life's puzzles. Likewise, several writers of family theory have suggested that within family life there are underlying structures or patterns of interactions that direct what occurs in family life.

The metaphor of a system is easier to understand if one thinks of a mechanical device or group of devices welded together and designed to solve some problem in a factory. Think of a complex factory, for example, in which there are hundreds of steps performed by hundreds of machines to produce an item, like an automobile for example. Most systems like the automobile factory receive inputs (e.g., metal, plastic, paint, and glass), the parts of the system (e.g., the metal press, the paint robots, and the glass installing arms) work together to solve a central problem (i.e., to have an automobile exit the output door, completed and working and looking like it is supposed to). The workers in the factory are really extensions of the robotic arms and levers, moving in unison (if all goes well) to produce a specific goal. The patterns of interaction (e.g., the metal is pressed and cut before it is painted) are all thoughtfully mapped out, timed, and executed according to a massive collaborative effort by all involved.

In the world of systemic thinking, the idea is that you can observe the movement of the actors, how they communicate, what comes into the system, what happens to the system (whether it be factory workers or family members) and based on those observations one could deduce what the goals of the system are and how effective that particular system is at achieving its apparent goals.

Like Freud trying to discover the underlying patterns of the mind, the researcher or therapist who works with family systems theory tries to understand the

Chapter 2

underlying patterns of family life by watching how families solved problems, how family members communicated with one another, and how they allocated resources. So, family systems theorists are fond of saying, "a system is a group of interacting parts that comprise a whole."

Families have goals. This view of the world reflects not only the system perspective but also the social-exchange and conflict theory ideas from above. All of these approaches assume that the system is goal seeking: families have goals they are trying to achieve. Therefore, two key terms of the systems approach is that a system is a group of interacting parts (family members and the patterns of interaction that occur) and that the family entity has goals it is trying to attain. Further, the family entity uses strategies that are pattern-like to make those goals happen. That is, they are more likely to do the same routines over and over than they are to try some new approach to achieve goals and deal with problems that might affect goal achievement.

The family as a whole. This brings us to an important idea proposed by systems thinking researchers and family intervention workers: It is impossible to understand family life without viewing the family as a whole (Hall & Fagan, 1956; Broderick, 1993; Klein & White, 1995). In Freudian psychology and other general social science approaches, the unit of analysis is almost always an individual, with other family members playing a supporting role in the story. In a systemic view of family life, the primary story is about what the whole family is doing and the focus on a particular individual (even if she/he is the person with the most obvious "problem") is secondary to understanding how family life works. Indeed, solving an individual's "problem" often involves changing patterns that involve other family members.

Often when researchers examine family life, the interaction in families is viewed as larger than any one person or even any one rule or pattern. Okun and Rapport (1980) summarize this idea below:

> *The system in an integrated coherent entity that is more than the mere composite of independent elements. This wholeness transcends the sum of the system's component elements. A family consisting of Mother, Father, Sally, Johnny, and David Brown is viewed as a total interactional process that characterizes them as the "Browns"; it is not view as the sum of Mr. Brown, Mrs. Brown, Sally Brown, Johnny Brown, and David Brown. ... Despite this wholeness, a change in one part of the system may cause a change in many parts (subsystems) of the larger system and in the larger system itself.* (pp. 8-9)

We cannot understand the "Browns" simply by understanding each individual member of the family. We must also understand the relationships and interactions

> PRINCIPLE 2.1: THE FAMILY UNIT AS A WHOLE.
>
> *When using a systems approach to understanding family life, one has to view the family unit as a whole and, therefore, not use the individual as the primary focus of interest.*

that occurs with this family entity (or systemic unit). Another way to say that is that each role found within the family is dependent on the others. For example, one cannot be a mother unless there are people to "mother."

Equilibrium.   Another useful term that comes from the systems perspective is equilibration or equilibrium. Of course, this idea refers to the balancing act that families must perform. As family entities attempt to reach goals, they have to respond constantly to the changes that happen in their world. Money comes in, children get sick, the local factory announces layoffs, the mother is depressed, etc. Family units are not static systems. A closed system, like a watch, can be wound and then you do not have to bother with it until it needs winding or a battery. On the other hand families are interactive systems that require constant adaptation, change, and response. One cannot get a family organized, arranged, thought out, and defined and then walk away as you would with the clock. Instead, on a daily or even hourly basis family members are changing and influencing the other family members. Therefore, family units try to reach goals by keeping life's events in balance. We have to change the rules, adapt our traditions, and alter how we get daily chores done.

Morphostasis and morphogenesis.   These are two forces that occur each day in family life. According to the family systems way of thinking, as various events occur (such as a child is injured on the playground), family entities try to keep the rules of everyday living intact and keep life moving along. Morphostasis means that we want there to be continuity and sameness. The other pull is that families realize that there is constant genesis or creation and change. So, when the child is injured on the playground, we collectively ask if the old way of doing things will work today? Does someone else need to make the dinner, who can help with homework tonight while someone takes her to the doctor, or who will call her friend and tell her she is not going to be able to play? Later in this book, we will talk much more about family crises and how families adapt to events that change the nature of family interaction as the Browns try to keep the daily events of life running smoothly and at the same time re-create who they are to meet the changes that occur as people get older and the family alters. (See Chapter 8 for a more detailed explanation of these ideas.)

Boundaries.   System boundaries occur where two or more systems or subsystems interface, interact, or come together. They are borders of a system. Sometimes these boundaries can be very solid and rigid and other times they are very permeable.

Chapter 2

Boundaries occur at every level in the system and between systems. Often, we understand where a boundary is by listening to the rules families construct about where people can and cannot go, what they can and cannot do, and who is allowed in the family and who is not allowed to leave. For example, in some families, they may have a very open system and family members are allowed to come and go without much restriction. So, we say the boundaries are more permeable. In fact, in some families they are so permeable they are like a sieve. Other families are more protective and they construct boundaries that resemble castle walls. The "drawbridge" is only lowered for certain events and a castle-family member has to return on time or trouble will ensue. Likewise, there may be strict rules about who can enter other family members' rooms or study areas. We will speak more of this issue in the chapter on rules and patterns of interaction.

Pauline Boss (1998) has illuminated another type of boundary issue. As a family scientist, she has researched the idea of boundaries in many settings and recently applied her work to the problem of families who have a member with Alzheimer's disease. In her book, she shows how the physical and mental awareness of family members can greatly influence our ideas about family membership and responsibility.

Subsystems. Within the family system there may be smaller units of analysis. Another element that researchers speak of is the idea of subsystems within the family realm. There are several possible subsystems and include the spousal or executive subsystem, the parent/child subsystem, and the parental subsystem (in which the husband and wife relate to each other with regard to a parenting role). One of the key tasks of subsystems is boundary maintenance.

Family therapists have long known that a sure sign of a family in difficulty is when their subsystems are not kept separate and distinct (Minuchin, 1981; Minuchin & Nichols, 1993). For example, when family members build coalitions across subsystems, the family's ability to achieve goals is weakened. If a parent builds a stronger relationship with a child than she does with her spouse, then the family system is weakened. If a parent (in this case often the father) blurs the boundaries between himself and a child emotionally and sexually the entire family system is weakened and can even be destroyed as is often the case when incest occurs.

The concept of the subsystem helps us understand that the primary "parts" of the system are not the individuals but instead are the interactions between and among the various subsystems within a family group. The individual influences his partner, and in turn, the response of those two people influences how they allocate resources, make decisions, and monitor their children. The great American playwright Arthur Miller once said "all human interaction is 98% historical." He was referring to the simple idea that the patterns of previous interactions and decisions live on and direct the next thing we say to a family member in the next situation. The study of those patterns of interaction is a characteristic of the study of the family using a systems approach.

Equifinality. One of the more unique concepts used in family system thinking is the idea of equifinality. Simply put, equifinality captures the idea that "many beginnings can lead to the same outcome, and the same beginning can lead to quite different outcomes" (Bavelas & Segal, 1982, p. 103). In other words, any outcome you can imagine can be brought about by multiple causes. Further, since there are so many events that can cause a given outcome, paying attention to this idea turns our attention away from worrying about those causes as much as some other theoretical orientations do.

For example, we know from various studies on parent child interaction that over parental involvement can lead to two very different outcomes in children. Being an over-responsive parent can push children to overachieve and it could push some children to underachieve. Friedman (1985) listed several research ideas that seem to lead us to the conclusion that one beginning could have many different outcomes. Having an alcoholic parent could produce children who are diametrically opposed to drinking or children who abuse alcohol themselves; if a parent takes a stand on some ideological issue (a strong religious conviction, for example) children may see the parent has a hero or see them as a controlling, demanding dictator.

Likewise the same effect could have come from very opposite causes. For example, the death of a child could bring a family close together and their level of functioning could dramatically increase, or it could devastate them and great distance and unresolved negative feelings could result.

When one thinks more systemically, the search for causes moves to the back of the stage. At center stage are the search for outcomes and their related processes. In the example of the death of a child, a family systems person would not focus on the events of the child's death but rather on how the family entity responds and tries to adapt. The focus would be on the strategies they use to resolve the loss.

When using a family systemic way of thinking one asks what questions rather than why questions. The systemic way of viewing family life is to focus more on what can be done once some event happens rather than a post mortem approach to find out why something happened. By examining how families and family members respond to daily life, we can make guesses about what they value, how they solve problems, and how they think about the world. Armed with those insights, family systems thinking researchers believe they have a better chance of helping families cope with life's difficult events than if they only focus on why the child died, why the farm lost money, why the unmarried teen got pregnant, etc.

Imagine a family floating down a river in a raft. The river is in a scenic wilderness. The surroundings all contribute to the experience of the family. Specifically, the slope of the river as it cuts through a canyon will determine how fast the water is flowing. While the family members may note these determining factors such as the speed of the water, the number of rocks, the position of the raft in the river, it is the rowing that is the focus of their attention. No one pays too much attention to why a rock is there…it is there and must be avoided. Only in a few instances (like if my mother were there) would be family members be rehearsing why they came here in the first place.

> PRINCIPLE 2.2: FAMILIES REACHING GOALS
>
> *Family members are more effective in reaching their goals when they focus more on the "how and what" part of life than spending their energy on the "why" and causal aspects of daily life.*

And, no one would be thinking much about how the family formed and why they were born with children who could not row better (although it might cross someone's mind). Instead of focusing on causes, the most effective families learn to focus on the problem at hand.

As you can see from the example above, our focus has shifted from thinking about the researcher to the family itself. Both family researchers/therapists and family members themselves can benefit from the principle of equifinality. Certainly, there is a never-ending list of causes that one could examine in the river example. However, strong families and researchers who use this perspective spend most of their energy focusing on rowing better, spotting rocks earlier, and having some fun while the event is in progress. According to this perspective, researchers have less impact when they focus on the reasons why the family is rafting in the first place. And, families are less effective when family members evaluated, rehash, rehearse, and criticize family activity instead of learning how to row better, so to speak.

THEORIES OF CHANGE AND FAMILY DEVELOPMENT

One of the giants and founders of family science research was Rubin Hill. As early as 1949 he developed the idea that a family was composed of social roles and that the nature and assignment of these roles changed over time (Hill & Hansen, 1960). Theorists who use this perspective make several key assumptions found below.

The first assumption found in this approach can be labeled the *Change Assumption*. The change assumption states that any living system (be it the individual or a complicated family group) has a path it follows and that all living entities change over time. The job of the researcher is to note those changes and find out how they influence individual or family decisions.

The second assumption we learn from family life course theory is that change over time in family life has to be examined from a number of different levels. This idea

> PRINCIPLE 2.3: CHANGE HAPPENS
>
> *Individuals, family structure, and interactions among family members change over time.*

surfaces in many theories about the family and has several different labels. Basically, the idea is that individuals live in some type of family group. Obviously, there are exceptional cases in which some children do not grow up in some type of family group, but that is clearly atypical. Family groups (whatever the make-up) are social by nature. By that we mean that a primary purpose of families is to care for, nurture, and facilitate an optimal outcome for each member. Again, a basic notion of this theory is that family groups organize around the idea of well-being. In every culture and in every historical time period, there are no examples of cultures that we know about where the individuals have not banded together in these intimate family groups and their overall goal was to help each other "do better." Said differently, in every culture we know about, families exist in some form and are not established with the intent of destroying each other.

At the next level of complexity is the community. Each community in the world is composed of clusters or groups of families that are more alike or homogenous than they are different. A small community of families living in Northern England are probably more alike than different and the same would be true of a community of families living in Egypt, Bolivia, or Japan. While the similarity begins to fade the wider we cast our community net, it also true that families living in the U.S., generally, are more similar in ideology, beliefs, and organization than they are dissimilar. Additionally, it is important to understand that individuals are connected to families, families are connected to communities, and larger communities are formed from collections of smaller local or proximate communities. Each level influences the other levels: to more fully understand the complexity of family life one must take into consideration how the larger and more distal community influences family life and how local family life influences the larger community. Chapter 4 explores this idea in depth but the principle of community life captures the core idea.

PRINCIPLE PRINCIPLE 2.4: FAMILIES ARE CONNECTED

Family development is influenced by the connections families have to their proximate and distal communities. Likewise, larger community life is influenced by smaller collections of families (i.e. one's proximate community) and by individual families themselves.

Another key assumption that is a feature of the family life course perspective is the notion of transitions. Transitions occur in families as they change and try to adapt the events that happen over time. (Klein & White, 1996, p. 128). This concept will be explored in depth in Chapter 8. But, the central idea simply states that the transitions we make in family life, such as getting married, having and raising children, divorcing and remarrying, create a path of possible events. And, depending on

> **PRINCIPLE 2.5: ANTICIPATING TRANSITIONS IN FAMILY LIFE**
>
> *When a transition occurs in a family life that is unanticipated or does not occur when it was generally expected to occur, that transition is more likely to have a negative influence as that family attempts to achieve its goals.*

the paths one chooses, other events are more likely to result. For example, once a child is born into a family, family members find a new set of paths that appear before them that were of little concern before the child was born. In a few short years, the child may be attending preschool, parents may begin thinking ahead about other school plans, the child's future, and how their family will be a part of the child's future.

There are two very important principles that emerge from this simple idea. First, is the idea of *off-time transitions*. Younger unmarried women who conceive and bear a child are less likely to contribute their personal and family goals than are those young women who have children within a range of years that is more "on-time."

> **PRINCIPLE 2.6: EPIGENESIS OCCURS IN FAMILY LIFE**
>
> *What we do in life early on, has a significant impact in our lives later on.*

Epigenesis. A second important idea is the notion of epigenesis. Again, this is a simple idea that is useful and powerful in understanding everyday family life.

What we do in life early on has a significant impact in our lives later on. The choices we make early in our lives effect who we are, the type of family we raise, and the life we will lead later on. This does not mean we cannot overcome the choices we make in times of family transitions, however, those choices have the power to strongly influence our futures. For example, if a young couple decides to have several children early in their marriage, for better or worse, it will not only have an economic effect on future choices available to them, but can influence the resources available to their children, family activities that are chosen, where they can and cannot live, and even the educational pursuits of the parents.

In sum, family developmental theory is a useful perspective and some of its ideas help us understand important family processes. Throughout this text, two of its most powerful ideas will be referred to frequently. Those two ideas are: first, family life has a course and that course can have many paths.

Second, as family members make transitions, the choices they make within those transitional times can (and usually do) have influence on future opportunities and choices available to each family member.

RATIONAL CHOICE/ SOCIAL EXCHANGE THEORY

One of the more frequently used theoretical ideas in family science is called Rational Choice or Social Exchange Theory. At the heart of this perspective is the idea that each individual seeks to maximize individual self-interest. That is not to say that all people are necessarily "selfish" per se. But, it does assume that each person acts with his/her personal welfare in mind as a primary motivating force (Klein & White, 1996).

PRINCIPLE PRINCIPLE 2.7: FAMILIES CAN MAXIMIZE RESOURCES

Individuals maximize self-interest by rationally making choices that result in the most personal reward, and individuals avoid choices that are not rewarding or are otherwise costly.

The rational person goes about the task of maximizing. That is, he or she maximizes his/her position in life by avoiding situations in which the rewards of the situation are less than the costs. By definition, a reward is anything that is "perceived as beneficial to an actor's interests" (Klein & White, 1996, p. 65).

Likewise, costs are defined as outcomes that are not beneficial to one's interests. For example, when we make a decision to buy a car, choose a spouse, name a child, or select an occupation, those who subscribe to this point of view suggest that we weigh the costs and rewards and choose what we believe to be in our best interest at the time of the choice. This is called a rational theory because it assumes that each of us has the power to use our intellect in the selection process. It also assumes that (unless someone has a serious emotional problem or is under extreme distress) that we do not make choices that are deliberately bad for us.

An Example of Self-Interest Theory
From Anna Karenina by Leo Tolstoy (1993, p.265)

And this irritated Levin.
'I'll tell you, then,' he began with heat. 'I believe the mainspring of all our actions is, after all, self-interest. Now I, as a nobleman, see nothing in our local institutions that could contribute to my prosperity. The roads are not better and could not be better; besides, my horses carry me well enough over bad ones. Doctors and dispensaries are no use to me... 'I believe that no sort of activity is likely to be lasting if it is not based on self-interest. That is a universal principle, a philosophical principle'...

Another way to say this is that we make choices that seem to assist us in reaching goals we have selected as important. The concept of rationality does not suppose that people make good choices all of the time (or even most of the time). Nor, does this approach assume that goals that have been consciously or implicitly selected are appropriate or worthy. Instead, it assumes that people weigh their choices and balance up the costs and rewards and try to do the best they can at the time.

Social exchange theory also helps us understand the nature of relationships. As will be explained in Chapter 6, when relationships are based on a principle of equity they will thrive and be more likely to achieve the desired goals. Equity means that partners in a relationship work toward a balance of resources that each brings to the relationship and a climate of fairness their relationship. When the balance is absent and one person has more resources (such as money, talents, or physical goods) it is assumed that the relationship will not be as effective in reaching the goals they set. For example, we know that people who are of the same social or economic status tend to choose each other for marriage (Chapter 6) and how decisions are made, resources allocated, and time used is reflected in the resources each person brings to the relationship (see Chapter 11).

PRINCIPLE 2.8: EQUALITY IN RESOURCES

When partners in a relationship are more equal with regard to the resources they bring to the relationship, it is more likely the relationship will be stronger and is more likely that the goals of the relationship will be achieved.

There are two important criticisms of this approach that need to be mentioned. First, this perspective has a difficult time with the concept of altruism. Altruism reflects the idea that sometimes people seem to act (protect a child, for example) without calculating the cost/reward ratio. A perpetual discussion by those who write about social exchange ideas is the struggle to explain behavior that seems to not be "rational" or in other words behavior that seemingly does not result from a cost/reward calculation.

Feminist writers have focused on this notion to show that this approach undervalues the contribution women make in relationships. For example, Sabatelli and Shehan (1992, p. 396) suggest that social exchange theory does not do a good job of considering the part played by family members whose mission in the family may be to create solidarity as the expense of individual gain. This is really an extension of the problem that social exchange theory has explaining seemingly selfless acts of contribution. That leads us to a brief discussion of the notion of tautology.

The concept of tautology is the label given to reasoning that is circular and there is no way of proving your assertion (Klein & White, 1996). In the case of social exchange theory, every aspect of the theory assumes that people act only when a reward is forthcoming (or to avoid cost). Therefore, it is impossible to find examples of someone doing something that is not rewarding (according this theory). Scholars frequently bemoan this type of tautological thinking because it does not seem to be very helpful in understanding more complicated human interaction. In other words, it does help us to simply know that a "reward is something that is rewarding."

Family as an entity.   Another difficulty with this approach is the idea that many family scientists are becoming more interested in studying the family as an entity. That means we want to see the family as a whole unit rather than trying to imagine all of the calculations that apparently occur in each family member's mind. Social exchange theorists have only recently begun to talk about how this theory can move from only describing the behavior of individuals to describing the complex behavior of several people in a closely knitted group like a family.

Like all theories, this one falls short of explaining everything we wish it would in family life. However, there are some aspects of family life that are easily explained and understood, understanding the language of social exchanges. For example, I will suggest later in this chapter that families, like individuals, have goals and do maximize resources to attain those goals. The language for that construct comes from social exchange theory and it suggests that a unit, like a family, moves forward with a belief about what they would like to accomplish and, for the most part, they do not deliberately set out to fail.

CONFLICT THEORY AND FAMILY SCIENCE

The primary essence of this theoretical approach is to answer one central question: "As family members come and go, age and change, how is order achieved in such seemingly complicated and chaotic situations." The question of obtaining order out of chaos is one that has been asked for several hundred years (cf. Hobbs, 1651/1947). At first glance, one might think that conflict theory is simply about why people argue and fight.

That is too simple and does not capture the intent of this theoretical perspective. Instead, conflict theory is the struggle that we all have (in and out of family groups) to survive. This theory suggests that there is a natural state that humans live in that is rather unruly, nasty, and carnal. All men and women are in a collision with each other because in life resources are scarce (e.g., money, time, space, etc.) and each person wants to not only survive but feels an inner push to compete for those resources and have the freedom to choose a personal direction. One person may want to buy a new car and the other wants to keep the old car and use the extra money to pay off debts.

A key idea in understanding conflict theory comes to us from German philosophers such as Friedrich Hegel who viewed the human condition as one of struggle. He suggested that while each of us is primarily self-interested (as in the exchange perspective from above), the process of struggling was a good thing. He did not say that fighting or having wars was an effective strategy. However, when we try to solve life's difficult problems (like how to spend family income, who should sleep in what room, or who should do the dishes) and a family member suggests who should do the dishes, the resulting exchange can either build strength in the family system or it can tear it down. If prolonged conflict ensues and the balance of power is uneven, then families will be less likely to meet their goals. When families struggle together and are successful at reaching a consensus then they become stronger.

This process idea has the following elements. First is the original idea and we call this the thesis ("Sandra, I would like you to do the dishes tonight"). The thesis or original idea always comes attached to the other side of the coin, the antithesis. The anti-thesis or antithesis is the opposite point of view in which someone says, "No, I don't think so, it is your turn to do the dishes"; or "I think it would be better if we spent the tax refund on tires for the car"; or "Our apartment is not as big as you would like, you will have to share your room with your younger brother." In this way a dialogue or dialectic emerges, or in other words, a struggle. And when members of a family group (in our case for this text) struggle together and do make decisions that consider both the thesis and antithesis, the hope is a synthesis will emerge. When a synthesis occurs, it assumed that this creates strength and the family is more effective. When there is no synthesis or consensus and agreement, the family is weakened and is less likely to meet their goals.

ACTIVITY 2.1 - FIND AN ARTICLE AND REPORT ON THE THEORY

Step 1. Go to the library and find an article about family life. This article can be from current popular periodicals (e.g., Psychology Today) or from professional publications (Family Relations or Journal of Family Issues).

Step 2. Read the article and report here on the main points presented in the article.

Step 3. Find the theoretical approach that best fits the information in this article. Tell briefly what that theory is and then tell how those in your article seem to be using this theoretical approach. It may be that more than one theory is presented. If you cannot tell what theory is being used, carefully describe what you assumptions you think the authors are making about family life.

Scarce resources.   At the core of this theoretical idea is the notion of scarce resources (Klein & White, 1996; Sprey, 1979). Resources are more than just money, however (Klein & White, 1996). Resources can be problem solving skills, talents, abilities, or even the ability to control or authority in a family. This theory also indicates that in most cases conflict is inevitable. That is, there is almost always an imbalance of resources or power in family relationships, and therefore conflict emerges.

The first principle, therefore, of conflict theory is the inequity principle and it states:

PRINCIPLE 2.9: INEQUITY CREATES CONFLICT

Conflict arises in families when resources are not evenly distributed. And, they are almost never equitably distributed.

Many of the constructs and ideas that emerge from this perspective are used to describe how larger groups of people struggle together (e.g., a labor union and factory) to resolve their conflicts. However, in terms of the family, there is one more idea from this perspective that needs to be restated from above. This is the idea of struggle and synthesis. It is assumed that all families struggle as they allocate resources. Those families who are better able to meet their goals are ones who share resources more equitably and are better able to experience true consensus and synthesis rather than prolonged conflict when allocating family resources.

Some constructs from conflict theory will be used in later chapters. In particular, we will refer to these ideas when we examine in the chapter on communication.

PRINCIPLE 2.10: FAMILIES STRUGGLE WITH RESOURCE ALLOCATION

It is assumed that all families struggle as they allocate resources. Those families who are better able to meet their goals are ones who share resources more equitably and are better able to experience true consensus and synthesis rather than prolonged conflict when allocating family resources.

It is also important to note that from this intellectual tradition has emerged a strong gender oriented feminist critique of family life. In this view, social historians, family scientists, and feminist writers illuminate the idea that men have traditionally controlled most of the tangible resources and have typically had more power in family life. Therefore, when the power is unbalanced and the resources not distributed equally, families are not as effective. This imbalance ensures the privilege of some (usually the males) in the family at the expense of others. This issue will be more fully addressed in Chapter 4 on Gender in Family Life.

SYMBOLIC INTERACTION THEORY

Symbolic Interaction Theory is also a widely used perspective in family science. Originally, those writing from this perspective were describing individual psychological processes about how individuals place meaning on the events that happening to them. For example, when a researcher uses this perspective he or she may ask someone why they got a divorce or inquire about who is responsible for the financial decisions in a family. Researchers who begin with these types of questions want to know "what the family member thinks about the specific event being asked"? In other words, what does it mean or symbolize and how does the meaning or interpretation of their view of what happened effect how they reacted. The assumption is made that the meaning we bring to the situation has a significant impact on the decisions we make and the ways we interact with other people

Symbols. For example, when we ask an Irishman what the word "da" (the common Irish word for father) means to him, he may have a complicated and involved response that includes elements of his biological father, someone who was supportive and involved, and/or a strict authority figure. The symbol "da" represents a very complicated collection of feelings, thoughts, and ideas. These ideas may be tied to his own experience with his own da, images he has collected from movies, books, and television, and even from watching other fathers interact with children. In terms of a family science application, scholars have for many years been asking family members what certain aspects of family life mean to them. A basic principle that we use when we search for the meanings family members place on the events, outcomes, and activities they experience is the idea of perception as reality. Family members define the activities, behaviors, and outcomes of family interactions. And, the way they define those activities, behaviors, and outcomes is real for them. In other words, one's perception of an event is that person's reality and the perception has the power to contribute to consequences and outcomes.

In several places throughout our text, we will explore the above idea and show how our perceptions and definitions of events and activities in family life become expectations and goals that direct what we do and how we evaluated family life. For example, sometimes how we act or perform in family settings does not match our expectations nor the expectations of others. Consequently, we feel less satisfied with how we are doing with that particular family role.

Roles. An important concept in symbolic interaction theory has been the development of the idea that each family member adopts and "plays" certain roles within the family. For example, a very important topic in the study of family life

JOURNAL OF THOUGHTS 2.3: HOW ABOUT THAT CONFLICT THEORY?

1. In the space below, tell the difference between arguing and fighting and how your author has described conflict theory.

2.   How is this theory useful?

focuses on father involvement. Some family scientists approach this topic by asking first "what are the roles that fathers are expected to perform in families in the U.S." Some have suggested that the most common response to this question is that fathers are providers, protectors, nurturers, and that these larger ideas form to construct a father's identity as he evaluates his performance within that particular role (Marsiglio, Amato, Day, & Lamb, 2000).

Another example of how this theory can be used is found in Chapter 11. When we study families experiencing crises, we often want to know how they define the event. Even the death of a family member could have several different meanings to different family members. It becomes critical in studying family life to know how each person is affected by life's events, how events are defined generally by the family (as an entity) and how a family is generally affected by the struggles and challenges of life.

Our perception about our role performance in family life influences not only how we feel about our family experience but it is important to note how much consensus there is among family members about the collected idea about how a role is performed (Burr, Leigh, Day, & Constantine, 1979). This is a good example of a family level idea that is used in the symbolic interaction tradition. Let's return to our father involvement research.

One example of a research study that could be done would be to find out how all family members (a multi-perspective research approach) felt about the what was expected of the father in a family. The following principle would suggest that when family members have more agreement about what a father should do in his father role, there would be less strain on all family members as he performs that role. One of the problems with the changing nature of family life is that many of the roles we have assigned to us (or we choose voluntarily) are changing rapidly.

A young father may not have a clear idea of what he should be doing as a father because the people around him (i.e., family and community members) do not have much consensus about what it is he should do in that part of his life. Therefore, this theory would suggest that as a young father enters the fathering role (let's say at the birth of a child) he might feel anxiety and strain as he considers what he should do.

In roles where there is high consensus about what a person should do in the role, we would expect that the person would have much less anxiety as he/she takes on that new role.

PRINCIPLE 2.11: CONSENSUS DECREASES STRAIN

They more consensus family and community members have about what should occur in a family role, the less strain a family member will have as they enter and perform that role.

Chapter 2

In summary, symbolic interaction theory helps us understand that humans are thinking, choosing, and deliberate creatures. We humans place meaning on what we see and the events that impact us. Those who study families using this perspective pay attention to those meanings that family members hold. Additionally, family scientists attend to the roles performed in family life and the ease of adopting and/or exiting a role (e.g., becoming a parent, losing one's parent, changing partners, gaining a partner).

The View of Family Life Used in This Text

All of the theories examined above can be used to describe and understand family life. From rational-exchange theories we learn that individuals and groups of people (such as families) have a goal of maximizing self-interest. Within that idea, we expect families and family members to rise above individual interest and contribute to the well-being of the group. This is difficult for many and is a constant struggle for some.

We also note that family members and families change over time. This added complexity adds rich variety to family life as children get older and eventually leave the nest. Relationships change and effective families are ones who figure out how to adapt to a changing and chaotic world. But regardless of the changes, families (as entities) try to do the best they can (for the most part) and they make the best decisions they collectively can. It is my position that most families try to succeed and very few (only in excessively troubling situations) set out to fail. Families work each day at trying to find the best way to allocate the scarce resources they have in ways that meet the deeply held goals and ideologies they subscribe to.

Additionally, family life can be thought of in terms of a system. The interactions that occur within that are pattern-like and can be studied. The individuals within the family system are symbol-making, thinking individuals who bring personal meaning and definition to the world in which they live. It is critical to consider the ways in which family members view the family experience they create. As these individuals inevitably struggle together and make daily decisions about how to solves life's daily problems, they either learn how to reach consensus and equity or they are unskilled in this attempt and long-term conflict erodes their ability to make decisions effectively. The task for each day is to find ways of rising above selfishness and conflict and create effective family units that turn chaos into productivity and success.

It is quite clear that some families seemed to be very skilled at accomplishing this feat, while others struggle and even fail at this daunting task. As you read the following chapters about family processes and daily life, you will begin to form a position statement about family life. It is your task at the conclusion of this chapter to

JOURNAL OF THOUGHTS 2.4: COMPARE THE THEORIES

1. Which of the theories presented best represents how you think of the world?

2. Maybe you are attracted to pieces of several of those ideas. Which idea do you like and why?

begin writing some of your ideas down about how families can better succeed at the difficult task of family life. Activity 2.1 is designed to assist you in thinking about your view of family life and how that view was formed.

Chapter 2

STUDY QUESTIONS

1. What do we mean by the idea of reductionism?

2. What is a theory and why do we care about them in the family science?

3. Explain what is meant by equilibrium in a family system?

4. What is a "family system?"

5. Give an example of equifinality and tell how this idea can work in family life.

6. Look up the word entity and see how this term can be applied to a family.

7. What the difference between a thesis and an antithesis?

8. Why is the idea of roles so important in the study of the family?

KEY TERMS

Reductionism
Entity
Roles
Families and goals
Equilibrium
Morphostasis and morphogenesis
Boundaries
Subsystems
Equifinality
Resources
Thesis, antithesis, synthesis
Symbolic interaction
Conflict theory
Development

PART II

Foundational Family
Processes

CHAPTER THREE

Individuals in Families:
Biosocial Beginnings,
Gender, and Personality

Chapter Three

Main Points:

1. Much of who we are is a biologically inherited.

2. Additionally, several general family issues seem to be influenced by bio-social factors.

3. Certain hormones influence family development across the life span. The areas influenced include: early child development, parenthood, mate selection, and relationship quality and stability.

4. Gender matters: men and women bring differences to family life.

5. Gender differences can create power differences that influence family life.

6. Individuals bring personality traits into new relationships.

7. Personality traits can influence relationship stability, how we solve problems with our partners, and how we organize family life.

Individuals in Families: Biosocial Beginnings, Gender, and Personality

INTRODUCTION

A glance at family texts published even a few years ago would reveal a startling discovery: Biology was completely ignored as a feature of family life. More recently, there has been a significant shift in the family scientists' thinking about the role of biology as a feature of who we are, what decisions we make, and how we conduct family life. Until recently, most family scientists operated on the assumption that adults were primarily rational and social. It was assumed that most of the time, when a decision was made (or not made), it was because the family group got together, struggled, and came up with some type of conclusion based on how family members felt about the dilemma, cultural norms, family rules, expectations, and other social factors.

In recent years, however, family scientists have begun to explore the links among family behaviors (e.g., choice of mate, decision to parent, parenting style, sexual activity, and even divorce) and the hundreds of chemical (i.e., hormonal) and genetic messages that travel through our circulatory and nervous systems.

Hormones.   Hormones are powerful chemicals that regulate body functions and influence how we think. Additionally, they interact with the genetic messages found deep within our cells. We can no longer ignore these powerful messages as part of the study of family science.

In the next few pages, a few basic ideas about how genes and hormones influence family life will be discussed. A main point of this chapter is that genes, hormones, and our immediate environments work together to help shape who we are and the decisions we make. Keep in mind that the research presented in this section is relatively new. Advances are being made daily and so it is likely that some of the findings reported may be out of date before this text is even published.

The basics.   The endocrine system, an essential part of the human body, comprises various glands (e.g., thalamus, hypothalamus, thyroid, pituitary, and adrenal).

These and other glands produce hormones that send messages to other glands, to organs, and to the brain. Hormones regulate body functions, trigger other hormones, and stimulate a variety of inner responses including both physical responses to our environment and mental responses, or thoughts.

Some of the more common hormones that are mentioned in family science research are testosterone, dehydroephiandrosterone (DHEA), oxytocin, estradiol, and cortisol. Testosterone occurs in both men and women, but men produce about twice as much of it as women do. Men produce testosterone in the testes and adrenal glands. In women, the ovaries and adrenal glands secrete testosterone. Higher levels of testosterone are linked to some important personal characteristics of men. These include how men participate in competitive activities, which seem to be linked to gaining, maintaining, or losing social status (Booth, Carver, & Granger, 2000; Mazur & Booth, 1998).

DHEA is produced by the adrenal gland. Its primary function is to stimulate other glands that, in turn, produce other hormones. However, the production of DHEA has been linked to such important family issues as alcohol use, smoking, and higher levels of emotionality (Booth, Carver, & Granger, 2000).

Oxytocin is an excellent example of a hormone that may directly influence parent–child interaction. One study found that varying levels of oxytocin were linked to childbirth (timing and response by mother) and to lactation in women. Additionally, these researchers showed that there may be a link between oxytocin, the prompting to lactate, and eventual quality of interaction between mothers and their newborn babies (Turner, Altemus, Enos, Cooper, & McGuinness, 1999).

Estradiol is found primarily in women. In one study of levels of estradiol in younger women, it was found that this hormone seemed to be directly linked to sociability. That is, women with higher levels of estradiol were more likely to seek out other women (and men) as confidantes and were more likely to build stronger affiliations with others (Fleming, Ruble, Krieger, & Wong, 1997).

Cortisol is a very interesting hormone found in abundance in both men and women. This key stimulator regulates heart rate and other features of personal metabolism. It is linked to memory and other human survival mechanisms such as the "fight-flight" response. When we perceive danger, for example, the endocrine system produces higher levels of cortisol, which then prompts us to run or to stand and fight. As will be seen below, cortisol levels in men and women can have a significant and direct influence on how people respond to family crisis and decision-making situations.

Genetics. One of the fastest growing fields of scientific study is the work being done on our genetic foundation. Deep within each human cell is the DNA that contains the entire code for the growth and development of a person. There is incredible variation with the human species. People differ in hair color, size of fingers, and how well their eyes focus on distant objects. There are a host of visible traits that define who we are. There is also a staggering array of difference among the unseen

traits. These include blood types, how effectively our immune systems operate, mental abilities, and personality traits. Our genes even play a role in inheritance and predispositions to some physical and psychopathologies.

It is important to note that our genetic heritage rarely determines what we will become. Instead, our genes push or influence us in certain directions. Likewise, the environments in which we are raised (e.g., single-parent home, rural farming community, or inner city) do not determine who we are. Our genetic heritage and our environments, including our parents and where we grew up, and other situations contribute to who we are. Additionally, we make choices that may be quite independent of (albeit greatly influenced by) our genetic, familial, and community profiles. Social scientists have struggled for decades with the important philosophical question that asks how much each of these influences matter.

In the mid-twentieth century, many psychologists decided that the genetic world was of little importance, and that the individual was shaped and fashioned by his or her surroundings and the people with whom he or she came in contact. Today, many researchers and educators are paying more attention to the genetic messages in each individual, the hormonal responses that are, in part, triggered by genetic profile. Of course we also believe that one's environment is a crucial aspect of the puzzle. However, many social scientists are paying more attention to the inner biological person than ever before.

Human Genome Project.   The National Institutes of Health have funded the Human Genome Project. This project has a yearly budget of $3 billion. Scientists from every country are feverishly mapping human DNA in search for genetic codes that may promote cancer, heart disease, cystic fibrosis, antisocial behavior, and a host of other human problems (Committee on Science, 2001).

The study of *behavioral genetics* (Booth, Carver, & Granger, 2000) studies genetic influence on individual behavior vis-à-vis environmental influence. In a classic example of this type of research, a well-known family scientist examined antisocial behavior in twins (Reiss, 1995). It was discovered that identical twins (who share 100% of their DNA code) were similar in their antisocial scores (.81 correlation) while fraternal twins (who only share 50% of their DNA code) were not quite as similar (.61 correlation). Using this relatively simple kind of research we can take a closer look at the influence of genetics and how it relates to environmental influence. Using a simple statistical procedure in this study, Reiss reasoned that about 60% of the influence to be antisocial (for these twins in this study) came from their genes, while only 40% came from these children's close environments.

Other studies using similar approaches have examined such things as intelligence, memory ability, impulse control, and risk-taking behavior (for further reading in this area see Booth, Carver, & Granger, 2000; Reiss, 1995; Plomin, 1995; and Rowe, 1994).

Sample research.   In this section, a few interesting research studies are highlighted to show the kinds of human/family interaction that may be tied to genetic and hormonal influences.

Cashdan (1995) studied how women respond to sexual decisions presented to them based on their levels of testosterone (which are a result of genetics). It was found that women with higher levels of testosterone (who were consequently more dominant in relationships) were less likely to "need a partner," less likely to be selective in choosing a partner, and were generally more sexually active. On the other hand, women with decreased testosterone levels were more selective in choosing mates and more likely to be purposeful in their partner selection activities. For example, they paid more attention to grooming and dressing in ways that would attract men. Cashdan concluded that women with lower levels of testosterone organized dating and mate selection around activities that would assure their male partners that the women's offspring were also the partner's offspring.

In the same vein, testosterone levels seem to be associated with other family-related activities. Udry, Morris, and Kovenock (1995) found that women who had higher testosterone levels were more likely to display nontraditional family behaviors. These nontraditional behaviors included such things as not caring about getting married, how many children they wanted, and how much they enjoyed playing with or being around children.

Following the birth of a child, hormone levels in women (who experience higher hormone levels during pregnancy) return to normal levels. Fleming, Ruble, Kreiger, and Wong (1997) found that women who had increased levels of estradiol (which triggers oxytocin production) were calmer and attended to their babies more.

SPOTLIGHT ON RESEARCH 3.1: PERSONALITY AND MARITAL ADJUSTMENT. DOES YOUR PERSONALITY PREDICT HOW WELL YOUR LONG-TERM RELATIONSHIP WILL TURN OUT?

Bochard, Lussier, and Sabourn (1999) studied the personalities and marital well-being of 446 couples. These were French Canadian heterosexual couples who had been living together for about 9 years on average. About one-half were living together and the other one-half were married. They had just over one child on average per couple. They wanted to know the answer to seven basic questions: First, overall, do one's personality traits predict marital adjustment? Second, do one's personality traits predict how your partner rates the adjustment of your relationship? Three, is it true that if a person reports a highly neurotic personality trait, that the marital adjustment score would drop? Four, does being an extrovert in some way boost your marital adjustment score? Five, how important is the personality trait of openness to marital adjustment? Six, how important is agreeableness to the adjustment of couples? And last, are partners who are more conscientious (as a personality trait) more likely to have better adjusted marriages?

These researchers found that, indeed, personality mattered in marital relationships for both men and women. One of their key findings that in order to study the question of personality and marriage adjustment it was critical to study the personalities of both partners. Here are some of their findings:

1. These women scored higher on neuroticism and openness than did their partners.
2. Women were scored lower on the over measure of how adjusted they thought their marriage was.
3. Women who scored higher on the neuroticism scale also scored significantly lower on the marital adjustment scale. People who score higher on the neurotic scale may be chronically subjected to negative emotions. When any partner has a high neurotic score, it is likely that the relationship will suffer.
4. The only other trait that had meaning in these researchers analyses was the degree to which women reported being agreeable. Women high in agreeableness also scored higher on the marital adjustment scale. Perhaps a spouse with a higher agreeableness score would be more likely to seek consensus during times of disagreement.
5. Like the women, men who were neurotic were much more likely to report lower marital satisfaction scores.

6. Unlike the women, however, the other three of the four primary personality traits (openness, agreeableness, and conscientiousness) strongly predict marital adjustment. Simply, men who are neurotic were not very martially adjusted. Men who were agreeable, open, and conscientious were much more likely to report higher levels of adjustment.

7. Finally, these researchers found that the personality of one partner had a powerful effect on the level of adjustment reported by the other. This study supports the idea that marriage partners do influence each other help shape the daily life climate of family life.

This pattern of hormonal secretion (again, triggered by genetic predispositions) may be linked to how mothers feel when breast-feeding. Think systemically here. Breast-feeding increases important hormone production; the hormones create a sense of calm and attention to the child. That, in turn, increases the skin contact, which results in more hormone secretion. Researchers are beginning to look much more carefully at the bonds created in parenting in connection with hormonal secretion related to interaction with the new baby.

Uvnas-Mosberg, Widstrom, Nissen, and Bjorvell (1990) found a similar pattern in men. Following the birth of a child, men experienced a drop in testosterone, which seemed to promote more caring and nurturing behavior.

In another fascinating study, it was found that children who experience higher levels of family conflict, quarrels, and fighting had elevated cortisol levels (Flynn & England, 1995). In turn, higher levels of cortisol in children can lead to more sibling fighting, more incidences of social withdrawal, antisocial behavior, increased social anxiety, and decreased impulse control (Granger, Weisz, & Kauneckis, 1994). In other words, family environment mixed with genetic propensities for hormonal production of cortisol can lead to less than desirable results.

For many years, family scientists have pleaded with parents to decrease the levels of contention, spanking, fighting, and hostile behavior in families. Only recently have scientists begun to discover the biological mechanisms that figure in these important equations.

Our genetic profile and hormonal configuration may play a significant role in mate selection. Let's assume for a minute that deep within the genetic codes of our existence we, as humans, want to survive. The genetic codes for survival may include subtle messages that scientists have just begun to understand. One study (Wedekind, Seebeck, Bettens, & Paepke, 1995) suggested that each person has a unique "immunological finger print." That is, each of us has a genetic profile made up of certain proteins found within cells that attack pathological germs and viruses. As it happens, the proteins produced by the immune system can be detected by humans in the odors associated with sweat. These odors, according to this research team, are a signal to men and women: We do not consciously categorize the odors nor do we even think about them. But according to these researchers, humans can somehow detect the presence of these odors and the smells tip us off as to who has a different immunological pattern than ours. The implication becomes apparent when two people have a child: The child is more likely to survive if it has inherited genes from two genetically diverse immune systems. When we have diversity in our immune systems, we have a greater chance of having the appropriate immune system response to a new and threatening disease.

Finally, a ten-year study done by the U.S. Air Force shows that unmarried men have much higher testosterone levels: Following marriage, the levels significantly decrease (Mazur & Michalek, 1998). Higher levels of testosterone are associated with aggression, violent behavior, and competitiveness. These researchers suggest that once men marry (and decrease their association with other males) the activities that promote higher levels of testosterone decrease and men become more nurturing, loving, and caring for their spouses.

In this section, we have suggested that a key element of who we are and how we act in social situations is tied to an interaction among genetic heritage and how our bodies respond to changes in hormone production, all within the context of close environments. The research in this arena is relatively new and exciting. Much of it, however, points to a much more complicated picture of family life than previously imagined.

OTHER ELEMENTS OF INDIVIDUALITY

There are two other elements of the individual that will be discussed in this section. In addition to the strong influences of biosocial factors, we are influenced by, first, *gender* and second, *personality*. These two features of the individual combine to influence close relationships. While one's *sex* is biologically identified, one's *gender* refers to the roles, attitudes, and beliefs one associates with being male or female. The societies in which we live influence and shape these roles that, in turn, guide how we behave as either men or women. So, the one of the connections we hope you will make in this chapter is that your biological self, your personality, and your gender guide and help define who you are. In turn, who you are plays an important role in your choice of a partner and, consequently, what type of relationship and family you create. The combination of individuals found within couples creates a profile that becomes the core of the potential family system.

GENDER IN FAMILY LIFE

The study of gender is an important key aspect of understanding family life. In the section below, this topic is introduced and several terms reviewed.

JOURNAL OF THOUGHTS 3.1: THOUGHTS ON GENES

1. In the following space write your thoughts. Think about the genetics research found in this chapter and in other places and what implications this research may have in the future. Write your initial comments below.

2.   If you could change some characteristic of who you are, what would it be? List and comment on the things below that you like about yourself (body or mind) and those you wish you could alter. Would you have these alterations done if you could? Are there any reservations you have about making those kinds of changes?

Individuals in Families

Elements of gender. To understand how our gender is formed and shaped, let's examine a few studies that illustrate the process. In Western society, female babies are usually treated more gently than are boys (Fagot & Leinbach, 1987). Children are socialized to perform in gender-appropriate ways. By appropriate, we mean whatever the parents think is appropriate. Parents usually teach their children about cultural norms and behavior similar to behavior they were taught as children, or in ways that represent certain ideologies or beliefs about the "right" way a child "should behave." For example, boys are usually more likely to be involved in active play with their parents, especially their fathers (Fagot & Leinbach, 1987; Park et al., 2001). In a fairly well-known study, the researchers brought a baby into a small group of adults (both men and women). One group was told the baby was a boy, another group was told it was girl, and the third group was not told the sex of the child. The experiment was to see if the different groups would treat the baby differently just because its sex. The group that did not know the sex of the child reported higher levels of uncertainty and frustration. They searched for clues about whether the baby was "strong" or "soft" as a way to tell its sex. Additionally, when the baby became fussy, the group who were told it was a boy labeled the baby as "angry" while the group who thought the baby was a girl thought its fussiness was "frustration" (Condry & Condry, 1976). In these simple and unnoticed ways, parents tell us when we are young what our crying means, how active we should be when we play, and how aggressively we should respond to stimulation. And they tell us different things depending upon whether we are male or female.

For the most part, parents are unaware they are treating their children in gendered ways. Additionally, recent research suggests that babies' biological-hormonal states resulting from sex characteristics may push boys and girls to act differently when stimulated. This prompts the parents to then treat the baby more like a boy (or girl) and the cycle of socialization continues (for a review of the emerging literature on biosocial influences in family life see Booth, Carver, & Granger, 2000).

The result of how our parents socialize us, how we respond, and how they respond again is that men and women often develop characteristics that are gender specific. Oakley (1985) identified several of these results. First, she suggested that children differ in what they are exposed to. Girls are far more likely to be exposed to "mothering" activities and are encouraged to become "mother's helpers." Boys, on the other hand are discouraged from such feminine pursuits. Second, Oakley found that children are channeled to gendered play activities and toys. For example, girls are given dolls and boys are given trucks. Third, we label children's activities with gendered tags. If a girl wants to play rough and tumble games she is labeled as aggressive, while a boy doing the same thing will be characterized as active. Fourth, parents often treat children in different ways from birth onward; they speak more softly to girls, tell them they are beautiful, and sooth them. Boys, on the other hand, are tossed and tickled and told to be big boys.

A father in church recently took the small fist of his young infant, made it into a ball and helped the baby pretend to punch him in the face. The child seemed delighted.

One wonders how delighted the father will be in a few years when the child does that on his own.

Research on fathers has shown that men are major players in socializing children to become gendered. In one study, Fagot and Leinbach (1987) demonstrated that men in families push boys more than girls to set high standards for achievement. Also, men seem to focus on developing emotional stability in girls, while they center on developing task completion and toughness in boys.

From these beginnings, we cooperate in the formation of who we are. Who we are is partly genetic, linked to sex characteristics, and partly taught by our families. How we respond to our gender may also be due to deeply held characteristics of our personalities.

Power and gender. In the 1960s, two prominent family scientists (Blood & Wolf, 1960) suggested that historically men in the United States were in control of families because of a long history of patriarchal control. These researchers interviewed several hundred wives and claimed to have discovered that an egalitarian style of marriage is the marriage type that was emerging in the United States. However, several other researchers pounced on Blood and Wolf's findings and suggested that there was still a great deal of inequality in relationships (see Monroe et al., 1985, for a review). Most family scientists assume that historically men had the final say in marriage and were controlling and dominating. While we are probably not as egalitarian as Blood and Wolf thought we were, we do seem to be moving significantly toward increased power for women in relationships. John Scanzoni, a well-respected sociologist, has suggested, "Husbands and wives are equal, but husbands are more equal (Scanzoni, 1988)." He has labeled this equality difference by claiming that, in U.S. society today, men are the "senior partner" in most marriages.

As was mentioned above, men and women are socialized and treated differently from birth. This differential treatment carries into adulthood and marriage. Women who work earn less than men, so men are more likely to control more the family finances (Kalmuss & Straus, 1982). Husbands usually are older and have higher levels of education. While men and women are socialized to accept different roles in relationships, there is a long-running debate about what is the ideal.

As you read the above information, keep in mind that the reason it is presented in this chapter is that the choices one makes about the above issues—marriage, employment, childrearing—should play a significant role in selecting a partner. The way you view gender and power in relationships will guide how you decide to organize your family, divide household tasks, and direct what happens during daily family life. So, take a few minutes now and fill out the worksheet labeled Activity 3.1. This worksheet asks you the following: How equal should a marriage be (specifically your marriage)? Who should do the various tasks? What should happen if the role divisions are not what you think they should be? How should the roles and responsibilities in marriage be divided? If you are a woman, do you expect to be a "junior" partner in the relationship? If you are the man, do you see your role only as provider, defender,

ACTIVITY 3.1 - ROLES IN FAMILY LIFE

Fill in the following with your answers:

1.   How equal should a marriage be (specifically your marriage)?

2. Who should do the various tasks?

3. What should happen if the role divisions are not what you think they should be?

4. How should the roles and responsibilities in marriage be divided?

5. If you are a woman, do you expect to be a "junior" partner in the relationship?

6. If you are the man, do you see your role only as provider, defender, and protector? Or, are you interested in a relationship based on equal division of providing, childcare, household tasks, and financial decision-making? (Women should respond to this question about what they expect in men.)

and protector? Or, are you interested in a relationship based on equal division of providing, childcare, household tasks, and financial decision-making? These may be some of the more important questions one asks as relationships begin.

PERSONALITY

The third theme of this chapter is that your personality and the personality of your current or future partner(s) is a key element in understanding how people select mates, how well the relationship thrives, and whether or not it will survive. Before you continue, turn to the activity marked 3.1 and fill out the questionnaire about your personality. Alternatively, you may want to access the personality assessment found in alternate Activity 3.2. Activity 3.2 is a web-based activity that provides more information about a particular way of viewing one's temperament.

Defining personality. What is your personality? What do you think of when you say that "she has a certain personality" or personality trait? Is everything about you your "personality?" Can your pet spaniel have a personality? How about your pet snake? In a study of personality and gender, Pines (1998) found that men described themselves more likely to be attracted to a woman's physical appearance, while women seem to focus more on such things as intimacy, commitment, and security. Would you say that these findings are about gender differences (something that is learned from society) or about personality differences (something much deeper that comes from the core person you are)?

When we talk about personality we are speaking of the attributes or distinctive characteristics of a person. In the case of your pet snake or even your car, it has attributes or characteristics that make it different from other pets or cars. One of the authors has a special guitar that is his long-time friend. He bought it when he was a teenager. It has special dents and scratches that make it different from other guitars and it sounds different than any other guitar he has played. It has a chunky, raw, and homey sound that generates a certain mood when he plays it. Although it is a special guitar, he probably should not get carried away and give it a persona. The guitar has attributes, but not thoughts and feelings.

So, is personality just another term for person? What is a person if not the collection of that person's special attributes? Brody and Ehrlichman (1998) define personality as "those thoughts, feelings, desires, intentions, and actions that contribute to the important aspects of individuality" (p. 3). Those collections of thoughts, feelings, desires, and actions make up who we are and form a kind of profile. Think of a dozen or more attributes on which a person could score high or low. Imagine a graph with the attributes listed along the bottom and the scores charted above. Some of the attributes might be introversion, attention to detail, cheerfulness, musical ability, and physical dexterity. Each of us has a different profile with different scores on hundreds of characteristics that make up who we are.

Chapter 3

The purpose of this part of the chapter is to explore just a few of those attributes that make up our personality. The reason we are exploring this aspect of individual psychology is that many people have wondered if the type of personality they are has anything to do with how well they get along with one another in close relationships, specifically with other family members. For example, if someone is introverted and shy, is it better for him or her to seek out a partner that is engaging, extroverted, and reaches out to others? Or, should we encourage people to seek out partners that are more like they are? Of course, two of the primary goals in family science are try and help people make better relationship choices and, once in a relationship, find ways of making those relationships stronger. By understanding the qualities, differences, and special nature of each person, we believe one can build a stronger relationship with his or her partner.

Additionally, many researchers continue to pursue the idea that who we are (i.e., our personalities) can be tied to genetic foundations. Our personalities may also be tied closely to how we are treated with regard to gender as we grow into adulthood. Families are composed of individuals and the unique profile of each individual within a family contributes to how that family solves problems, makes decisions, and organizes life.

We are not interested (at least in this chapter) about all of the attributes one brings to one's life. Most of who you are probably does not affect family life much. However, there are a few characteristics that seem to matter more than others. Additionally, we focus here on the person instead of the single attribute. Early in the study of personality (cf. Allport, 1937) researchers suggested that it was much more effective to examine the "the unique individual (as) the point of intersection of a number of quantitative variables" (Eysenck, 1952, p. 2). So, rather than study whether being shy (a quantitative single variable) influences work performance (for example), the study of personality is about how one's profile of characteristics (the collection of many attributes) collect together within each individual.

Additionally, family scientists are just beginning to ask questions about what happens when there are different types of people with different personality profiles coming together in the context of family life. We suggest the obvious: families are composed of individuals who are interesting, unique, and wonderful in their own right. The study of family life examines what happens when the individual joins with another individual to form a (relatively) permanent relationship. While the relationship is usually built on commitment and long-term goals, the ability of the relationship to survive over time lies in the individual and his or her desires, sense of obligation, and investment in that relationship. Certainly, our personalities, our genetic make-ups, and how we respond to issues of gender influence our commitment decision.

The rest of this chapter is divided into two sections. The first is an explanation of several personality traits that have a long research tradition in the field of psychology. We will explore five personality traits that seem to reappear in many differ-

JOURNAL OF THOUGHTS 3.2: THINKING ABOUT YOUR PERSONALITY

Do you like who you are? Is who you are unchangeable? Imagine that you can change some element of your personality. Provide an example below of something you think you could change about yourself that falls into the category of personality (e.g., introvert/extrovert).

How would go about changing it? Where would you begin?

Chapter 3

Why don't people change very much in their lives? What keeps them from being different even when they really want to change? Record your thoughts below.

ent forms, but that nearly everyone agrees are essential and fundamental attributes of one's personality. Second, we will make some suggestions about how to use this information in with the context of family life.

The big five: OCEAN. Several researchers and writers (cf. Brody & Erlichman, 1998; John, 1990; McCrae & Costa, 1991; Goldberg, 1990) have identified a way to access five primary attributes of human personality. These attributes have a fairly long research history and many social psychologists agree that there is good reason to pay attention to these five items. Goldberg (1990) surveyed a large number of people and administered 1,400 items to them using a test similar to the one given in Activity 3.1. His work was based on other research (Norman, 1963), which began to collect any kind of word people use to describe the personality of another. Norman looked for words like *anxious, quiet, shy*, and *creative*. Goldberg then used a statistical procedure called *factor analysis* to numerically determine how people rated themselves when they saw these words. He found that there were common threads in the ways people linked certain words together into clusters as they described themselves. As he read through the clusters of items, he labeled the themes in those groups of descriptors.

Researchers who follow the work of Goldberg and others believe that the essential aspects of personality can be captured by five global terms they call *markers*.

Openness is the first factor. This refers to how open you are to experience. People who score higher on this part of the test are thought to be more creative and imaginative; they seek variety, and are more likely to focus on intellectual and artistic pursuits. The openness described here is about openness to life's adventures. Obviously, if one is more closed to experience, one would rate one's personality as less creative and less interested in seeking the new and different aspects of one's surroundings.

Conscientiousness is the second factor. This aspect of personality describes how organized we are. Think for a moment about how much you plan daily. Do you carry a day planner? Do you have a small electronic computing device that beeps you every few minutes telling you where you should be? How thorough are you? How much do you fret over assignments and tasks that must be done? Conscientious people are organized and preplan most aspects of daily living. They usually love yellow posting notes and make lists to remind them where their lists are.

Extroversion: How out-going are you? When you go to a party, do you "work the crowd"? Extroverts need to shake everyone's hand, say a few words to every guest, and connect with larger numbers of people in every setting. At a party, they are likely to be more energized at the end of the party than at the beginning. Gatherings provide extroverts with vigor. At the end of a good party, an extrovert might take several hours to "come down" from the energy created by the experience.

On the other hand, introverts are more quiet, solemn, and restrained. If they do go to the party (and they may do anything to get out of going), they may find a

corner to sit and talk with one person, or two at most. Instead of speaking with people superficially about a number of things, they usually find one person to explore a topic in depth.

Agreeableness: If you scored high on this item, it means that you are warmhearted, trusting, and kind. It also means that others would probably rate you as compassionate. That means that you would understand the feelings of others and be empathetic. If you are lower on this scale, it may mean you are more suspicious, less trusting, and perhaps more unsympathetic to the plight of those around you. *Empathetic role taking* is an important idea here. People who score higher on this measure are more likely to feel what others feel. People with lower scores are usually focused on how they feel and not what is happening to those around them.

Neuroticism: The final trait describes how much a person sees her/himself as emotional, anxious, and high-strung. A person who is less neurotic is less emotional, even-tempered, and self-assured.

Application: Please understand me.   David Keirsey (1998) explains that one of the most important messages in the study of personality is that it provides an important mechanism by which we can become more accepting and approach relationships with greater generosity. He suggests that each of use can learn that personality traits are neither good nor bad, they are just a part of our makeup. Of course, some change is possible, and some change and refinement of habits and patterns of life are not only possible but highly desirable. But at the core level of existence, it seems that most people change little during their lives. That is, their core personality and sense of who they are changes only slightly in most cases. While we may change what we believe in, what philosophies of life we subscribe to, and even change significant patterns of daily living (such as eating and drinking patterns), the core person that we are changes very little.

Therefore, our goal in relationships is not to change our partners, but instead to understand them. Keirsey has several axioms of relationship power that flow from

ACTIVITY 3.2 - YOUR PERSONALITY AND TEMPERAMENT TYPE

This is an optional activity that will cost you extra. You can complete this in one of two ways.

1.   The first way is to go to the following website
         http://www.keirsey.com/cgi-bin/keirsey/newkts.cgi

      For $15 you can take a personality inventory that will tell you about your specific personality and how it relates to famous people with similar personality profiles as yours.

2. Second, you can purchase the book *Please Understand Me II: Temperament, Character, Intelligence* by David Keirsey. Again, this will cost you about $16 and is a more in-depth look at temperament. Once you have purchased the book, find the inventory located in the front, take it, and calculate your score.

3. When you have completed this assignment do the following:
   What are the four letters used to describe your personality in the inventory?

What does each one stand for? How extreme are you in each of the four categories?

Comment on how the inventory does or does not capture the essence of your personality/temperament.

Your response? How does it make you feel to read about yourself? What did you discover? What was a surprise?

Record any other thoughts you may have about this activity.

our understanding of personality study. First, we should not assume that our goal in a relationship is change the other person into a clone of who we are. Sometimes this requires courage and patience. Many of us become impatient with our spouses' and partners' non-conformity to how we see the world. Suppose we are an introverted person. Some people believe it is their duty to change their partner into an extrovert (because they are). They believe that the other person is defective if they do not approach life in the same way they do. Relationships are strengthened when we learn to accept the nature of others. That does not mean that we have to accept abusive behavior, irresponsibility, or violation of deeply held values. But it does mean that we recognize that each of us is a unique person whose way of approaching the world is valid and important.

Second, when we begin to think in terms of acceptance rather than change only then can we really deeply bond and develop stronger loving relationships with others. On the other hand, if our primary goal in relationships is to try and change others into copies of us, it pushes people away and alienates them.

According to Keirsey (1998), one of the more destructive relationship problems occurs when a person in a newly forming relationship takes the new partner into his or her life with idea that the new partner could be a fine match with the change of a few traits. And the person believes it is his or her job, duty, or even right to set about changing that other person. Instead, our primary job in relationships is to understand one another and discover the different ways that person sees the world and solves the problems of life.

The above ideas seem to be borne out in a research study done about our selection of marriage partners. Perhaps one of the more well-documented theories of mate-selection is the information that has been collected about assortative mating. Assortative mating is a theory that suggests that "birds of a feather flock together." In other words, when we are dating and looking for a partner we choose someone who is like we are. That is probably true when it comes to personality characteristics (Barnes & Buss, 1985; Botwin, Buss, & Shackelford, 1997; Bouchard, Lussier, & Sabourin, 1999; Blum & Mehrabian, 1999). However, it seems that women are more attuned to that idea than are men (Botwin et al., 1997). Additionally, according to findings in that study, women expressed a definite preference for men who displayed a wide variety of socially acceptable personality characteristics (such as agreeableness and emotional stability). Men, on the other hand, were satisfied with fewer of these socially desirable traits and were probably focusing more on physical attributes. In addition, two other findings were reported. First, it turned out that finding one's ideal partner (with regard to personality traits) was probably more important that finding someone with identical personality traits. That is a finding that is worth reading again. How we get along with a close companion in marriage may be directly related to whether that person matches our ideals. Interestingly, however, having a mate that does not meet your ideal later on does not dampen one's marital or sexual satisfaction. In other words, having a mate that meets or exceeds one's ideals can help but does not significantly detract. However, it did detract from marital satisfaction if one's partner was not similar to the personality of the other mate.

Second, Botwin et al. found that three specific personality characteristics were key elements in predicting future marital and sexual dissatisfaction. These were identified by a lack of agreeableness, emotional stability, and intellectual openness. This is an exciting area of research that will continue to grow in the future.

Our last example of research about personality and family life comes from the communications literature. Chapter 7 covers the area of family communication in depth. However, a study done by Geist and Gilbert (1996) illuminates how communication and personality issues can be linked. In this study, couples were asked to fill out a number of questionnaires about their personality characteristics, how much relationship hostility there was, and to comment on the type of problems they argued about. The results of this study were that personality matters a great deal in how we argue with one another and how those arguments are resolved. Husbands who were more extroverted were more likely to express anger and contempt during times of relationship difficulty. The same was true for wives. Women who were more likely to report higher scores on the neurotic aspect of the personality scale were also more likely to berate themselves and consequently their husbands. Their own feelings of inadequacy probably spilled over in how they judge and criticize those close to them. These researchers also suggest that introverted wives may have difficulty interpreting and therefore understanding the needs of their husbands. Again, this example shows that our understanding of personality and gender can assist us in knowing why people do what they do in relationships. An often-used catch phase is "first seek to understand." Relationships can be enhanced when we take that idea to heart, even though it is particularly difficult for those who have personality traits that make that task difficult.

SUMMARY

In this chapter, we have discussed three aspects of the individual that are fundamental. First, we suggested that family relationships are probably more influenced by our biological make-up than family scientists have previously thought. Second, gender orientation describes a core element of who we are and how we approach relationships and life in general. Last, it was suggested that another foundational element of human interaction is the personality each of us brings to relationships. As an application of all of these elements that make up the individual, it was suggested that relationships are stronger when we approach them from an attitude of understanding instead of a position of wanting to change others into copies of ourselves. Relationship strength is about patience, understanding, and being generous and kind. Relationships do less well when based on power inequity, attempts to control and change, or intolerance and close-mindedness.

Individuals in Families

1. Name three different hormones that could play a part in some aspect of family life as described in your text. Tell what they do and give an example of the research about these hormones.

2. Explain how it is possible that we are influenced by the odor of another person with regard to attraction and interaction.

3. What is the difference between gender and sex?

4. According to your text, what does the research say about how parents may treat different sex children differently?

5. What is personality?

6. How can the personality of individuals influence relationships in families?

7. What do we mean when we say that our goal in relationships is to understand, not change, one another?

Key Terms

Hormones
Glands
Testosterone
Oxytocin
Estadiol
Cortisol
DHEA
Genetics
Human Genome Project
Behavioral genetics
Personality
Temperament
OCEAN
Gender

CHAPTER
FOUR

*Generations in
Family Life*

Generations in Family Life

Main Points:

1. Principles about generational processes tell us that generational ties matter in family life.

2. The Generational Alliance Principle tells how it is helpful to have clearcut generational boundaries in family life.

3. The Generational Transmission Principle captures the idea that families tend to transmit their style of life to each new generation.

4. Genograms are tools that can help us understand generational processes.

5. There are several ways we can use these ideas of generations to help others and ourselves.

Generations in Family Life

INTRODUCTION

The birth of a person is a beautiful event because it creates the most valuable thing that exists. It creates a new person, a new human being. It also creates something else that in its own way is beautiful, important, and powerful. It creates generations because a birth makes someone a child, someone a parent, someone a grandparent, etc.

The main aspect of generations is that they are the links that connect parents and children, but they also include much more. They include the ties to others who are connected to the parents and children. For example, they include ties with aunts, uncles, cousins, and siblings. They also include the connections people have to the traditions, patterns, emotions, values, ways of relating, and standards that have become the heritage and life style of each family.

Generations as a basic process of family life. Generational processes are one of the basic parts of the family realm because they are part of the foundation, the bedrock, the core of what it means to be "family." Most aspects of family life are built on these processes.

Also, generational processes are unique to family life because they only occur in families. We don't have generations in schools or in neighborhoods. We don't have them in friendships. We don't have them in corporations or careers, and we don't get them from governments, laws, or social conventions. They exist only in families.

Generational processes have a significant influence on family life: They influence how we think, how we feel, what we believe, how we relate to others, what is important and unimportant to us, whether we think the world is a friendly or unfriendly place, and how we use our environment to help us learn and cope. They influence our aspirations, our values, our struggles, and our resourcefulness. They influence the attitude we have toward other people, property, deity, learning, conflict, intimacy, anger, love, hate, and life.

There are many reasons generational processes influence us so much. One reason is because some parts of them are permanent. They are fixed and inalienable. The word *inalienable* means that we cannot annul, escape, or cancel them. For example, a parent cannot decide to not be the biological parent of a child they have given birth to. Children cannot decide to have a different set of biological parents. We can make some changes in generational arrangements through legal processes such as adoption and custody, but these only change some of the generational connections. They change the legal and social relationships, but they don't change the biological, the natural, and the experiential parts; and they only partially change the mental, interpersonal, striving, heritage, lineage consciousness, and emotional parts of generational connections.

A second reason generational processes are important is because, even though some parts of these connections can be changed, it is very difficult to change them, and most of us don't: We just live with them as they are. We don't know how to change them, or it doesn't occur to us to try. We don't have the resources or will power to change them, or we don't want to pay the emotional and interpersonal price we'd have to pay to change them.

A third reason generational processes are influential is that they start making a difference at the earliest stages of our lives, at the stage when we are infants and small children, when we are so very dependent on the older generation. They also involve our deepest feelings of who we are, what we are connected to, and what is important. Also, we don't choose them. As an old saying goes . . . "we can choose our friends but not our relatives," and our connections with our relatives, unless we work very hard to change them, are extremely important.

Generational processes influence us in many different ways. One way is biologically since physical traits are inherited through genes that are passed from one generation to another. Another way is that there are emotional, intellectual, developmental, interpersonal, and experiential aspects of generational processes that influence us in many ways. This chapter focuses on these generational processes. The following principle summarizes this idea:

PRINCIPLE 4.1: GENERATIONAL PROCESSES

When generational processes are stronger, families are more likely to meet their goals.

Constructive generational processes help us have a sense of bond without bondage, closeness without being stifled, and a sense of identity. Many families have deep ideological goals about trying to create affection, love, and a sense of security in family members. It is through generational connections that these types of goals are, in part, facilitated. In addition, they also contribute to a sense of meaning and purpose in life.

James Coleman (1988, 1990) has suggested that the relationships that are inherent within systems like families actually create "capital." Think of the concept of financial capital. Having money is very important if you want to attain certain goals. In family life, the special generational connections we have with other family members

JOURNAL OF THOUGHTS 4.1: WHY IS THE CONCEPT OF GENERATIONS IMPORTANT?

1. Think of the relationship you have with any parent (or parent figure). What is that relationship like?

2. Do you have a special relationship with any other relatives?

3. Why are these relationships special (even though they may not be pleasant)?

create social capital. Social capital results from the resources created when special relationships are enhanced. When problems arise or we are simply trying to get a homework assignment done, we are more likely to survive, meet the challenge, and get the task done if social capital has been created within the relationships we create. The relationships found within family life are special because they represent the connection of people who often mean the most to us and to whom we usually have the greatest responsibility.

On the other hand, weak generational processes can be very destructive. In fact, they can destroy family relationships. For example, many forms of abuse occur in generational processes. They can interfere with mental health, ruin marriages, and interfere with the healthy development of children in many ways. Sometimes within a system like a family, there are power imbalances in which the special relationships do not form and trust is destroyed. While the abusive aspect of these situations is deplorable, the loss of social capital makes these situations even more problematic. Crises are not as likely to be dealt with effectively, homework is not as likely to get completed, and the individual is left to struggle alone without the resource of those who could be of most help.

This chapter focuses on two generational processes that can either strengthen or diminish family life. Also, this chapter describes several strategies we can use to help them be more enabling. The two processes are generational alliances and generational transmissions.

GENERATIONAL ALLIANCES

The close alliance between mother and child is then implicated as a problem factor in the substance abuse. (Bartle-Haring & Sabatelli, 1998, p. 264)

During the 1950s, an early family researcher made an important discovery. He discovered that it is helpful in family systems to have some of the alliances be within generations and not across generations.

The term alliance refers to the connections and the boundaries between subsystems in a family system. An alliance is when two or more individuals in a family become unusually close or align themselves together so they are a clique or a semiunique unit in the family. As they do this, they change the boundaries in the family system. The boundaries in a family system are the barriers between parts of a system or between the system and its environment. What people do when they create an alliance is reduce the boundaries, or make the boundaries more *permeable*, between the individuals in the alliance and increase the rigidity or closed-ness of the boundaries between them and the others in the family.

Chapter 4

One of the important and strengthening alliances in families is when parents have a clear boundary between what they do as parents and what children do while they are growing up. This means it strengthens families and creates better social capital when the parents form an alliance with each other instead of one of the parents forming an alliance with a child. In ideal situations this means the parents are a cohesive, integrated, and coordinated team. They are supportive of each other and unified in the way they relate to their children, and the boundaries between the parents are few and permeable. At the same time, there are a number of more rigid or impermeable boundaries between the parents and the children. For example, the parental alliance is "in charge" in the family, and the parents set limits and guidelines for the children. This is what we mean by the parental alliance becoming an executive subsystem in the family. This smaller system within the larger one is responsible for family functioning providing rules, rituals, disciplining, correcting, and the of teaching of children.

Cross-generational alliance. Sometimes families choose to organize in ways that are not as effective in helping them meet the goals they have in mind. For example, sometimes there are unresolved conflicts or tension between the parents and one of the parents forms an alliance or coalition with a child. If one parent is an alcoholic, for example, and has difficulty being an effective parent, the other parent may turn to a child for help in running the home, disciplining the children, solace, and companionship. A fairly frequent pattern of this is when a father is unemployed for long spells or is emotionally distant from the family and the mother creates an alliance with one of the sons by having the son be a substitute husband in a variety of ways.

These cross-generational alliances (sometimes called inter-generational alliances) place the oldest child in an awkward position because the child is, in a sense, a member of two different generations. These cross-alliances can lead to emotional and interpersonal problems for the parents, the oldest child, and sometimes for some of the other children.

The principle that is involved in these family processes is the Generational Alliance Principle:

PRINCIPLE 4.2: GENERATIONAL ALLIANCE

It is helpful in family systems to have clear-cut generational boundaries. When boudaries are clear, families are better able to meet their goals. When cross-generational alliances and coalitions exist family members find it more difficult to achieve personal and familial goals.

JOURNAL OF THOUGHTS 4.2: WHAT ALLIANCES HAVE YOU SEEN?

1. First describe what a generational alliance is.

2. Describe any such alliances you may have experienced in your family. It does not have to be you.

3. Have you seen such alliance create negative interactions in family life? Describe and comment on the examples you have seen.

4. What were (are) the effects of these alliances? Does your personal family data support the ideas in the chapter?

Generations in Family Life

Research about generational alliances. The theorizing and research in the field since the 1950s has added a great deal of evidence in support of the Generational Alliance Principle. For examples of research that highlights this idea see the work of James Framo (1970), Salvador Minuchin (1974, 1981), Jay Haley (1976, 1987), and Murray Bowen (Kerr & Bowen, 1988). More recently Baydar and Brooks-Gunn (1998) examined data from a large national data set called the National Survey of Family and Households (NSHF). In their study, they wanted to know about the positive side of generational alliances with regard to grandmothers. As the welfare reforms of the 1990s began to take effect in every state, it was projected that there would be increased numbers of low income mothers to become employed (Baydar & Brooks-Gunn, 1998, p. 392). One of the primary emphases of the welfare-to-work legislation is that there are limits on the amount of money and number months a family can receive assistance (Cherlin, 1999). Therefore, researchers expected that grandmothers would take a more active role in caring for children, creating increased generational alliance between children and grandparents.

In the Baydar and Brooks-Gunn study of 13,000 families across the U.S. it was found that grandmothers play a significant role in raising children, are not detaching and are not as disengaged as some have believed. This was particularly true of lower income families in higher poverty situations who need less expensive child care. These researchers found that many grandmothers are involved in the daily lives of their grandchildren, act as parents, and have a true cross-generational alliance. In fact, it was found that 43% of the families in the study had a grandmother who was involved in caring for the family's children on a regular basis (Baydar & Brooks-Gunn, 1998).

While the above study did not explore the dynamics of how cross-generational alliances actually work in these families, it would seem that families would be stronger if there were some mechanism to change who is in charge. In other words, some families may be able to successfully cope with cross-generational alliances of this type if, when the mother or father returns home, the grandmother perceives her "shift" as being over and turns the parenting responsibility back to the parent(s). On the other hand, a less desirable example of cross-generational alliance would be that the parents come home and the grandparent wants to remain in charge of the children, compete with parents for control, and confuse everyone about who is in charge.

The cross-generational alliance principle is also used frequently in therapy settings. One example of how this principle is used is the way Mara Selvini Palazzoli and her co-workers in Italy use it (Palazzoli et al., 1989). They work with families who have anorectic and psychotic problems, and the first part of their treatment program is to try to strengthen the parental alliance. They have developed a number of ingenious strategies to increase the cohesion between the parents and increase the status and influences of the parents in the home. They have the parents keep secrets from the children, have the parents go on unannounced excursions, and exclude the "problem" child from the therapy sessions, and do many other things to help families strengthen the parental alliance. They have found that this strategy helps the families cope with their challenges much more effectively.

Early teen pregnancy is another topic that remains high on the list of public policy issues. How would the Generational Alliance Principle play a role in helping us understand this issue? In many cases, the non-married young woman who has an unanticipated baby often lives with her parents (or with her mother only in many cases). Kalil (2002) conducted a study in which they wanted to know if after an expected child was born to a young mother (and she lived with her mother and/or father) would the interference and/or assistance from the parents increase the chance that the young mother would become depressed. Again, the researchers speculated that this type of living arrangement would increase significantly with the implementation of the new welfare system. Young mothers would not receive as much government support and, therefore, would not be as likely to live on their own. So, they live with parents creating the potential for a cross-generational alliance situation. In this study it was discovered that having a mother in the household with the new mother was not something that contributed to the young mother experiencing more depressive symptoms. What did create more symptoms was the climate within the home. That is, when there was more conflict about child rearing, finances, and child care issues the depression in the young women significantly increased.

One can easily see the picture. The young mother is caught in the middle of an important life transition; is she the mother or is she a child? The parents are probably trying to help her spend money more wisely and help her to see better ways to take care of the new baby. She may see these attempts at help as intrusive especially when the parents create conflict over the money and care issues. The boundaries of generations become blurred and when that is combined with conflict, trouble is sure to result.

While family science researchers have begun to examine the effects of generational problems and strengths, there is much more that researchers still need to discover about this principle. For example, we don't know yet whether it is more helpful in some kinds of families than others. For example, we suspect that it is more important when families are raising children and less important in the relationships between adult generations. Additionally, we know little about situations in which a cross-generational alliance may actually be essential as the family tries to survive the loss of a parent.

Generations in Family Life

Generational transmission. Scholars in a number of different disciplines have researched the process of generational transmission in recent years. Generational transmission is the process of transmitting from one generation to the next such things as ways of behaving, ways of feeling, ways of relating, ways of defining reality, and ways of coping with intimacy and distance. The main principle the researchers have developed is the Generational Transmission Principle:

PRINCIPLE 4.3: GENERATIONAL TRANSMISSION

Families tend to pass on ideals, beliefs and paradigms to the next generation.

Families tend to transmit some ideals more readily than others. For example, researchers have found that there is more generational transmission with regard to ways of loving and maintaining intimate relationships than such things as political ideas, careers, leisure interests, and social class behavior (Troll & Bengston, 1979; Klonsky & Bengston, 1996; Stenberg, 2000).

Also, Peter Steinglass and his colleagues (1987) have done years' worth of research on families where alcohol abuse is found. He found that negative family attributes (such as alcohol abuse) are more likely to be transmitted when behaviors are a part of family rituals. Somehow the power of the ritual and special feeling of the moment can have great influence in transmitting a variety of family values, including some that may be destructive.

One aspect of the above principle is that it reinforces the idea that family life is "the best of times and the worst of times." For example, when families have patterns of relating in kind, loving, empathic, intimate, understanding, and facilitating ways, these patterns are passed on to new generations of children. When families interact harmoniously with each other and cope with life's challenges in helpful, creative, and humane ways, these patterns are passed from parents to children and it helps the children become well rounded, creative, constructive, resourceful people who can accomplish their goals and establish and maintain intimate, beautiful, peaceful, loving, harmonious relationships with others.

Unfortunately, the "worst of times" part of generational transmission is also very real, and it has so much effect in our society that we cannot escape it. When families have traditions of unwholesome, harmful, abusive, and unfortunate patterns, these too are passed from parents to children. The worst forms of human abuse, exploitation, discrimination, prejudice, hate, vengeance, and animosity occur in families, and frequently they too are passed from one generation to the next.

Ironically, the privacy that is so important for the positive and constructive dimensions of human growth, intimacy, and wholesome bonds also tend to allow, protect, hide, and preserve the heinous parts. The fact that most of what happens in families is "behind closed doors," is in the privacy of the home, is in the hidden part of the iceberg means that the unfortunate parts of the human experience can be perpetuated in ways that are fairly invisible to outside observers.

Research about generational transmission. Most researchers who write about how generational transmission influences the quality of marriage have focused on how problems such as divorce and pathology are transmitted. However, we should realize that the processes are the same for healthy, constructive, and desirable aspects of marriage. Thus, since we can assume the principle is valid, we can assume that patterns of effective communication, ways of coping with differences, and methods of handling anger are also transmitted. Patterns of loving, caring, being close, creating bonds and meeting the challenges of life in a supportive and helpful way are also transmitted across generations.

Intergenerational welfare recipiency. One of the more studied topics in family science is how poverty and welfare use is transmitted across generations from parent to child. This topic has also been the subject of many prominent literary figures such as Charles Dickens and William Faulkner. They usually describe poverty as couched in a world of shame and misery. Sociologists (cf. Stenberg, 2000; Duncan, Hill, & Hoffman, 1988; McLanahan & Bumpass, 1988) have been very interested in the transmission of poverty from one generation to the next. According to Stenberg (2000) there are three main theories used to explain why poverty seems to always be with us. First, some suggest that welfare damages one's self-reliance and weakens people's ambitions (Seccombe, 1999). Others suggest that when someone is in poverty there are fewer sources of human capital for a child to draw upon and he/she cannot connect to right people. It then becomes difficult to pull one's self out of a poor situation. The third idea is that of rational choice. That is, the welfare system itself gives people incentives to not want to do anything differently (Seccombe, 2000).

One would assume that if there are strong intergenerational aspects to the transmission of poverty, the policies in effect would not have as great an effect as would the training or ideology prevalent in a family. Stenberg (2000) conducted an in-depth study of families in poverty and receiving assistance in Sweden. He found that even when he took several important factors into account (such as race, or type of community, or advantages) there was still a strong intergenerational transmission of receiving welfare. He states, "This study indicates that the intergenerational inheritance of welfare appears to be driven by an interaction between poverty and other social and personal problems. It is not a result of a particular social policy" (Stenberg, 2000). I often hear from people who believe that welfare causes more welfare. Based on the above study, one would have to look to other explanations about how one generation transmits this behavior to another.

Abusive and nonabusive behaviors. The presence and absence of abusive behavior is a second area where research has documented that human behavior tends

JOURNAL OF THOUGHTS 4.3: WHAT DO YOU BELIEVE ABOUT WELFARE?

In the following two pages, write about your views, biases, and feelings about receiving help from the government.

1. First, list 20 words that first come to mind when you hear the word welfare.

2. Have you known anyone who has taken government assistance? This would include housing assistance, food stamps, AFDC, TAN-F, community action assistance, etc.

3.   Do the people you know personally match up to the word descriptors you listed in the first part of the assignment? Why or why not? What are your biases (and we all have them) about welfare recipients?

4.   It is an established fact that people who were raised in families in which government assistance was received are more likely to get it themselves. Why is that? What is your theory about how that happens?

to be repeated generation after generation in families. For example, the best predictor social scientists have been able to identify about whether someone will be physically abusive is whether abusive behaviors occurred in their parental home (Milner & Wimberly, 1980; Pagelow, 1984). Also, the rates of sexual abuse in the general population are difficult to identify, but a number of research studies suggest that sexual abusers have been abused more than non-abusers (Pagelow, 1984). This suggests that generational transmission is probably an important factor in the perpetuation of physical and sexual abuse.

There is a cautionary note that must be sounded here. Johnson and Ferraro (2000) have suggested that it is unfair to suggest that the cycle of violence is inescapable. Often, in texts and in research reports, we read how violent behavior is passed from one generation to the other. This leaves the reader with the idea it is an ironclad finding and that no one who was the victim of violence can escape it. Actually, the studies on the transmission of violence from parents to children is sometimes weak and not very convincing (cf. Johnson & Ferraro, 2000 for a review). Most researchers freely admit it happens and is a problem to which we should attend. However, even the most generous estimates of this phenomenon (Straus, Gelles, & Steinmetz, 1988) suggest that about 20% of the sons of violent parents in turn are violent to their own spouses and children. That means that 80% are not. Additionally, in this nationally renown survey of violence, we really don't know much about what the 20% do that labeled them as violent.

Substance abuse. Substance abuse also is a serious problem. One form, the abuse of alcohol, has also been studied extensively, and again, the data suggest the intergenerational factor is very important. Michael Elkin's experience illustrates this process.

> *Of the more than one hundred families in whose treatment I participated, nearly all turned out to have at least one person who suffered from alcoholism. Some of these parents were out of the home and some were recovering, but the correlation between teenage drug abuse and parental alcoholism was almost invariable.* (Elkin, 1984, p. 10.)

It is important that we also think about the positive side of this issue. Families apparently also help transmit the ability to have self-control and to cope with the stresses of life without abuse and excesses. Families who have traditions of moderation and of coping with extreme difficulties in humane ways help new generations learn these desirable ways of coping and adjusting.

THE GENOGRAM: A TOOL FOR UNDERSTANDING FAMILY PROCESSES

Thus far this chapter has demonstrated that generational alliances and generational transmission are two important parts of all our lives. With these insights as givens, we can then move to the next concern that is important to family scientists. It is: how can we use these ideas to help families and individuals better attain their goals?

What is a genogram? A genogram is a tool developed by family scientists to help identify and measure intergenerational characteristics of families. Individuals, families, educators, and ministers, therapists, and counselors frequently use them. Genograms are charts or graphs that diagram the biological and interpersonal relationships of people across several generations. They also identify significant events in intergenerational relationships that can have an influence on the families and individuals.

Genograms can be helpful in several ways. Each of us can make a genogram for our own family, and they can help us better understand the desirable and the undesirable influences that our earlier generations have had on us. This can help us enjoy and appreciate the desirable effects, and sometimes find ways to minimize and change some of the undesirable effects. We can also use genograms as family scientists to help others better understand their lives, their families, and the options they have to grow and improve their lives.

How to make a genogram. There are four parts to a genogram. The first part is the chart or diagram, and a simple chart is shown in Figure 4.1. McGoldrick, Gerson, and Schellenberger (1999) developed a set of standardized symbols and methods for constructing these charts, and many of their conventions are used in this chapter. Figure 4.1 shows a fairly simple genogram for the family of a person I've named Sandra Jones, and this figure illustrates how to diagram some of the basic parts of a genogram.

Each family member is represented by a box or circle. The boxes are used to indicate a male and circles show females. A genogram chart is usually created to understand a particular person, and that person is known as the *Index Person*. Double lines are used for that person, as shown for Sandra Jones. It is helpful to put names and years of birth and death on a genogram, and the best method the authors have seen is to put them just below the box or circle. If there is just one year shown, it is the birth year and means the person is still living at the time the genogram is made.

The children are arranged with the oldest child on the left and youngest child on the right. Thus, in Sandra's family, she is the oldest child. Her younger brother Mark was born in 1969, and the youngest child, Kyle, was born in 1970. The dotted lines above Kyle show that he was adopted. Sandra's parents were married in 1965 and the marriage is shown with the horizontal line connecting them. Sandra's father, Marvin, was born in 1942 to Peter and Joyce Jones, who were married in 1940. Peter Jones died in 1945, and Joyce did not remarry, so the genogram shows that Joyce raised her son as a single parent. The other aspect of their family that is shown is that they had a stillborn child in 1943. The "X" inside a box or circle indicates a person died prematurely.

Generations in Family Life

Figure 4.1.   A Genogram Showing the Family of Sandra Jones in 1980.

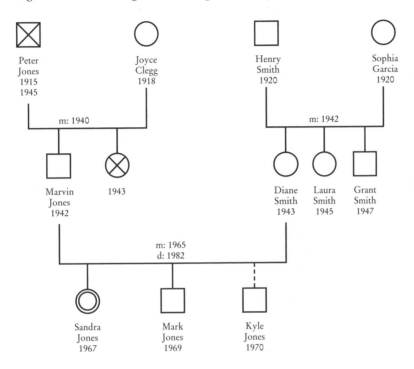

Figure 4.1 shows that Sandra's mother was the oldest of three children. Her parents were the same age as both of them were born the same year, and they were married in 1942.

Families are seldom as simple as the information in Figure 4.1 shows. They usually have a number of complications, and the method of diagramming some of the complications that can occur are illustrated in Figure 4.2. This figure shows the same family five years later. Sandra's parents were divorced in 1982, and the year of their divorce is placed just below the year of their marriage. Marvin, Sandra's father, remarried quickly as he was married to LeAnne Brady in 1982. Sandra's mother, Diane, was married in 1983 to Philip Page.

The dotted lines show the residential patterns of the step-families. Sandra and her youngest brother Kyle live with her mother and her step-father. Sandra's brother Mark lives with his father and step-mother.

Figure 4.3 shows how to diagram a number of additional complications that can occur in families. In this diagram, the step-family residential patterns are not shown because Sandra and her surviving brother are now married and have their own families. Sandra's brother, Mark, died in 1987, and since he was only 18 at the time an "X" is placed in the square.

Sandra was married to Jeff Brown in 1987, and they have given birth to two sets of twins. The older twins are fraternal twins, and one of them, Janet, died as an infant. The younger set of twins, Aimee and Nicole, are identical twins.

Figure 4.3 also shows how to diagram relationships where two individuals are a "couple" but they are not legally married. Sandra's youngest brother, Kyle, had a relationship with Lori Rice. They met in 1987 and separated in 1989. Lori had an abortion in 1987, and it is shown with a vertical line and small "x." Later, Kyle was married to Brenda Strong in 1991, and Brenda experienced a miscarriage in 1992.

Figure 4.3 also shows that Sandra's step-father Philip Page died in 1987, and her mother married Bradley Derrick, a man who was 20 years older than she was in 1989. This marriage was Bradley Derrick's third marriage. He was married to his first wife, Ruth Dietzel, for a very short time, and they had a daughter named Jill in 1945. Bradley's second marriage was to Deborah King in 1926, and they had a son named Scott. Thus, Jill and Scott are step-siblings, half-brother and sister. Jill was married to Harvey Zinn in 1966 and they had a son in 1967. Thus, when Sandra's mother Diane married Bradley in 1989 it created some unusual family relationships. In addition to getting a step-father, Bradley, the remarriage also gave Sandra a step-sister named Jill

Figure 4.2.   A Genogram Showing the Family of Sandra Jones in 1985.

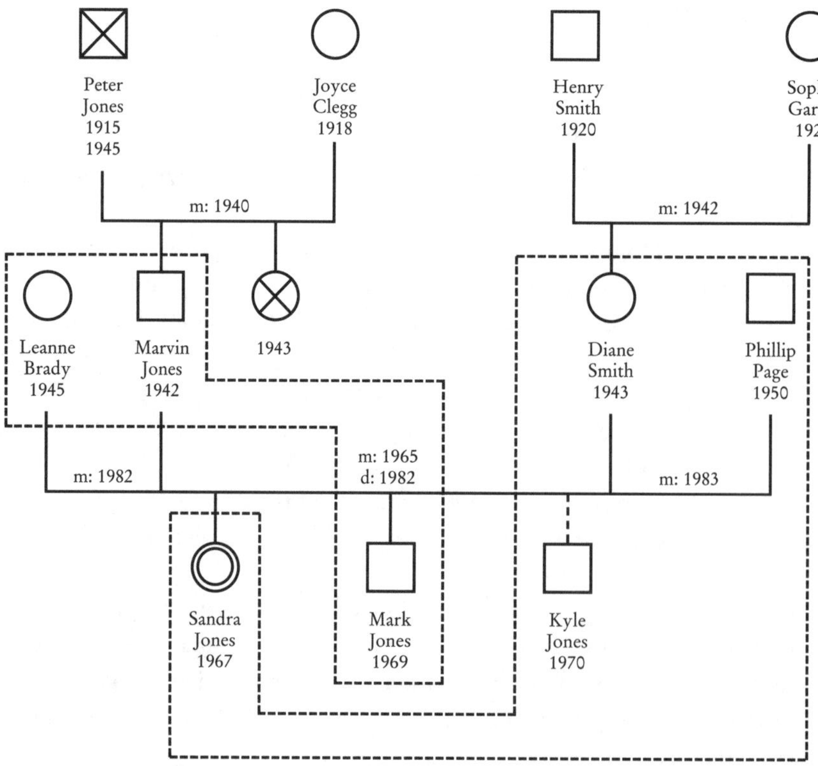

Figure 4.3. Genogram Showing the Family of Sandra Jones in 1999.

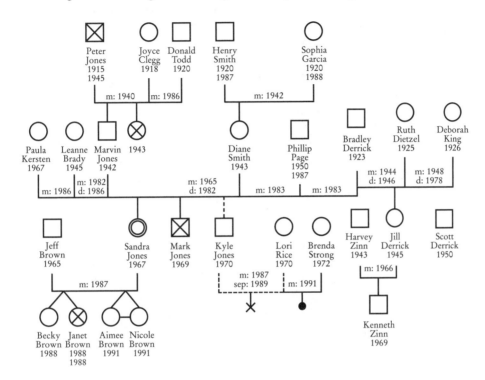

who is 20 years older than she is, and she has a nephew, Kenneth Zinn, who is one year older than she is. Another unique aspect of these relationships is that they did not begin until the year after Sandra was married.

On the other side of Sandra's family, Figure 4.3 shows that her father was divorced again in 1986 and married Paula Kersten who was 19 at the time, the same age as Sandra. Thus, Sandra then had a step-mother who was the same age she was. Also, Sandra's paternal grandmother, Joyce, remarried at the age of 68. Her new husband, and Sandra's new step-grandfather, was Donald Todd. The genogram also shows that Sandra's maternal grandparents died in 1987 and 1988.

Genogram charts are sometimes helpful in giving us insights about what is happening in the lives of individuals and families, and they can help us find ways to cope and adjust to many of life's challenges. For example, we would expect that the period between 1986 and 1988 was a challenging time for Sandra and her family. During this period of time her 18-year-old brother died, two grandparents died, and her stepfather died. Her youngest brother had a temporary relationship that included an abortion, and her father was divorced for the second time and married a woman the same age as Sandra. Shortly after this marriage Sandra was married. With that many dramatic events happening in Sandra's family situation, it would be likely that she would have a number of emotional reactions that she and her new husband would find themselves dealing with. Many people find a genogram chart such as this helpful in putting these events in perspective, understanding the emotional reactions, and working through the many feelings that would be occurring.

How to make a family chronology. The second part of a genogram is a family chronology. This is a chronological listing of major events experienced in a family. A family chronology should include desirable and unfortunate events. For example, events such as graduations, serious illnesses, moves, changes in careers, changes in family composition such as a grandparent or other relative moving in or out, periods when there were drinking or other substance abuse problems, runaways, special honors or awards, times when a parent is gone for extended periods of time, times of financial affluence or difficulty, accidents, and periods of unusual closeness and love would usually be important events if they were to occur in families, and they should be included.

Many families experience some very unfortunate events. These are such things as a member of a family being in prison or a mental hospital, serious illnesses such as cancer and incapacitating strokes, affairs, suicides, physical abuse, sexual abuse or incest, and homes burning. These events have an important effect on individuals and families, and they should be identified. Care should be taken in describing them to be sure that confidences are not breached, and sometimes it is best to describe some of them in general terms. For example, saying something like "Paul and Sarah not close" could mean many things to the person making the genogram, and that is what is important.

Sometimes there is a tendency to focus on the tragic and traumatic events in writing the chronology of family events, but this tendency should be avoided. Unusual positive events should also be described because they influence families and the individuals in them. Some examples of these are such events as a member of the family being on a championship team, getting special awards or recognitions, developing unusually meaningful friendships, having a special musical or artistic performance, special trips or vacations that are memorable, or being elected to a high office.

The following family chronology for Sandra Jones lists some of the information from her family life to show how a family chronology is written.

A Chronology of the Jones Family

1915-   Peter Jones born.
1918-   Joyce Clegg born.
1920-   Henry Smith born.
Sophia Garcia born.
1939-   Henry Smith moved to Mexico.
1940-   Peter Jones and Joyce Clegg married.

(continued on page 135)

Generations in Family Life

ACTIVITY 4.1 - MAKING A GENOGRAM

This activity is to make a genogram of your family. A genogram is a variation of a family tree. It also is like a "road map" of a family. Most people enjoy making a genogram for their own family, and there are a large number of benefits. People usually learn a great deal about themselves, their family, and family processes in general. Also, as they look at their own family, they get a clearer understanding of what the family "realm" is and how it is different from other realms. People also usually acquire new insights about how they fit inside their family, how their family has influenced them, how they can influence their family, and how they can help themselves and others attain the goals they desire and value. They also usually acquire greater appreciation for their parents and grandparents and their relationships with them. Most people also have a better understanding of their family history, their culture, their environment, and the potential they have for future relationships and experiences.

This activity has four parts. The first three parts can be completed simultaneously, but the fourth part should be done after the first three parts are completed. The first part is to make a genogram chart. See your text reading for explanations of and how to make one, and these pages should be read carefully. Several details to pay attention to are:

1. The chart should include four generations if possible. If information cannot be gathered on four generations, three generations is ok. You may include some or all of your cousins and aunts and uncles who have had an impact on your family, but the chart doesn't need to include any aunts, uncles or cousins if it makes the chart too complicated for one page. The "rule of thumb" is to include enough people that the page is fairly full of people.

2. The chart should be neat. This means a pen and ruler should be used, or it should be printed with a computer rather than merely making a pencil sketch. It is usually best to make a few pencil sketches first to see how to arrange the circles and squares so they all fit in a coherent way.

3. The figures in your text show the conventions that are usually the best in making a genogram.

4. Sometimes families are different at different times. For example, the residential pattern may be unique when there is a foster family arrangement. You may make a diagram for the way your family was at one particular time, or, if you want to be more thorough, you make several different diagrams to describe your family at different stages.

5. The charts should be on an 8 1/2" x 11" piece of paper. Be sure to put your name on the chart.

The second part of this activity is to make a Family Chronology. You can find an explanation of how to do this in your text.

The chronology should be typed or printed on a computer, and it should include such important family events as major life-cycle changes, moves, relationship shifts, losses and successes, migrations, people living with the family or moving out, major illnesses, increases or decreases in fame or fortune, religious conversions, major career changes, etc. Only record the information you don't mind sharing with the instructor. A thorough chronology would begin with some events in the great-grandparents' lives and have over 40 events described in it.

Examine the sample Family Chronology shown for the Sandra Jones family in our text. It illustrates how a family chronology is written, and shows the type of information that is usually included.

The third part of this activity is to describe and analyze the chart and chronology. Assemble as many facts as you can about the family and see what information they provide about your family system. In the class presentations, emphasis is given to three principles, and you ought to give these a special emphasis in your analysis. These three are:

1   Generational transmission: Are there patterns or characteristics of the family that occur in more than one generation? If so, what is being transmitted? [You may want to do Activity 5 to help you see these items. Activity 5 is a slightly more involved and different way to do this, and it will provide additional insights.] Is there generational transmission with members of the family other than yourself? Is there transmission of desirable or undesirable characteristics or both? How has this transmission influenced your heritage?

2. Generational alliances: Are there any alliances or coalitions that can be identified, and are they transmitted? Are there any healthy alliances, and are there any unhealthy alliances? Are there any other patterns in the affection or rejection that are informing? How have these patterns influenced your family heritage?

3. Generational bonds: What are the patterns in the intergenerational bonds in your family that provide new insights? For example, are the bonds strong or weak, or stronger in some branches than others? What effects have these patterns had in your family heritage?

Note that the information in the text divides this third part into two aspects. In this activity we combine the section beginning on page 81 about "Describing Family Relationships" and the section beginning on page 82 about "Describing Family Processes" into one part.

The fourth part of the activity should occur after you have completed the first three parts. Take a few minutes to think about what you have learned by doing this activity. Summarize what you have learned by completing this activity and attach it to your chart, chronology and analysis. If you did not learn anything, spend a page discussing what you could do to learn more about the role of generational processes in families.

Chapter 4

134

Generations in Family Life

1942- Marvin Jones born.

Henry Smith and Sophia Garcia married.

1943- Diane Smith born.

Stillborn child born to Peter Jones and Joyce Clegg.

1944- Peter Jones has a severe stroke.

1945- Peter Jones died.

1952- Henry and Sophia Smith move from Mexico to South Carolina.

1965- Marvin Jones and Diane Smith married.

1967- Sandra Jones born.

1969- Mark Jones born.

1970- Kyle Jones born and adopted by Marvin and Diane Jones.

1982- Marvin Jones and Diane Smith divorced.

Marvin Jones and LeAnne Brady married.

1983- Diane Smith and Philip Page married.

1986- Marvin Jones and LeAnne Brady divorced.

Marvin Jones and Paula Kersten married.

1987- Sandra Jones and Jeff Brown married.

Mark Jones died at the age of 18.

Philip Page died.

Henry Smith died.

Kyle has affair with Lori Rice.

Lori Rice has an abortion.

1988- Diane Jones has mental breakdown.

Sophia Garcia Smith died.

Twins, Becky and Janet Brown born. Janet died.

1989- Kyle and Lori broke up.

1991- Twins, Aimee and Nicole Brown, born.

Kyle Jones and Brenda Strong married.

1992- Kyle and Brenda Jones have a miscarriage.

A thorough family chronology involves events from at least three different generations, and it usually has over 50 items. The above list has 35 items to illustrate how a family chronology is made, but it doesn't include many events that would be important in the family life of Sandra Jones.

Describing family relationships. The third part of a genogram is a description of the relationships between family members. These are usually fairly simple and straightforward descriptions, and some of them can be drawn on a genogram chart with the symbols shown in Figure 4.4. Usually it is not possible to diagram all of the important information about relationships on a chart because it becomes too complicated and confusing. Therefore, most of the time it is necessary to write the information about relationships on a few additional pages of paper.

Figure 4.4. Symbols That Can Describe Relationships in Families.

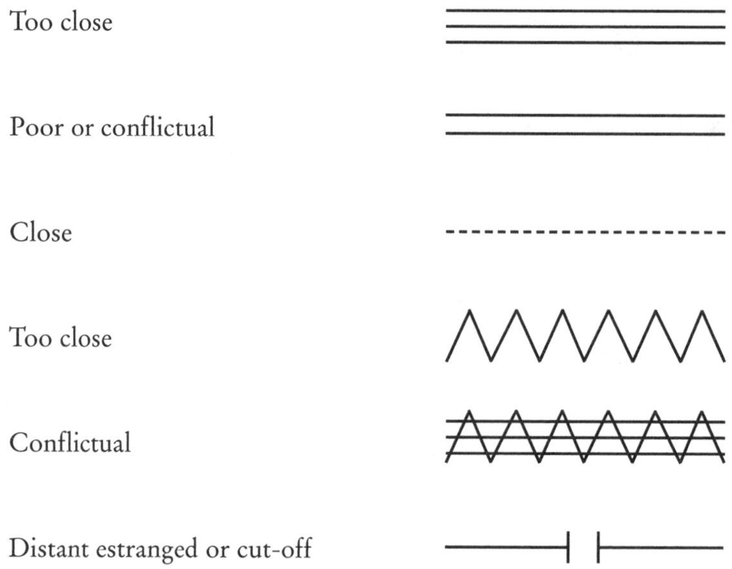

Too close	≡≡≡
Poor or conflictual	=
Close	- - - - -
Too close	/\/\/\/\
Conflictual	XXXXX
Distant estranged or cut-off	—⊣ ⊢—

Another way to describe relationship information is to make the basic chart and then make several photocopies of the chart. It is then possible to diagram some of the relationship information on the duplicate copies. Also, sometimes it is helpful to show the relationships at several different time periods in a family life cycle.

The following list of questions illustrate the kind of information that is usually included in the relationships part of a genogram:

1. Who was close to whom?
2. Which individuals had conflictual relationships?
3. Which individuals were "left out"?
4. Who tended to be the family scapegoat if there was one?
5. If there was a "favorite" child of a parent or grandparent, who were they?
6. Who were the leaders, the followers?
7. Who was the family peacemaker, troublemaker?
8. Who was distant from the family?
9. What were the alliances, cliques, or coalitions?
10. Who was "overfunctioning" or "underfunctioning?" Overfunctioning individuals take upon themselves a lot of responsibility to make sure the rights things get done. Underfunctioning individuals take little responsibility and initiative as they let others get things done.

Generations in Family Life

Describing family processes.   The fourth part of a genogram is a description of circumstances or processes that can help us understand how generational relationships influence a family and the people in it. Several examples of processes that can be helpful are things such as cliques, alliances, and coalitions in families, ways children are treated differently by the parents, favorite relatives, conflicts that are not resolved, ways of solving problems, in-law pressures, marital harmony or difficulties, feuds between family members, who helps out when help is needed, and difficulties coping with life's challenges.

The following list of questions helps identify some of these processes:

1. How did the family react when a particular family member was born or died? Who took it the hardest? The easiest?

2. Have there been any job changes that influenced the family? How do people feel about their jobs?

3. How do people in the family get along with relatives? Are some relatives especially difficult, close, or helpful?

4. Have any members of the family had a drinking problem? What about trouble with medications or other substances?

5. Who is supportive or helpful of other family members? Who is unselfish, and who is selfish?

6. In what does the family take pride?

7. What are the leisure time and recreation patterns in the home, and how do the various members feel about them?

8. Were any individuals especially successful in school? Did any have problems?

9. What are the talents and special gifts those members of the family have?

10. Did the family have any special "program" or "plans" for a particular child?

11. Did sibling positions or relationships influence any of the children?

12. How involved was the family with churches, clubs, fraternities, or other organizations?

13. Were any life cycle transitions (births, deaths, moving away from home, marriages, etc.) especially gratifying or difficult?

14. Did any members of the family have unusual ways of gaining recognition or success?

15. What were the successes, failures, traumas, satisfactions, and themes in the home?

16. Were there any coincidences of life events?

17. Did any economic or political events such as economic depressions or wars influence the family?

18. Were there any triangles inside or outside the family that had an effect on people?
19. Were there any "black sheep" or "family skeletons?"
20. Were there any resources such as inheritances or unusual brilliance or beauty that influenced the family?

Another helpful strategy in completing a genogram is to have the index person tactfully do "research" about his or her own family history by interacting selectively with relatives. Many people find it helpful to get more "involved" with their extended family by attending reunions, weddings, funerals, and other family gatherings and by observing others and observing their own emotional reactions to what they experience. It is especially informing to be around extended families when important emotional feelings are occurring, such as at a birth, a marriage, a death, a special achievement, a crisis, or an illness.

It usually is not very helpful to get involved with relatives to try to "straighten them out."

Interpreting a Genogram

You are encouraged to make a genogram for your own family. Making one for our own family provides an "experiential" type of learning that does not occur in any other way. We learn to better understand some of the interesting, informative, and subtle aspects of our own family situation. We also learn in a first-hand way how our generational connections have an influence on us, and how we may influence our posterity. It takes several hours to make a good genogram, but my former students and many colleagues who have made genograms for their own families have found that it is an interesting, helpful, and useful learning experience. None of us should try to use a genogram to help someone else until we have made one for our own family first.

The payoff with a genogram is that it usually gives us a lot of new information. When we are making a genogram of our own family, it usually helps us better understand why we have some of the feelings we have, why we believe some of the things we do, why we have some attitudes, and why we relate to people the way we do.

This information often helps us and others become more effective in managing our lives, and it may help us cope more effectively with life's challenges and difficulties. It often helps us better attain the things that most of us want in family life. Most of us want such things as closeness, understanding, love, richness, fulfillment, commitment, healthy development, support, communication, empathy, and intimacy, and the insights we get from our genogram may help us better reach these goals.

If we are using a genogram as an educator or therapist to try to help someone else learn and grow, it can have the same effects. The other people often gain insights about why they feel, act, relate, and think the way they do, and they can then use their new insights to better attain their goals.

My experience with genograms has identified several strategies that are helpful in interpreting them. One strategy that usually helps is to try to identify some positive things first. This can be done by looking for events, patterns, relationships, and processes that have helped create strengths or things that are valued and desired. All individuals and all families have some strengths, good aspects, and admirable characteristics, and finding some of them builds morale and motivation. Even the most troubled and problem-ridden families have assets. In fact, sometimes the individuals and families that have had the most challenges have an unusual number of strengths.

Another strategy that usually is helpful is to be tentative and hypothetical in trying to understand what a genogram means. This means it is wise to state ideas as hypotheses or guesses about the effects of various relationships or processes. Some examples of this are: "It may be that . . ." "It's possible that. . ." "It could be that. . ." "Maybe. . ."

There are a few cautions that are helpful when we try to use a genogram to help someone else. Some people have very painful experiences in their families, and the strategies they have used to cope with some of their experiences are sometimes to forget and avoid them. In some of these situations, they may be very uncomfortable when they begin to think about their earlier experiences, and forcing them to think about them may do more harm than good. Therefore, people's feelings, desires, and wishes should be respected, and they should never be forced or coerced to face or deal with aspects of their family life they are not ready to deal with. Their personal wishes and desires should determine what they do, and only when they are emotionally ready should they try to think about or understand how their earlier family experiences have influenced them.

USING KNOWLEDGE ABOUT GENERATIONAL PROCESSES TO HELP PEOPLE

Even though the study of generational processes is only a few decades old, family scientists have begun to discover ways to use some of the new ideas to help people attain their goals. We can use these ideas in our own family situations, and we can use them in a number of professional and avocational settings. For example, family therapists, family life educators, social workers, medical doctors, lawyers, and the clergy can use these ideas.

Liberating families from undesirable generational effects.   Conservatism is the process of trying to protect ideas and practices people think are valuable. It is attempts to protect and maintain traditional ways of doing things people think are worth keeping. Liberalism is the opposite, trying to liberate people from conventions, practices, and ways of doing things that are oppressive and undesirable.

We usually think of liberalizing as liberating people from political and economic oppression. When we think about events such as the civil rights movement, and the women's movement we also ought to realize that the family realm can be excessively dominating and oppressive. One goal of family scientists should be to help liberate people from the undesirable bondage and oppression that occurs in families.

When undesirable patterns are being passed from one generation to another, there is a technique that can help liberate families from these patterns. It is to be a transitional character.

> *A transitional character is one who, in a single generation, changes the entire course of a lineage. The individuals who grow up in an abusive, emotionally destructive environment and who somehow find a way to metabolize the poison and refuse to pass it on to their children. They break the mold. They refute the observation that abused children become abusive parents, that the children of alcoholics become alcoholic adults, that "the sins of the fathers are visited upon the heads of the children to the third and fourth generation." Their contribution to humanity is to filter the destructiveness out of their own lineage so that the generations downstream will have a supportive foundation upon which to build productive lives.* (Broderick, 1988, p. 14)

There are many things people can do to help them be a transitional character. Eight of them are: (1) deliberateness, (2) distinctive family rituals, (3) maintaining emotional distance, (4) marrying later than average, (5) reading good books about family life, (6) joining organizations that can help, (7) getting an education, and (8) getting a philosophy of life.

Deliberateness.   A group of researchers at George Washington University have discovered that deliberateness can influence generational transmission (Bennett et al., 1987). They conducted a series of studies of the transmission of alcoholism in families, and one of the factors they found to be important is the amount people deliberately try to plan their own family identity, rituals, and ways of living.

In one of their studies they had 12 couples who had a high level of deliberateness and 75% of them were able to be transitional couples by interrupting the transmission of alcohol problems. Of the 31 couples who were low on deliberateness, 77% of them transmitted from their parents the pattern of having alcohol problems (Bennett, Wolin, Reiss, & Teitelbaum, 1987).

Distinctive family rituals.   A second idea that was developed by the George Washington researchers has to do with family rituals, traditions, and routines. They discovered that families who do not allow a parent's alcohol abuse to disrupt important family rituals are less likely to pass their severe drinking problems to their offspring.

They found that when alcoholism becomes intertwined with family rituals and traditions such as birthday parties, dinners, family reunions, and holidays, the alcoholism tended to be transmitted to the next generations. However, when the alcohol problems were kept separate from the family traditions and rituals, the alcoholism did not tend to be transmitted to the next generation. They called this process the distinctiveness of rituals because families that were able to keep their family rituals and traditions "distinctive" from the problems they were having with alcohol were able to disrupt the transmission processes.

In one of their research projects, they studied the alcohol transmission in 25 families. They found 5 of the families were clearly distinctive and 5 were clearly not distinctive, and, even though the numbers in the study were small, the pattern was clear. In the 5 distinctive families none of them transmitted the alcoholism to the next generation, but in the 5 non-distinctive families four of the five families had alcohol problems in the next generation (Wolin, Bennett, Noonan, & Teitelbaum, 1980).

Get an education. An education can broaden ideas, insights, and ability to relate and make decisions. If people take classes on topics such as family science, parenting, and marriage preparation, these can be very helpful. However, getting a broad and general education is probably also helpful because it teaches people to think more clearly, examine their ideas and beliefs, and make wise choices. Therefore, a broad or general education is probably more beneficial than technical or job-oriented training.

Reexamine your philosophy of life. Many people who grow up in troubled families may not have a philosophy of life with which they are comfortable. In these situations, it can be helpful to be creative and deliberate about acquiring a set of basic beliefs about what gives life purpose and meaning. This can help clarify personal values, ideals, aspirations, purposes, and beliefs. In the following chapter on ideology in family life, readers and students are encouraged to develop more intentional ideological approaches to family life. This is sometimes painful and taxing, but has great payoff.

Some people find it helpful to become involved in spiritual or religious activities as a way to develop their personal philosophy of life. Others find that becoming part of a different type of close-knit community is helpful to them. Either way, if people can find something they can believe in deeply, and they then build their life around these beliefs, it may help them learn how to relate to others in meaningful ways.

PRESERVING DESIRABLE GENERATIONAL PROCESSES

Many of the things that are transmitted across generations are very desirable. For example, many people grow up in healthy families, and they learn the subtle values, goals, feelings, and attitudes that give meaning, purpose, and a sense of direction to their life. They learn ways of trusting, loving, being close, serving, supporting, communicating at the deepest and most meaningful levels, and ways of helping infants and elderly in ways that give purpose and joy to their lives.

Many people acquire a set of bonds in their family that are multifaceted and strong and provide loving, intimate, close relationships that are of infinite value. They form lifelong connections with their siblings, parents, grandparents, and their own children and their children. These kinds of connections involve so many feelings that are so complicated, deep, and fundamental to a healthy life that they provide a richness and beauty that is difficult to describe.

Even those who grow up in families where they want to "do some things differently than their parents" learn many things from their parents that they want to continue in their own life. They also, except in extreme situations, have bonds and feelings for their family that last their whole life.

Creating Healthy Generational Alliances

There are a number of strategies that can be used to create healthy generational alliances. Some of these strategies are simple things. For example, the parents in a family can help the parental sub-system be the executive subsystem in a family by periodically having "planning sessions." These sessions would help them be a board of directors of the family or an executive committee. The small children would not attend these sessions, and in them the parents could discuss the ways they are relating to the children, ways they are disciplining them, what's going well, and what needs to be changed. Sessions such as this can help them make plans together so they are a coordinated team. If they have disagreements about how to structure the family or relate to the children, they can use sessions such as these to try to find common ground and compromise. As the children mature, the family system can gradually change so the older children have an increasing access to the executive subsystem and influence it an increasing amount.

Another idea that can help families create healthy generational alliances is for the parents to have a "social life" as a couple in addition to the social activities of the family. This can include "dates" with each other, vacations as a couple, and joining social organizations together. These activities can help the bonds in the marital relationship by showing how the couple subsystem is a unique and important unit in the family.

Unfinished business. Another concept that can help families deal with generational processes in healthy ways is called unfinished business. Unfinished business refers to the need to deal with unresolved issues, feelings, injustices, and conflicting loyalties in a family.

Generations in Family Life

A book titled *Invisible Loyalties* by Ivan Boszormenyi-Nagy and Geraldine Sparks (1973) helped the family science field begin to understand the role generational loyalties have in the healthy and unhealthy development of individuals and families. According to Boszormenyi-Nagy and Sparks, each generation has ethical obligations and loyalties to the generations that preceded it and to the generation that follows it. For example, parents have ethical obligations to their children to provide affection, care and nurturance. They also owe their children a secure and loving home, economic support, and security while the children are small and dependent. These obligations create a complex web of invisible loyalties and obligations from parents to children.

A set of invisible loyalties and obligations exists from children to parents. When parents fulfill their obligations to their children, it creates a obligation in the child generation to be appreciative for the valuable and essential things they receive from their families. It also creates invisible loyalties that children feel toward their parents and they develop feelings of appreciation, respect, bonds, closeness, and admiration for their parents.

Boszormenyi-Nagy and his colleagues believe that network of intergenerational loyalties in family systems is not something created by cultures or societies. It is a "natural" part of the family realm that exists because the generations are so intricately intertwined emotionally, mentally, and experientially (Boszormenyi-Nagy & Sparks, 1973). Cultures and societies, however, influence and shape some of the ways these networks appear and whether they are healthy or unhealthy.

The research of Boszormenyi-Nagy and his colleagues help us realize that these patterns of invisible loyalties in the family realm deal with deep feelings and emotions, and they are extremely important to most people. Therefore, when families have healthy patterns in their web of invisible loyalties across generations it provides a helpful reservoir of emotional stability in life. It also helps provide emotional and interpersonal bonds that help people deal effectively with the challenges and obstacles of life, and it provides a deeply experienced sense of meaning, purpose, and lineage consciousness that extends across the generations.

Another aspect of these invisible loyalties is that they gradually evolve and change as the family progresses over time and the family members mature and move to new stages of life. For example, young adults gradually shift their primary family loyalties from their parental family toward their spouse and the children they want to create and raise with their partner. As they make these shifts, they develop new loyalties and some of their old loyalties change and become less important. The old loyalties that diminish deal with obedience, reverence, allegiance, and indebtedness, and the new loyalties deal with subtle, invisible, intangible, but extremely important things such as emotional dependence, connectedness, fidelity, nurturance, and creating together a sense of home, meaning, growth, and sense of one's roots.

There are some family situations where the disruption in the ledger of invisible loyalties becomes tragic and disruptive. For example, when serious misbehavior occurs such as child abuse, incest, negligence, alcoholism, violence, manipulation, exploitation, and substance abuses these destructive behaviors create serious disruptions in the invisible loyalties in a family system. In these situations it takes a long time for the members of a family to find ways to balance the ledgers and help the individuals and families become free from the hurts and fears and resentments. Fortunately, many of the people who have experienced these tragedies in their families are able to face their feelings and they eventually work through their emotional responses in ways that are productive and enabling.

Many families do not have these serious tragedies, but most families, and maybe all of them, find it necessary to deal with unfinished generational business at certain stages of their life. For example, it is fairly typical for ledgers to become imbalanced during the launching stage of the family life cycle. It is natural for the younger generation to be striving to gain freedom and control over their life and for the older generation to be hesitant to let the younger generation have control because they are aware of the limitations in their judgment and experience. The result is often that there is considerable conflict during this period of the life cycle and the invisible loyalties become trampled and twisted and out of balance.

When this occurs in family systems they have unfinished business, and they would be wise to try to deal with it. The unfinished business is that there are resentments, frustrations, and animosities at the same time there are feelings of connection, loyalty, and love. When this occurs it is helpful for families to try to find ways to work through the negative feelings and inequities so they do not interfere with the ability of the individuals to move on to their new stages of life and new responsibilities. When young adults have deep resentments and conflicting loyalties in their relationships with their parental family it is difficult to begin their own family without the scars from the earlier family system interfering with the new family. Thus, it is helpful to find some way to take care of the unfinished business.

There are many ways the younger generation or the older generation can take care of unfinished generational business. Sometimes it helps to try to talk about the feelings with parents, children, or siblings. In other situations it is neither possible nor wise to talk directly with the people who have been unjust because it would just make the situation worse. In these situations it sometimes helps to think about the unique circumstances that helped make it difficult for the parental generation to be as wise or fair as desirable. This sometimes helps people cope at least somewhat with their negative feelings. It also helps in some situations to accept the fact that the parents also are frail and limited in their humanness and they may need acceptance and understanding, or in some circumstances tolerance and even pity. Sometimes it is helpful to adopt a forgiving attitude and conclude the parents probably had reasons for what they did and it will not be helpful to continue to feel resentful. Sometimes it is helpful to get professional help to work through these types of unfinished business.

Generations in Family Life

SUMMARY

This chapter described how generational processes influence families and people. Two principles were introduced. The *Generational Alliance Principle* states that there are several boundaries between parent and child generations that are natural and desirable; and when families maintain these boundaries it contributes to the healthy development of the members of the family. Conversely, when these boundaries become blurred it interferes with healthy development.

The *Generational Transmission Principle* states that aspects of the family realm are transmitted from one generation to the next, and this includes the good, the bad, and the ugly. Three areas where there is considerable evidence that transmission occurs are: marital stability and instability, abusive and non-abusive behaviors, and mental health and illness. The chapter described how to make and interpret a genogram, and then described strategies that can be used to conserve desirable generational ties and transmissions and liberate people from undesirable generational ties and transmissions. Readers were encouraged to make a genogram for their own family because learning how to make and interpret genograms can help them deal effectively with their personal life and learn an effective method of helping others to cope wisely with their generational processes.

Chapter 4

STUDY QUESTIONS

1. What is the genogram symbol for divorce?

2. What is the symbol telling the reader who the person of focus is?

3. Name four ways a genogram might be used in clinical and/or counseling settings.

4. What is the generational transmission principle?

5. What is the definition of a generational alliance?

6. Why do we care about cross-generational alliances?

KEY TERMS

Genogram
Cross-generational alliance
Generations
Social capital
Intergenerational transmission
Invisible loyalties

CHAPTER
FIVE

Ideologies in Family Life

Chapter 5

Main Points:

1. An *ideology* is a set of ideas or beliefs. The ideological part of a family system is different from the generational and emotional parts, and all three are important.

2. Some aspects of family ideology are more abstract than other aspects. Many family scientists think about three *levels of abstraction* in family systems: *Levels I, II, and III.*

3. *Family paradigms* or *ideologies* are an important part of the Level III ideology in families and are the enduring, fundamental, shared, and general assumptions families develop about the nature and meaning of life, what is important, and how to cope with the world they live in.

4. There are four general types of family paradigms: open, closed, random, and synchronous paradigms.

5. *The Exaggeration Principle* says that when families encounter stress they have a natural tendency toward exaggeration of the processes created by their paradigmatic beliefs.

Ideologies in Family Life

INTRODUCTION

This chapter deals with a fundamental and important part of family systems—their *ideology*. Before we can understand the role of ideology in families, we need to understand what this term means. The root of the word *ideology* comes from the Greek term *ide* that means *idea*. Therefore, the term ideology refers to the body or group of ideas that exist in a group, society, or social movement. Thus, when we focus on family ideology we are focusing on the cognitive or intellectual aspect of family systems that is reflected in their beliefs, thoughts, myths, symbols, ideals, aspirations, values, world-view, philosophy of life, or doctrines.

It is helpful to realize that the ideological aspect of a family is different from the generational and emotional aspects. One difference is the emotional part is *experienced* as sensations or emotions rather than *thoughts*. It is not as much an intellectual process as it is an affective, emotional, or somatic process. Also, the generational processes discussed in chapter 3 are not part of the "idea" part of family systems. They are connections, continuities, discontinuities, and other processes that occur between parents and children—even when families are not aware of them intellectually. When families develop ideas or beliefs about their emotions or their generational processes, these ideas are part of their ideology, but the emotions and generational processes themselves are fundamentally different as they are not ideological.

LEVELS OF ABSTRACTION IN FAMILY LIFE

Some parts of family ideology are relatively abstract beliefs, and other parts are fairly specific and concrete ideas. These differences in abstraction are important because the abstract ideas play a different role in systems than the less abstract beliefs.

Definition of abstraction. To understand what this means, we need to first understand what the term *abstraction* means. Abstraction refers to whether something is relatively specific, tangible, and concrete as opposed to being relatively general, intangible, obscure, and disassociated from being specific. An example of abstraction is that when we think of our personal family life we are not thinking about families in "general" because we are thinking of one particular family. However, when we think of "family life" as a way of organizing humans it is a more general idea. A different analogy is that one kind act is situation-specific, concrete, and not abstract. Kindness, on the other hand, is a more abstract and less situation-specific idea, so it is a more abstract concept.

Several illustrations from other parts of life further illustrate what the concept of abstraction means. When we think about apples, oranges, and lemons, this thinking is less abstract than when we think about fruit. Thus, fruit is a more general or abstract term. When we think about congress changing a law this is less abstract than thinking about changing a constitution or changing the basic form of government. When we think about a family rule it is less abstract than thinking about how a family makes or changes its rules.

Abstraction is a continuum that varies between the two extremes of no abstraction (concrete, specific) to highly abstract (general, unspecific). Like distance or height, it is a gradual continuum that varies in degree. It doesn't have categories or units. With many continuous variables we find it useful to create measuring devices that divide the continuous variables into units, and many of these measuring devices are widely understood. For example, we use inches or meters to divide distance into units or categories.

The levels approach.   Family scientists in the 1970s developed a method of dividing the abstraction of family processes into two levels (Watzlawick et al., 1974). The lowest level was called *first-order* or *Level I*. The Level I processes were thought to exist in contrast to a higher level which was called *second-order* or *Level II* processes. Additionally, family scientists identified family processes that are more abstract, and they are now known as *Level III* processes. When this typology is applied to the *ideological* part of family systems, it has the following meanings.

LEVEL I IDEOLOGY

Level I ideas are simple, fairly visible skills and rules that are more specific and concrete. Most of the "rules" and skills families have fall in this category. For example, rules about calling to let others know when we will be late and how to act at the table are Level I rules. A typical family system has thousands of these specific "ideas" about how family systems ought to operate. For example, most families think they ought to put beds in bedrooms rather than in living rooms, and they think it is ok to show physical affection to each other—as long as it is appropriate. Of course, families do differ in what they think is appropriate: Some families express affection a great deal and others express it less. Most families have ideas about where people should and should not eat, and how family members should dress. Some also believe that lawn mowers and garden tools should not be left in driveways, electrical appliances should be kept safe, and toys should not be left on stairs.

Ideologies in Family Life

In addition, families have skills that help define how competent they are (Beavers, 1982; Gontang & Erickson, 1996). Family competence according to these authors is the ability level families have to perform skills that are crucial as families choose between individual needs and group needs. Families struggle with the need for each family member to enhance their individual development and wants. At the same time there is a group agenda. So, for example, we want to know about how families decide if they should put extra money into the 'new couch' fund, or should it be spent on a new baseball mitt wanted by a younger child. Important to this notion is the idea that by observing their choices we learn several things about a particular family. First, as they make Level I decisions about allocation, we can begin to find out what they actually value (not just what they *say* they value).

Second, we can observe how skillful they are at implementing the choice. Families that are more competent and experience better outcomes are more balanced and flexible. That is, they find ways of successfully balancing the needs of the child *and* the larger ideological goals of the larger family group. They know how to be flexible and show concern at this basic level of interaction.

Third, many Level I ideas in family systems are so obvious small children understand them. For example, most family members learn that it is not ok to use someone else's toothbrush.

Fourth, some Level I ideas are more subtle and unspoken. For example, a family may have an implicit idea that "dad can criticize other members of the family but the other members cannot criticize dad." Or, some members of a family may think that "Stephen is the mother's favorite child" but the mother may think she has no favorite. More competent families have Level I skills that promote openness, generosity, and communicate caring. Families who struggle are more likely to be rigid, less caring, and more authoritarian about these Level I interactions.

Fifth, by observing the skills and rules families adopt to solve daily problems, we can begin to get some idea about deeper strongly held ideologies they subscribe to. If the family decides to save the extra money and not buy a baseball mitt, that decision and how it is carried out is an important piece of information about what that family thinks is important.

LEVEL II IDEOLOGY

Level II ideas are more abstract than the specific ideas in Level I and less abstract than the highly abstract ideas in Level III. Thus, this level refers to ideas that are at an intermediate level of abstraction. Watzlawick and others (1974) described this more abstract level of analysis, and they used two different ideas to discover there are two levels.

One of the ideas they used is part of the "Theory of Groups" developed by French mathematician Evariste Galois (Borceaux, 2001). The idea is simply that thinking about a member of a group of things in a system is thinking at one level, and thinking about the group itself is thinking at a more abstract level. When the group thinks about itself we call this a *meta-level* thought

The second idea that comes from Watzlawick is that changes in the whole group is a different "type" of change than changes to a part of the group. This idea provided the basis for realizing that changes within a family are different from changes in one person in the family.

Watzlawick et al. (1974, p. 9) used the example of an automobile with a standard shift to illustrate shifts in levels. When you are driving a car in the lowest gear, you can only go so fast. When you are in that low gear you can only go faster or slower within a limited range using the gas pedal. If you want to travel faster than that, you have to shift to another gear.

Changes with the gas pedal are Level I changes. Shifting gears provides the driver with a new range of speed and power. We call this a Level II change. This type of change puts us into a higher level of speed.

Disciplining children can illustrate these differences in families. When parents want to change the behavior of a child, they may decide to use disciplinary behaviors to accomplish the goal. Let's say they decide to use physical punishment as their main mode of operation. If they only do a Level I change as the problem behaviors in the child get worse, they would simply spank harder… step on the gas, so to speak.

If they wanted to try a new strategy they would have to shift gears and try something completely new like using natural or logical consequences. This is usually very difficult for parents. We usually don't change our strategies when we discipline children or cope with stress, instead, we just "turn up the volume" of the strategy we already use.

LEVEL III IDEOLOGY

The Level III parts of family ideology are at the opposite extreme of abstraction. They are very general ideas basic to the way we think and believe. So, Level III thoughts are usually highly abstract. For example, some Level III deep ideologies a family may hold are like general summaries they have of the way the world operates. Some families may believe that the world is a hostile place to be feared, others might believe that the world is a garden of opportunities to be experienced and embraced. Sometimes these beliefs deal with values such as the nature of reality and how to cope with it. Some think the world is basically simple and others believe it is complex. Some families believe they have control over their destiny and others think they have little control over what happens to them.

Abstract ideas are difficult to articulate and define clearly because they are, by their very nature, general and diffused rather than specific and concrete. None-the-less they are an important part of family systems because some of the abstract beliefs are

JOURNAL OF THOUGHTS 5.1: WHAT IS AN IDEOLOGY?

1. What does the word "ideology" mean?

2. Tell about different themes or ideologies orientations you have seen in the families you know (yours or others).

3.   Draw a diagram that shows how an ideology is the root of nearly everything that results in family life. This can be an abstract drawing or a process-like model that shows the flow of action that results from what we believe.

the framing and basic assumptions that have a broad and pervasive influence on the more specific beliefs and behaviors in families. People's abstract beliefs influence their major goals in life, the ways they try to attain their goals, and how they behave.

It is also important to note that families have a difficult time changing these deep beliefs. Sometimes in a severe crisis they may rethink whether or not there is a God, or really examine who they are. But, most of us rarely even think about these deeply held ideas that direct our lives.

To summarize. Thus, it is helpful to think about three different levels of abstraction in family systems. Level I refers to specific and concrete things. Level II refers to things that are at an intermediate level of abstraction, and Level III refers to highly abstract things in families. These ideas about levels of abstraction are used in the later chapters to think about several different aspects of family life, but in this chapter they are applied to abstraction in family ideologies. However, before these ideas can be developed in more detail, it is important to describe another aspect of family ideology. It is that at least some parts of family ideologies are constructed rather than just copied from the culture or society.

FAMILY IDEOLOGIES

Noted family therapist and researcher David Reiss wrote a book called *The Family's Construction of Reality* (1981). In this well-know scholarly book, he developed a concept that helps us understand the deeply held Level III ideas described above. He called these ideas *family paradigms*, another term for Level III ideologies. A family paradigm (or deeply held family ideology) is the enduring, fundamental, shared, and general assumptions or beliefs that families develop about the nature and meaning of life, what is important, and how to cope with the world they live in (Reiss, 1981, ch. 4). And a key to understanding family life was his notion that the members of a family shared these paradigms. As a family entity, he showed in a convincing laboratory setting that there was a shared, deeply felt, enduring meaning that families created.

He showed that all family members, despite the disagreements, conflicts, and differences, constructed and shared these beliefs or ideologies. Indeed, the core of an individual's membership in his own family is his acceptance of, belief in, and creative elaboration of these abiding assumptions (Reiss, 1981, p. 1).

Awareness of family paradigms. Family paradigms are rarely explicit or conscious in families. Also, these ideologies or paradigms are the fountainhead from which the rest of family life seems to emanate. When we believe the world exists in a certain way, we organize the rest of our life's activities to reflect that notion. For example, if a family believes the world is a hostile place, they would have more strict boundaries, tighter rules about daily events, and take more care about activities outside the safety of the home.

The time when paradigms come the closest to being conscious is when families make major transitions like divorce or remarriage. In times of crisis, our true inner beliefs are more likely to show through. During these periods, especially when the very existence of the family is threatened, they turn to their most basic shared beliefs to help them "manage" their way through the crisis. When these periods of crisis are resolved, the basic beliefs recede into the assumed foundation of daily life, and attention can again be given to everyday and routine challenges.

Family ideologies are like an "iceberg" that is beneath the surface, hidden from the view of outsiders and hidden, at least most of the time, from the families themselves. Observers of families have difficulty learning about a family's paradigms and usually have to settle for guesses about what they believe.

Another researcher suggested that invisibility of family paradigms is so complete that usually families are not aware of them. He suggested that the ideology remains a rather invisible property of the family not of individual family members. But, the ideology that a family holds is so pervasive and powerful that is becomes a template for the actions, decisions, and strategies families use to attain goals (Constantine, 1986, p. 16).

HOW DO FAMILIES CONSTRUCT PARADIGMS?

We are just beginning to learn about how families construct, modify, and maintain their deeply held beliefs. Apparently there are at least two different stages in the construction of paradigms. The first stage occurs during the courtship and formative stage of the family life cycle, and the second stage occurs when families experience serious crises.

Formative period. When a couple comes together in a relationship, one of their relationship tasks is to decide, consciously or unconsciously, what their new family will be like. In most situations the two individuals grew up in a family that had been through its formative period and constructed its basic ideology or paradigms. As they grew up the beliefs their parents held were assumed to be the "normal" way of viewing the world.

However, as children begin to form their own family, they have a series of choices. How will their new family be like their parents' family, and how will it be different? How will it be like his parents' family, and how will it be different? Also, how will it be like other families they have been exposed to?

Most couples go through a formation stage that can last for several months. During this time they talk with each other at great length about what they want their relationship and family life to be like.

Ideologies in Family Life

Most people have never even heard of such things as "family ideologies or paradigms," and they are largely hidden from view, there aren't many books to read or checklists to look at to help a couple decide what their family paradigms ought to be.

These discussions are usually exciting and filled with discovery. Somewhere along the way, most couples bond and join their thoughts. The two individuals discover what they share as common. They may also redefine who they are as they attempt to create something new.

Because this experience is so personal and affirming, some believe they are the first to "see the sunrise" and may believe that they are going through a process that is different from what other couples go through.

This sense of richness and depth that is almost universally experienced probably is partly because each couple goes through a process of constructing their unique set of meaningful and basic assumptions about what the world "really is" like for them. This process is a combination of consciously and unconsciously selecting some aspects from the family each person grew up in, other families that are respected, and developing some entirely new assumptions and beliefs (Steinglass et al., 1987, p. 308).

Family scientists believe that the first paradigms of a new family are borrowed and invented. As various aspects of the relationship are identified, talked about, tested, and revised they come and go in consciousness. They remain conscious as long as there is uncertainty, ambiguity, and conflict, and when they are resolved they slip into the implicit, implied, unconscious part of the gradually growing family paradigm.

Changing established paradigms. Reiss devoted much of his writing to help us understand the ways family crises influence paradigmatic beliefs. He found that the strategies families use to recover from crisis are found in the collective part of the family we have been calling a paradigm or ideology. That is, the individuals in a family share some idea about how best to solve the problems they encounter. They interact in certain ways that (they believe) will be effective in resolving their crisis. When the crisis is very severe, the family sometimes changes. They may even have to change the foundational, core ideologies they have in order to get through a crisis situation.

So, when family life is uncomplicated there is little reason to even think about one's beliefs. Instead, the paradigms provide a sense of meaning and order, and they are used as the guiding beliefs in selecting goals, making decisions, and managing resources. However, in times of crisis, the typical pattern is for families to begin to question old ways of thinking and doing things and to construct new ways of defining the stressful situation and new strategies for trying to cope with the stress.

Apparently, the usual pattern is that the longer a family experiences difficulty in coping with a stressful situation, the more the parts of their ideology are called into question, eliminated, or revised; and new definitions and perceptions emerge. If the new constructs are effective in coping with the stress, the general and abstract parts of the new beliefs are assimilated into the family paradigm.

Unfortunately, there is also a "worst of times" aspect to these processes. Some families are rigidly attached to some of the ideas they hold and they do not have the flexibility, creativity, or other resources to change. This inability to change can keep a family in a state of chronic difficulty until they can get outside help.

THE ROLE OF PARADIGMATIC BELIEFS IN FAMILY SYSTEMS

Family ideologies play a key role in the managing processes. You will remember from earlier chapters that families have goals. Simply put, the ideology a family has either helps or detracts from their ability to attain the goals. In fact, the deeply held goals and values they hold are really a part of the paradigmatic/ideological world. This idea is reflected in the following principle:

PRINCIPLE 5.1: FAMILY IDEOLOGY

Deeply held family ideologies have the power to either assist or detract from a family's ability to attain the goals they seek.

Several analogies illustrate the role of family ideologies. A family ideology is like the "north star" in a family's attempts to navigate. Another way to describe the power of an ideology is to imagine it as the family's constitution that is used to govern itself. Reiss described this role by saying that family paradigms are the "central organizer" that does the "shaping," "fashioning," and "guiding" of what families do when they regulate, order and transact with their environment (Reiss, 1981)

TYPES OF FAMILY PARADIGMS

The concept of family paradigms is so new that scholars have not conducted much research about them. One of the reasons for that is that they are very hard to measure and discover. A few scholars, however, have begun this process, and their ideas are helpful. For example, Kantor and Lehr (1975) and Constantine (1986) described four kinds of family ideologies that seem to appear repeatedly when counselors and therapists work with families. They labeled these four ideologies: *closed, open, random* and *synchronous* families.

Closed families. A *closed family paradigm* is when a family has a cluster of fundamental beliefs that emphasize continuity, steadiness and conventional ways of doing things. They believe that security and belonging are very important. They prefer stability whenever possible and are concerned about deviations from what they

Ideologies in Family Life

believe are the "right" ways to do things. The motto in closed families could be described as "stability through tradition and loyalty" (Constantine, 1986, p. 20).

When families have a closed paradigm it leads them to adopt goals that are goals well defined and have clear boundaries. For example, when a family adopts a closed ideology, the parents are more likely to be concerned about their children's friends, and there are many more locked doors, careful scrutiny of strangers in the neighborhood, parental control over the media, supervised excursions (Kantor & Lehr, 1975 p. 121).

Families with this paradigm tend to organize their time so it is predictable and stable. They pay attention to the past and to the future, frequently seeking to preserve or restore something that was, or attain or achieve something that has not been accomplished. They tend to have a well-understood pattern in using time, and the individuals tend to fit their schedules to the family pattern.

The method of making decisions in closed families tends to be relatively authoritarian. Tradition or aspirations are important, and what the parents think is important. These two qualities tend to create a more authoritarian power system and method of government than exists in open and random families.

Open families. When families have an *open family paradigm* they believe in a style of life that emphasizes dialogue, communication, patience, and a willingness to change. These families believe in adaptability and innovation and they are looking for new ways to do things. They believe in negotiation and collaboration as the fundamental ways to live and cope.

Families who have this paradigmatic orientation tend to behave and act in accordance with these Level III beliefs. Space in open families is more movable and flexible than in the closed type, and the individuals have more freedom in what they can do. They are allowed to self-regulate and they are more free to choose their own destinations as long as they do not interfere with rights and space of others. Frequent guests, unlocked doors, and lower levels of monitoring typify these families. The parents are much less likely to be intrusively involved in keeping track of family members movement.

The method of governance that is more consistent with this style of life is less authoritarian than the closed type. Therefore, there is usually more discussion, sharing of ideas, democracy, and flexibility. The approach tends to be to try to find consensus rather than to try to find what is "right" or proper.

Random families. When families have a random family paradigm their core ideology emphasizes discontinuity and they maximize change in a radical focus on the present. In the random paradigm, the guiding images are novelty, creativity, and individuality. The motto of a random paradigm family might be "Variety through Innovation and Individuality" (Constantine, 1986, p. 20). Random families are flexible with regard to traditions and established ways of doing things, but they tend to be fairly rigid in emphasizing individuality, little restraint, and high levels of freedom.

These abstract beliefs are used to manage family resources in ways that are quite different from closed and open families. The use of space has some predictability, but less than with closed or open families. For example, eating and sleeping may occur in many places. Expressions of anger, affection, and joy may occur in the street as well as behind the closed doors of the home.

The method of making decisions and governing tends to emphasize individuality. The family interests are considered, but what is important to the family is that the individuals are free to fulfill their needs and goals. Therefore, the individuals are

Ideologies in Family Life

JOURNAL OF THOUGHTS 5.2: YOUR FAMILY OF ORIGIN IDEOLOGY

1. Do the best job you can of identifying an ideology that exists in your family of origin. What are the themes and plans that go along with that ideology?

2. Give as many examples as you can that show what type of ideology existed in that family.

3. Has the ideology in your family ever changed? If not, comment on what you think it would take to change your family's ideology. If it has describe why it changed and what it changed from.

Ideologies in Family Life

quite free to "do their own thing," make their connections, set their goals, and arrange their schedules.

Time usage is irregular, and can be viewed very differently by different individuals or groups within the family. The preference is for evolving and spontaneous patterns that emerge from and out of what happens rather than because it is part of a plan or structure.

Patterns of getting energy are fluctuating and changing. Family members may engage in fueling operations singly or in groups, and they have great freedom to seek the type of fueling they want. Foods tend to be prepared more individually. Music and entertainment is more spontaneous and varied.

Synchronous families   The synchronous family paradigm emphasizes harmony, tranquility, and mutual identification. When families have this paradigm they believe they will be able to move through life with little conflict and they will be able to easily resolve the conflict that does occur. These families depend on family members thinking alike...not to control, but to avoid conflict. Many of these family decisions will be based on consentience (the root word here is consent and the word means a nonintellectual sense of unity) and they will try to function with consentaneity and try to act in harmonious agreement. Some have commented that families who adopt this ideology have a distinctly utopian, mystical, or magical flavor to their family climate. The motto of synchrony might be "Harmony through Perfection and Identification" (Constantine, 1986, p. 20–21).

Other ideologies.   The four ideologies discussed above are only the beginning of the many deeply held beliefs that families can have. For example, in the many years I have taught the course associated with this text, I have heard hundreds of hours of discussion by students about the themes, beliefs, and deeply held ideologies their families hold. Some of these include such ideas as "Education is to be revered above all;" "Our family will succeed in business;" "We will do everything we can to assure that our children make it to heaven;" and, "Our family members will prove themselves at sports at all costs."

The last one mentioned is particularly interesting. Not long ago in a class using this text, a young woman took about ten minutes of class time explaining how her family was a water-skiing family. At first, I didn't believe that what she was saying was really an explanation of how ideologies work in families. But, after a few minutes I began to see her point.

From an early age, her father had decided that she was going to be a world-class water skier. She explained the deep core ideology was about success and winning. She went on to say that attached to that winning notion was a very closed family ideal. She was not allowed to have friends unless the friends were willing to help with the water skiing workouts. The only magazines found in the house were about fitness and water skiing related topics. Schoolwork was even scheduled around practices. Meals in the home were designed for fitness and energy and every part of her life was regulated around ski meets, winning certain events, and progressing to the championship.

Additionally, the family finances were organized around this one idea (ideology, ideal, and paradigm). The family lived in Seattle and they purchased a home next to a lake that included a dock so that travel time for practice would be minimized. The mother took an extra job to make payments on a very expensive state-of-the-art ski boat. And, the family vehicle had to be one that could pull the boat and take the family on the weekly ski trips.

While this is an unusual example of a family ideology, it does illustrate how the principle works. Imagine for a minute if the girl was diagnosed with cancer and could no longer water ski. Or, and this was part of the story, imagine if one day she said, "That's enough" and refused to ski? The exaggeration principle (presented below) would suggest that instead of finding a new deep purpose or ideology, they would, instead turn up the volume of the old one and try to make it work. And, that is exactly what they did; there was a younger sister that became the next family skier. The young woman related how her family thought of her as a traitor and she was barely allowed to visit her home. The story was obviously a painful and traumatic one for her. Until she read the material for class, she really had not realized what had happened. What would you do to comfort her?

THE EXAGGERATION PRINCIPLE

Confronted by problems, families do the best they can to solve them. Again, they maximize their resources and try the best strategy they know to survive and attain the goals they have at their core. So, one strategy that most families try when something goes wrong is to try harder. "Trying harder" is itself defined paradigmatically: families try harder by doing more of the same. Instead of changing strategies or

Ideologies in Family Life

ACTIVITY 5.1 - YOUR FAMILY FLAG

The purpose of this activity is to metaphorically capture elements of your family ideology. You may focus on your current family, or you may think back on your family of origin. Be sure to specify which family you are considering during this activity.

On an 8 1/2" x 11" piece of plain paper make a sketch of a family flag. On this flag choose symbols that represent the key and central aspects of your family of focus. What is the core ideology of your family that can be represented in a few simple metaphorical symbols? Also, choose a motto for your family and integrate it into the flag. You may use colors to fill in your sketch. Remember to be simple and direct. Try not to make it too complicated.

Attach a one-page written explanation of the flag indicating how the symbols you have chosen represent deeply held family ideologies. Even if your family is composed of a few people or if it is complex and complicated, try to imagine some theme or idea that sums up your experience of living in that group. Each family has its own unique way of doing things and meeting the challenges of life. Do your best at capturing those core unique qualities and ideas.

Space to complete your family flag

changing their ideology, they turn up the volume of the strategy they already use. Thus, by using the available resources each family under stress has a natural tendency toward exaggeration of its own special character.

PRINCIPLE 5.2: EXAGGERATION UNDER STRESS

When families are under stress there is a tendency to exaggerate the family ideologies (paradigms). In other words, under stress families usually do not change strategies or ideologies...they exaggerate the one they are most used to.

A family paradigm represents a commitment to certain priorities that incline a family in one direction or another as it seeks to overcome difficulties. For this reason, as families of different types become over-stressed, they are prone to basically distinct modes of failure. A family's methods of managing its resources consist of essentially stable structures maintaining coordinated family processes. The regime is resilient and not likely to change fundamentally in response to stress, especially as it is guided by the family's paradigm. Paradigms are regarded as even more invariant features of a family and are, therefore, quite unlikely to change under even severe stress.

The stability of a paradigm can be appreciated if it is remembered that a family paradigm is the family's way of perceiving the world, including their problems, as well as their way of approaching and solving problems. Thus, the most likely response to any challenge from within or without is for a family to respond in a manner consistent with its paradigm and organization. The more difficult and intractable the situation, the more extreme are the measures that will be taken, extreme, that is, in a way consistent with the family paradigm. The longer an impasse is sustained, the greater the degree of typical exaggeration.

The closed family confronted by problems relies on tradition, authority, and loyalty to solve them. The more difficult the problem proves to be, the stronger are the attempts to control, to pull the family into line, and to maintain consistency against a threatening world. Thus closed families tend to become more isolated from the world, more strongly and intensely connected internally, and more rigid as they become increasingly disabled. The rallying cry is essentially "Fall in! Toe the line!"

The random family relies on spontaneity and creative individuality to find solutions to problems. As members work with increasing independence to find more creative solutions, family process becomes more chaotic, less coordinated. The random family tends toward greater separateness and chaos as it becomes more disabled. In the random family, the appeal is "Be more creative." "Find something new." (Which, it must be noted, does not imply a change of basic tactics; finding something new is what the random family does normally.)

Chapter 5

When initial attempts fail, the open family hangs in there, trying to hammer out a consensual solution. They gather more and more information and try harder to communicate. They become inundated with information and overwhelmed by hashing things through. As they question more and more of their basic rules, less and less is clearly known. They go around in circles. If problems remain insoluble they become more and more enmeshed in a process that generates chaos. Their rallying cry is "We've got to work this out. We'll talk it through again and consider it more thoroughly!"

The synchronous family relies on its essential agreement to enable it to solve problems in a coordinated way while acting independently. When this consentaneity breaks down, the family moves toward greater separateness. To remain coordinated and true to its paradigm, it narrows its scope and restricts its actions to those on which there is the closest agreement. Thus it becomes more rigid and stereotyped in its behavior while also becoming less connected. As synchronous families are based on similarity and do not deal as well with difference, which would contradict their synchrony, it becomes increasingly necessary to deny differences and problems, hiding these under a veneer of agreement and competence. As it becomes disabled, the synchronous family attempts to continue "business as usual" and insists, "There is no real problem. As always, we are really in agreement about this." Less and less happens as they become increasingly "dead" as a family or increasingly disconnected from their real problems (Constantine, 1986, p. 182–183).

According to Constantine's ideas, most of the time when families become disabled it is not the family paradigms that are the root of the problem. The family paradigms are the abstract beliefs, and most families have defensible, coherent, and healthy basic assumptions. It is the less abstract processes that occur at Level I and Level II that become disabled. In other words, it tends to be the management that becomes disabled rather than the ideology that guides the system. It is the family's strategies for clarifying goals, making effective decisions, and managing resources that become dysfunctional.

Strategies for using the Exaggeration Under Stress Principle. When families find themselves in deep trouble, they tend to seek help. Closed families are more cautious in whom they turn to and how they do it, but closed, open, and random families all seek help in their own ways. They turn to books, friends, relatives, educators, therapists, ministers, Ann Landers, psychiatrists, social workers, etc.

The strategy for using the Exaggeration Under Stress Principle to help families is to help them learn how to "borrow" management strategies from another type. For example, it is usually easier for a closed family to use open strategies than random strategies. And it is usually easier for random families to use open strategies than closed strategies.

JOURNAL OF THOUGHTS 5.3: YOUR FUTURE FAMILY IDEOLOGY

1. Now for some really hard (but interesting) stuff. I want you to imagine that you are on trial. In order to prove your innocence (for some crime you have committed) you have to convince the jury about the type of family paradigm your family adopted when you were growing up. Try to describe your family of origin (when you were 16, as an arbitrary age) in terms of the following: were you open, close, random, or synchronous? Provide some data, examples, or reflections to prove your case.

Chapter 5

(continue your example here)

Ideologies in Family Life

PRACTICAL IMPLICATIONS

The idea that *some parts of family ideologies are more abstract, central and fundamental than other parts of ideologies* provides a number of useful insights. For example, this idea helps us realize there is great flexibility in the way families can organize themselves and be successful. It is not usually unhelpful to think that families need to conform to one particular mold or style of life if they are to be successful. There are plenty of examples of successful families who are close, open, cautious, frugal, religious, adventurous, or whatever the overall core belief is. A real problem is if an ideology becomes too extreme in any of the many directions it could take.

Problems also arise when families get stuck in ways of doing things that are too narrow and restricted; their way of behaving can interfere with their ability to cope with new developmental, cultural, or technological changes. This can happen when family members are assigned roles that fit some predetermined ideal and there is a belief that to change how activities are done would be to damage the family.

Another practical insight these ideas provide is that families who are extremely and exclusively open, synchronous, or religious tend to attain their goals most of the time. They seem to get into trouble when unusual events occur such as an unanticipated developmental change or some new situation where the old methods don't work.

This also suggests that when families get into this type of difficulty, they usually do not need extensive therapy to get their life back in a workable and effective condition. They need to broaden their repertoire of ways to respond to meet a particular situation, and sometimes this can be accomplished as easily as talking to a friend or reading a book to get some ideas about new ways to respond.

Another practical implication of these ideas is that understanding ideologies help us understand why families do not change their basic way of life quickly, often, or easily. Sometimes when we try to help families we wish they would change easily and quickly. We naively want our therapy, advice or educational programs to make big differences in families. However, when we realize how earlier generations are involved in family paradigms, how slowly and gradually they are initially formed in courtship and early marriage, how they are intricately tied up with deeply experienced affective states, and how they are probably changed only by severe crises, it helps us realize that these basic assumptions are not fleeting and flexible ideas that can change easily. They are the most fundamental rudders in the ship of life, and once they are formed they only change slowly and only when there are very unusual circumstances.

Once we understand the nature of family ideologies and the role they have in family life, we can better understand what families are going through when they are experiencing enough stress that they are changing their paradigms. Also, we can adapt our attempts to help them so we focus on the parts of their systems that can change.

Chapter 5

Summary

This chapter described the three levels of abstraction that family scientists pay attention to in family systems. The three levels are called *Level I, Level II,* and *Level III*. Part of the Level III processes are what David Reiss has called *family paradigms.* Family ideologies or paradigms are the fundamental, general, abstract and guiding beliefs families construct about their world. Having this concept helps us better understand how family systems work and how we can help families regardless of the stage of life-cycle.

Ideologies in Family Life

SPOTLIGHT ON RESEARCH 5.1: FAMILY TIME AS AN IDEOLOGY

In the *Journal of Marriage and the Family*, Dr. Kerry Daly has written an excellent theory piece about ideologies in families and the time they use or want to use to promote family life (Daly, 1996). In this article, Daly suggests that there often a disconnect between what families see as important (their ideology) and what they actually do. Further, he suggests that family time is not the same to all families. Usually, those of us in the family science discipline ask families to spend more time together without thinking about what that really means.

There are three ideas in this article that are of interest to our discussion of family ideology. First, Daly suggests that our ideas about time and how we use it are greatly influenced by Western culture that promotes a more child-centered idea of togetherness. This ideology states that if we want families to be stronger and be able to meet their goals, they should spend more time together. That is becoming increasingly difficult as work schedules, complicated life expectations, and complex family structures emerge in the 21st century. He suggests that everyone has two families, the one we live with and the one we live by. Often these two do not meet in reality.

Second, he suggests that families are seriously pushed and constrained by the amount of time they use on family related issues. Further, there is difference in what children want from the time compared to what the adults say they would like to have. Parents report wanting more time to do activities, children simply want more time with their parents.

Third, his research found that most families were quite distressed about the amount of time they were spending with family members. Parents reported high levels of guilt about not being able to spend time with family members. He found that the primary strategy for this problem was to manage to find ways of managing their guilt rather than changing their ideology or their time available.

Your response: What types of struggles did your family experience when you were growing up? How was time use by children decided? Mostly by parents or by the child? Explain.

Ideologies in Family Life

STUDY QUESTIONS

1. Name all four types of family paradigms, give the definition of each, and provide an example of what each of those family styles would be like.

2. What is a Level III type of analysis when speaking of family life?

3. Compare Level III to Level II analysis of family life. Provide examples of each.

4. Explain why most of us never really think about Level III aspects of family life.

5. Provide four clear examples of how you could use the principles in this chapter to make family life stronger.

6. Is an ideology different than a paradigm? Explain.

KEY TERMS

Paradigms
Levels of analysis
Exaggeration Under Stress Principle
Ideologies
Abstraction

CHAPTER
SIX

*Discovering Rules and
Patterns of Interaction*

Rediscovering Rules and Patterns of Interaction

Main Points:

1. Some of the rules in family systems are social norms.

2. Many rules that are important in family systems are part of the culture in a society.

3. Rules have many purposes. They regulate the way resources are managed, regulate emotional distance, clarify boundaries, control the implementation of decisions, clarify how to deal with exceptions and violation of rules, etc.

4. Some of the rules in family systems do not come from social norms. Some family rules are simple and uncomplicated, but others form a cluster or complex set of rules that are called rule sequences.

5. Rule sequences regulate patterned ways of behaving.

6. Rule sequences usually have a cyclic or feedback-loop aspect to them.

7. Rules sometimes become developmentally inappropriate, too rigid, or disabling.

8. Usually the more implicit rules are, the better.

Discovering Rules and Patterns of Interaction

INTRODUCTION

Most families have thousands of formal and informal rules that regulate and direct family life. For example, think of the mail each family receives every day. When mail arrives, who goes to the mailbox and retrieves it? Where is it placed? Is it sorted and delivered to each person's room? Can anyone open the "junk" mail? Can parents open the children's mail? Are there certain types of letters that do not have to be shared at all? Most of the rules that govern these processes emerge without any fanfare or even much negotiation, but they have power to direct and dictate much of what we do. They influence where we sit when we watch T.V. or eat dinner. They direct which towels to use in the bathroom, where to store Christmas decorations, and who should replace the empty toilet paper roll.

Sometimes we think of family rules as *social norms*. Some of these rules come from accepted ways of doing things that we adopt from our culture, some are created as family life emerges, and some are developed in response to specific events in everyday life as we raise children and become involved in other complicated family activities.

RULES AS SOCIAL NORMS

Over the past 100 years, sociologists have been very helpful in showing how social norms are created and influence people. Social norms are beliefs that exist in a culture that prescribe certain behaviors and proscribe others. Thus, they deal with "shoulds" and "shouldn'ts" that get communicated to us by the groups of people we are around each day.

Social norms can apply to minor acts, like what utensil one uses at the dinner table, or to more major occurrences like who should be chosen as a sexual partner. Sociologists have developed several concepts that help us tell the difference between norms that deal with serious matters (those rules that become formalized over time are called laws) and those that deal with less serious behavior. They refer to norms dealing with behaviors considered especially important as *mores*, and behaviors that are preferred but more or less optional are called *folkways*.

Chapter 6

For example, in the state in which I live, there are many fathers who feel a strong pressure to take their children fishing. It is part of the news, frequently mentioned in conversation, and one often sees boats and fishing gear in people's yards. This is folkway. Or, in other words, it is a way "folks do things here."

Mores are customs or conventions that are essential to the maintaining of community life. They are a bit stronger than a folkway. An example of mores can be found in the choice and timing of dating behavior. From folkways and mores we learn who we are and how we fit into society. Folkways and laws have a powerful influence with regard to how we manage family business. Laws tell us it is not acceptable to discipline children with abusive strategies. Mores and folkways pressure us to dress our children in certain ways, and speak to our spouses in particular ways.

Children in their parental family learn many social norms that deal with the family realm, and the family of origin of a newly married couple has an enormous impact on what they adopt as the normative elements of their family life.

Additionally, family behavior may be greatly influenced by where the parents work, their religious orientation, and even the neighborhood in which they live. Every affiliation, and to some degree every past affiliation, of a family member has an influence on the norms that a family consciously and explicitly accepts as well as the tacit or "hidden" understandings, the "taken-for-granted" definitions that often are brought to light only when violated.

Since social norms are an important part of family processes, it is important to consider how families teach, adopt, and change the norms they use. Additionally, understanding the nature of social norms helps us understand some of the sources of stress in families. For example, a teenager might learn something new from their peers and try to introduce that idea into their own family.

There is one distinct property that clearly identifies the nature of a social norm/rule: they are simple. In other words, normative social rules are not complex. They do not describe behavior sequences, nor do they necessarily rely upon other rules as a requirement for their existence.

HOW RULES EMERGE IN FAMILIES

There are many ways rules find their way into family systems. Some are copied from the family of origin and are brought into the new relationship by either the husband or the wife. From the time of birth we assimilate and learn the rules we need to follow in order to live successfully within our families. Sometimes the old, well-used family rules follow us into our new relationships. When two competing rule systems (one from each partner) come together, a clash can occur. One of the purposes of courtship is to begin the process of rule discovery, negotiation, and creation. It is during this time that partners begin to adopt some rules from one person's family of origin, some from another, and discover they have some rules in common. The process of

Discovering Rules and Patterns of Interaction

courtship and marriage is a time when rules of family life are adopted and eventually submerge into the routines of daily living becoming the implicit rule structure of the family.

Families also acquire rules from the culture in which they live. They may be adopted by choice or simply assimilate beliefs and rules from external influences. For example, movies and television are sources of influence from which we may adopt bits and pieces of how to act in family life. This is a risky strategy because typically family life in such venues may be represented in ways that are unrealistic, over simplified, and even inaccurately portrayed.

A good example of this is the often-used portrayal of family life in shows that emerged during the 1950s and 1960s. Programs like *Leave it to Beaver* and *The Donna Reed Show* portrayed family life in ways that represented ideals rather than anyone's reality. But people watched these programs and thought of their own lives as deficient because they were not living up to a fantasy portrayal of what someone thought family life "ought" to be like.

Another excellent example of this type of inaccurate portrayal can be found in the Bill Cosby show of the late 1980s and 1990s. While certainly a funny program, I would often find myself saying, "How can he can solve all of these problems in a half-hour show"; or, "How is it his children have only superficial problems?" In that particular program, it was also inaccurate to portray this family, with house beautiful, and really low stress, where the father was a pediatrician and the mother an attorney. We rarely see them work or be confronted with competing family/work roles. Of course the problem arises when a young couple believes that the Cosby family in fantasy is how their life should be emerging in the harsh flurry of daily reality.

Third, family members adopt rules of daily life by negotiation. This process can include discussion about such mundane issues as who sleeps on which side of the bed, who sits where at the table, who puts their clothes in what closet, and whether to squeeze the toothpaste in the middle or end of the tube. Negotiation also is used for rules about deeper issues like who controls the money, the distribution of other resources, and the division of labor.

Multiple interactions. Many rules also appear through a series of multiple interactions (Haley, 1963; Galvin & Brommel, 1991). Through the processes of trial, struggle, error, conflict, and resolution, family members adopt what seems to work for them. By "work for them" we mean the processes that families find helpful in keeping the system in balance, free from chaos, and working in harmony. Eventually, they learn, adapt, assimilate, and accommodate. Not everything chosen is best for all members. Those within the system believe what they are doing is necessary to keep the system in working order. The process begins with the couple meeting for the first time, and continues on as a developmental process. They cannot avoid the process as it occurs with or without their approval or knowledge. Every transaction results in the creation, modification, or support of rules.

If your family was like most, you had informal "rules" about each of these areas. In fact most families construct hundreds of rules about how to manage their daily life. Most of the rules emerge without fanfare or proclamation, and they have a curious power to direct and dictate how we act to one another, how we come and go, what we say or do not say.

A good example of how silently these rules emerge can be found in the lives of practically any couple you survey. Ask them how they decided who would do the dishes, cook dinner, or make the bed in the morning. Most will look at one another and say, "ummm… we don't know." Even those who talk about these rules before they are married will often relate that things changed (albeit slowly and silently) over time without discussion.

RULE PURPOSES

One way to better understand rule behavior is to understand their purposes or functions. They have the purpose of maintaining regularity, providing system accountability, and providing boundary maintenance. They also educate and regulate personal distance within the system. These vital functions make norms a critical force in helping systems avoid chaos.

In their work on rules and communication, Cronen, Pearce, and Harris (1979) indicated that rules are an unavoidable and inescapable element of human interaction because individuals tend to act in rather unpredictable ways so, we are more effective when our behavior has regularities. Since the purpose of a system is to obtain goals,

Discovering Rules and Patterns of Interaction

ACTIVITY 6.1 - YOUR FAMILY RULES

Answer the following questions about the family in which you were raised:

1. Did family members usually sit at certain places during meals?

2. Did the members of your family "know" how much it was ok to touch each other, and what ways were ok?

3. Were there certain spots where dirty clothes end up before they were washed?

4. Did family members talk differently when visitors came? Did they choose different topics, or speak in different tones?

5. Was it taboo to speak about some topics?

seek balance, and maintain cohesion, if the behavior of each member were random and impulsive, the system could not flourish. Thus, families must demand of their members a certain amount of consensus and conformity about the underlying rules and assumptions.

Accountability. Rules hold system members accountable for actions within and outside of the system (Cronen et al., 1979). In Chapters 1 and 2, it was mentioned that families have expectations and unique sets of values about directions, activities, and goals. From those deep ideologies and values simple family rules advise members when they are not performing in ways that meet those generalized expectations.

Boundaries. Family rules also help family members know boundaries that exist between a family and its environment. Each family exists in a complex network of other family systems and external systems, and it has to maintain a certain amount of uniqueness and distance from the others or its own existence fades. Therefore, norms are developed to define the boundaries that represent the interface between each family and its environmental systems.

In addition, there are boundaries within the system. The executive subsystem (possibly the mother and father) interacts at a different level and is responsible for different tasks than the child subsystem. The boundary between two interfacing systems is defined by simple rules about boundaries (Okun & Rapport, 1980). For example, boundary rules dictate how permeable the family and subsystem boundaries can be and what the limitations of individual family members are.

If mom and dad are having a serious conversation and the door is closed, family members know not to interact. When the family is in a public setting they know it is inappropriate to speak of Sally's pregnancy and abortion. Family members know when (or if) it is appropriate to bring other children into the home. These types of rules maintain system boundaries. It is critical for each family member to know where the family and the outside world begin and end. Without implicit knowledge of boundary rules it is very difficult for the family system to be a system at all.

When family rules begin to be questioned and challenged, often it is the rules about boundaries that are being questioned. A healthy family system has effectively created functional and healthy rule systems that tell family members where the system begins and ends, where they can go and cannot go, and what they can and cannot do. This is assuming, of course, that the system has created a flexible and non-destructive rule system.

Distance regulation. One specific purpose of simple rules is that they regulate distance. Generally, family researchers use the term cohesion to refer to this aspect of family systems (Kantor & Lehr, 1975; Hess & Handel, 1959; Olson & McCubbin, 1982; Gavazzi, Anderson, & Sabatelli, 1993; Day, Gavazzi, & Acock,

185

2001). Cohesion means that each family establishes "a pattern of separateness and connectedness." Family rules tell us how and when we should be close and when we should be separate.

Another purpose of rules is to regulate how families allocate and exchange resources. These rules govern how scarce resources should be divided up within the system. This includes how family money should be spent, rules about living space, and rules about intangibles like time and affection. For example, if there is extra cash, dad may have first choice about whether he will spend it on a new tractor part or mom may have first choice about whether she will invest it. Rules of designated authority are rules about division of responsibility. Mother may be in charge of anyone who feels down. An older grandparent living with the family may be in charge of relieving tension when the pressure of an argument gets too intense. A father may be charged with the responsibility of the first reaction in times of emergency. At times of divorce or death, rule and role reallocation may occur to fill the void created by the absent family member.

Implementation.   Many of the rules we have in private life have to do with implementation. Rules of implementation exist for the purpose of implementing other rules and expectations. While a family may have a series of rules about a topic (how much schoolwork), they also have a series of rules that designate how they go about getting the work done. For example, suppose a family believes that having high grades is very important. They may have developed a series of implicit and explicit rules that direct the system to assist children in fulfilling the goal established by that belief. Rules of implementation are created to make sure larger rules are followed. The implementation rule might be: "If your younger sister is having trouble with math, you will help her. If she is having trouble with history, she is to suffer in silence, our family is not interested in history."

Exceptions.   Families may also have rules about *exceptions*. The exceptions allow the system to deal with the unexpected and regulate necessary behavior even when an important family rule cannot be followed. In the schoolwork example, an exception might go like this: "Jose is very athletic and we believe personal talents should be enhanced. But we also believe everyone needs to get better grades." In Jose's case, both of these things are not going to happen. So the rule exception in these types of cases emerges as: "We will let Jose choose where he will put the emphasis of his time."

Violation.   Another category of family rules is rules about violation. What happens in a family when a member gets bad grades and has violated the rule about good grades and achievement? What happens when someone does talk about death or negative ideas when the family has proscribed that kind of interaction? These actions will trigger another type of rule that specifies what is to be done following violation.

Discovering Rules and Patterns of Interaction

EXPLICIT AND IMPLICIT RULES

Some of the rules in families are *explicit* and some are *implicit* (Satir, 1972). Explicit rules are the beliefs that are recognized, acknowledged, and known by a family, and often they can be overtly talked about. Explicit rules are usually more formalized because they are made visible. An example of an explicit family rule is one that is made by decree: "All children who go on dates have to be home by 12:30 pm." Or: "Before a visit to your father, you must have your room clean." Such rules are a little different than daily requests that require a specific and perhaps a one-time response. They take on the form of regulating behavior over time, as a generalized guideline, meant to be in force "forever" or "until altered."

Another example of an explicit rule is: "Your grandmother and I have decided that all children should get some type of allowance, on a weekly basis." This type of rule has the necessary components. First, it implies that two or more people have discussed the need openly. Second, it has a long-term element to it, prescribing an action over time. Third, it is meant to regulate the flow of resources within the system or perform some other function. Also, it helps to maintain order and prevent debilitating chaos.

The members of a family do not recognize some rules and these we call the implicit rules. Implicit rules remain hidden and submerged from view. They are not discussed and have not been thought of or labeled by family members. This invisibility makes them very powerful. As invisible simple rules, they take on the status of something never questioned, or even considered as changeable. They are the way "things are."

An example of an implicit rule can be found in the way family members greet each other after a long absence. Do they hug, do they shake hands, or do they just smile? In this example, the norm reflects what the family has decided is appropriate about distance regulation: how close and affectionate should family members be.

Some families have implicit rules against sharing special feelings. They may go to great lengths to "help" family members learn ways to express or suppress how they feel. Suppose a family has an implicit rule that only good topics and feelings should be discussed. The belief may be that to talk about negative parts of life is a destructive process. The negative feelings and experiences may go unexpressed. The negative feelings remain unspoken, but probably not unfelt. It could be very dangerous for a family to create a system where significant and important feelings cannot be discussed.

Rule patterns. In the 1950s a group of family scientists led by Don Jackson and Gregory Bateson discovered that family systems have rules that are different from the rules families get from society or invent themselves (Jackson, 1957, 1965). These rules are patterns of behavior in family systems that are repeated so regularly that they are a governing or regulating part of the structure of the family systems.

The family scientists who have discovered these rules found that usually the rules "tend to be implicit and they are rarely, if ever, explicit or written down" (Ford,

1983, p. 135). Therefore, the only way to identify the family rules is to *infer* them from the repeated or redundant patterns in the behavior in a family. According to Jackson:

> *Again, we must emphasize the rule is an inference, an abstraction—more precisely, a metaphor coined by the observer to cover the redundancy he observes. We say a rule is a "format of regularity imposed upon a complicated process by the investigator." (Jackson, 1965, p. 11)*

> *Since we are always making inferences when we try to identify rules, it is usually helpful to precede each rule we think we see with the caution: "it seems as if...." (Jackson 1965, p. 592)*

In games such as bridge, the rules are mostly explicit and most of them are rules. In family life, however, there are many rules that are implicit. For example, if we observed a family in which family members rarely demonstrated their feelings in an open way, we could infer that "it seems as if..." they have a rule that they shall not demonstrate feelings overtly.

An example that illustrates the inference of hidden rules is what happened in a family where the wife was intellectually superior to the husband and every time something happened that illustrated her superiority, a child would become unruly or the husband would react with a biting negative comment. We could infer that "it seems as if..." the family has a rule that mother's superiority can't be talked about or demonstrated.

Another example of inferring hidden rules is that a family had a pattern that the only time the parents were able to act together was when they teamed up against a rebellious child. The parents never went out together and they maintained a pattern of discord most of the time. The father wasn't in charge generally in the family, but he gained control with occasional violent outbursts. In this family system, we could infer that "it seems as if..." the family has some rules that discord must be maintained at all costs, the parents shall not cooperate unless it is to gang up on the child, and the father shall gain power only by violent outbursts (Jackson & Yalom, 1965).

Another example of family rules is how often family members interrupt each other. Researchers have discovered that, contrary to popular opinion, interrupting is actually a healthy sign in the family realm. This was found in a series of research studies that compared a group of families who were having serious problems with a group of families who were not in a clinical setting. The researchers found that the clinical sample was more careful in the way they communicated with each other, and they interrupted each other less. The more healthy families, on the other hand, were more spontaneous and careless in their communication patterns and there was more interrupting (Alexander, 1973). Some other research found there are gender differences in the interrupting. Males tend to interrupt females much more than females interrupt males (Gottman, 1999).

This suggests there are some "rules" operating with regard to interrupting patterns in most family systems. These rules are not what we call "social norms" because they are in opposition to some beliefs. When most people are confronted with the finding that men interrupt more than women, they usually respond by thinking this is an undesirable pattern because it illustrates another subtle way males dominate females, and they then try to develop "social norms" to reverse the pattern of male dominance. The rules in this situation are the rules that govern the interaction that is actually in opposition to the more consciously preferred "agreements" or "understandings" that are the social norms.

An interesting example of a family rule is in a book by Lynn Caine called *Widows*. Her husband is dying of cancer and as the story unfolds he is dealing with the devastating feelings of knowing his life is about to end. Ms. Caine describes how this crisis debilitated their relationship. A source of major stress in her situation was a hidden rule that the subject of the husband's death could not be overtly talked about.

No one in the Caine family said "O.K., rule number 23: if a member of our family gets a fatal disease, no one is to come right out and talk about it. In fact, we should pretend the dying person is going to live and continue on as if nothing happened." Ms. Caine's family, however, acted as if the rule were formal, written, and unchangeable.

A very poignant and depressing part of Caine's story is her lamenting about her feelings following his death. She reports how much she wished she would have changed the rule or suspended the rule and talked to him about the end of his life and the hundreds of issues that needed to be resolved. But, the rule had prevailed and what was uppermost on their minds was never discussed.

This process was regulated by a series of rules about what could be talked about and what couldn't. The norms she wanted to live by were quite different from the implicit and hidden rules they had developed in their family system.

There are several aspects of family rules that are different from general norms. *First*, some family rules create and maintain patterns of behavior that are different from the values, ideals, and goals of families and the cultures the families live in. The rules that operate in triangling illustrate this difference. Most societies, sub-cultures, and families have a rule that family members should not "triangle in" lovers or children to escape from or stabilize unresolved emotional tensions in a marital relationship, but it occurs with an unfortunate frequency. When it happens there are always a number of unwritten and undesirable rules that govern, regulate, and stabilize these processes. The patterns of triangling in family systems are so predictable, so repetitious, and so redundant, that they could not be operating randomly, and therefore they illustrate the operation of rules.

Chapter 6

<hr>

A second way family rules seem to be different from normative rules is that family members are so unaware of their non-normative rules that it is almost impossible for most families to identify or describe them. It is usually an outside observer who is able to see them.

A third aspect of family rules is that, because they are not governed by the normative part of social systems, there can be great variability from one family to another. Imagine a situation in which the mother arrives home from a trying day at work. In the example below, she sees the kitchen in disarray, honey on the counter, and crusts of bread littered liberally on the table. The interaction that follows upon her arrival is predictable because of the family rules, but these rules are unique to each family and they are not determined by normative beliefs, even though they may be influenced by family goals, values, and ideologies. For example, if neatness and personal responsibility are valued, one series of responses tends to emerge. If independence and autonomy are valued, a different script tends to emerge.

The fourth of non-normative rules is that they cannot only be simple and non-complex (like normative rules) but they may also be complex and part of a cyclic pattern that is unique to a particular family. These complex sequences are explained in the next section.

The idea that family systems have non-normative rules is a helpful addition to the ways we think about family systems. When we understand this idea, it sensitizes us to aspects of family systems we don't have access to with other ideas. It also opens up a number of new ways to try to help families, but before the ways of using this concept are discussed, it is helpful to understand what rule sequences are.

Example: Family Rules
Family #1:
"Jason come in here this minute!"
"Gee, mom, keep your shirt on, no need to yell."
"I have told you, maybe a million times, that when you get something out it is your responsibility to put it away. Why do you leave these messes? Do you think I am your maid, and will just continue to pick up after you like you are some type of prince around here?"
"Sorry mom, I...."
"Sorry isn't good enough, get in here and clean this mess up!"
The family rule: make the child be responsible.

Family #2:
"Jason, I'm home."
There is no reply from the bedroom.
"Jason, do you know anything about this mess? The honey is getting on the floor, honey."
There is still no reply. She wipes up the mess, and continues on with dinner.

Discovering Rules and Patterns of Interaction

The family rule: Keep peace at any cost.

Family #3:
"Jason, could you come out here for a minute."
"Hi, mom, what's up?"
"The kitchen is a bit of a mess, I'm not to happy about the honey mess. I need to take a shower and relax for a minute. When the kitchen is clean, I would be willing to tackle dinner. Can you take care of it please?"
"I am in the middle of a math problem."
"Well, I am hungry, we won't start on dinner until the mess is gone."
Family rule: Insist on the logical consequences.

RULE SEQUENCES IN FAMILY LIFE

Jay Haley developed the idea that some family rules occur in what he called sequences (Haley, 1976). A rule sequence is when there is a connected series of rules that govern a complex pattern in the behavior of several individuals in a family system. These sequences tend to have a cyclic pattern to them, so they are sometimes called cycles. When they deal with negative or disabling patterns we often refer to them as *vicious cycles*. Another term for these sequences is that they often form a *feedback loop*. A feedback loop occurs when the feedback some family members get leads to the next step in the rule sequence. If the following situation were to occur regularly in a family, it would be an example of a fairly simple rule sequence:

1. When one parent has a bad day at the office, he or she comes home and is critical of the other parent.
2. The second parent takes the anger out on a child.
3. The child picks a fight with another sibling or kicks the dog.

Many rule sequences in families are healthy and enabling. For example, a family may have a pattern of the parents getting up a few minutes earlier than they would need to so they can visit for a minute with their child and express affection before beginning the daily routines. When the parents conform to this rule, it may tend to begin a cycle of other rule-bound behaviors in the family such as the children and adults being more pleasant, listening to each other, doing favors for each other, etc. When the parents do not follow this pattern (family rule), a different cycle might usually be precipitated in the family, such as the children and adults being less patient, more irritable, more short-tempered, or more critical as they begin the day.

Most families probably have many healthy rule-bound sequences covering such activities as time management, allocation of scarce family resources (i.e., space, money, affection), interaction with those outside of the kin system, and every aspect of

Chapter 6

general family functioning. We suspect there are hundreds or even thousands of these repetitious patterns an average family uses as they meet the usual problems of the day.

Some rule sequences are disabling and destructive. For example, the following situation illustrates an oversimplified situation where there is a father, mother, and child, and each of them is either competent or incompetent. Since these sequences tend to be cyclic, there is a series of steps that lead to the next and they eventually lead back to the beginning again. We could start the description at any point in the cycle.

Step 1. *Father—incompetent.* The father behaves in an upset or depressed way, not functioning to his capacity.

Step 2. *Child—misbehaving.* The child begins to get out of control or express symptoms.

Step 3. *Mother—incompetent.* The mother ineffectually tries to deal with the child and cannot, and the father becomes involved.

Step 4. *Father—competent.* The father deals with the child effectively and recovers from his state of incompetency.

Step 5. *Child—behaving.* The child regains his composure and behaves properly or is defined as normal.

Step 6. *Mother—competent.* The mother becomes more capable and deals with the child and father in a more competent way, expecting more from them.

Step 7. *Father—incompetent.* The father behaves in an upset or depressed way, not functioning to his capacity, and the cycle begins again. (Haley, 1987, p. 113).

Discovering Rules and Patterns of Interaction

There are several elements of this sequence that illustrate how rule sequences usually operate. *First*, the steps seem to occur in a cyclic pattern, and the pattern repeats itself over and over. *Second*, it is quite arbitrary where the cycle begins because it can begin with several of the steps. Punctuation is an attempt to identify where complex patterns begin and end, but it usually distorts the cyclic reality of these patterns.

Third, the strategy the mother uses to "change" the husband and child by increasing her expectations actually has the opposite effect. The more she tries to get them to improve, the more they go in the opposite direction. This points out how these repetitive rules may be painfully obscured from the vision of those who participate in them. A major element of family interaction patterns is that most of them are hidden from immediate view. Often, only an outside observer or a person trained to focus on systemic processes can piece them together.

Fourth, the details of the behavior may change in different situations, but when the pattern in the cycle is rule-governed it will reappear over and over again in different forms. It is critical to remember, however, that most of the time the family members are unaware they are choosing behaviors that are rule-governed or pattern-like. Most people are surprised when such rules are brought to light in counseling sessions or by a skillful observer.

These patterns help us understand that much of what goes on in families is systemic. The individuals are tied together and try to solve problems using rules of interaction that have somehow emerged over time, which may have worked in the past, and are now reemployed to respond to life's changes and challenges.

These rule sequences also help us understand the way different perspectives influence how we try to help families. A common approach to problems in the family realm is to focus on the individuals rather than the family system. In the above situation, a therapist with an individualistic orientation might encourage the mother to be more assertive or let the child "own her own problems." The therapist might tell the parents to let the individual consequences of individual behavior take over. A therapist with a family systems approach would probably have the family think about patterns in their rules and try to find ways to help the family have more flexibility in how they respond to disrupt the rule-bound sequence.

The rule sequences that exist in families sometimes involve three generations. The following example is a case study published by Jay Haley (Haley, 1987, p. 117). It is a situation where a single parent has returned to live with her mother after a divorce.

Step 1. Grandmother takes care of grandchild while protesting that mother is irresponsible and does not take care of the child properly. In this way the grandmother is siding with the child against the mother in a coalition across generation lines.

Step 2. Mother withdraws, letting grandmother care for the child.

Step 3. The child misbehaves or expresses symptomatic behavior.

Step 4. Grandmother protests that she should not have to take care of the child and discipline him. She has raised her children, and mother should take care of her own child.

Step 5. Mother begins to take care of her own child.

Step 6. Grandmother protests that mother does not know how to take care of the child properly and is being irresponsible. She takes over the care of the grandchild to save the child from mother.

Step 7. Mother withdraws, letting grandmother care for the child.

Step 8. The child misbehaves or expresses symptomatic behavior.

It is impossible to identify the beginning or the "causes" of the problems in these situations because they are ongoing cycles that have no beginning and no end. A systems theory perspective, however, suggests it is helpful to view these situations as rule-governed cycles. When we think of them this way it reduces defensiveness, helps us better understand the system characteristics that help maintain problems, and opens up several possibilities for improving the family system.

STRATEGIES FOR MANAGING RULES IN FAMILY LIFE

There are a number of important strategies that can help family members manage the rule parts of their family systems. Among them are developing a clear understanding of how and when to be adaptable, understanding developmentally appropriate rules, avoiding rule rigidity, and learning to avoid disabling rules.

Adaptability is helpful.   The idea of change is an important idea. When family rules are too rigid, the family may break instead of bend when the winds of stress come their way (Haley, 1976). If families are willing to be flexible or adaptable in their rules it is very helpful. An example of little adaptability is seen in what occurred after a mother died. Before her death the rules of family functioning were clear. Everyone knew the goals, and knew how to accomplish what needed to get done. When she died suddenly, the system went into almost complete shutdown. The system had no provision for flexibility. Therefore, when she died, there were great gaps left in the system's ability to function.

Before her death, she had taken care of the bills, managed money matters, run the household, maintained connections with other relatives, and made many of the decisions about the growing children. It was months before this family could reorganize, change the rules, reallocate responsibilities and begin functioning again. The vitality of systems lies in a balance between the chaos of undefined competing rules and the rigidity of inflexible and less adaptable rules. As Haley has suggested "it is the rigid, repetitive sequence of a narrow range that defines pathology" (Haley, 1987, p. 112).

The rule part of families can develop several different kinds of problems that need adaptability. Some of these problems are that rules can become developmentally inappropriate, rigid, or disabling. When problems such as these occur, flexibility and adaptability are important, especially as developmental changes occur.

Discovering Rules and Patterns of Interaction

Developmentally inappropriate rules. Families sometimes create rules that are effective for a developmental stage, and they find it difficult to change as developmental changes occur. An example of this is for a family to create a group of rules that the children must obey their parents. The rules could be appropriate when the children are young and immature, but as the children mature they increase in their ability to think for themselves, and it is developmentally appropriate to gradually let the children have increasing amounts of autonomy and control over their life. As they mature in these ways, the rules that they must obey become less and less useful and more and more inappropriate.

An example of a rule that is developmentally appropriate at one stage and inappropriate at another is a rule that children should go to bed at 8:30. The rule may emerge for several reasons when the children were young: Children need a lot of sleep when they are in grade school, parents need free time in the evening, having a set time allows for easy planning and makes the day orderly. However, if the parents were still trying to make the children go to bed at 8:30 when the children are in high school, it would be unreasonable and developmentally inappropriate.

There are several situations where it can be difficult for parents to changes rules about obedience. One situation is when the rules about obedience are tied in with emotional fusion or chronic emotional tensions in the family system. In these situations, the emotionality in the family system may be so powerful that it interferes with the ability of the parents to understand that the rules are becoming inappropriate, and they may put extreme pressure on mature children to continue to be obedient.

Another situation where it can be difficult for parents to change rules about obedience is when the rules are closely tied to family ideologies. When the parents in a family place a high value on obedience and conformity, they may be unwilling to let the system change so the children can become autonomous and independent.

A third situation where it can be difficult to change rules about obedience is when parents have high standards for their children and they have a child that is not meeting their standards. For example, if a child is a rebellious or independent child, or if a child gets into trouble often, the parents may be inclined to try to help the child by trying to enforce rules about obedience long after they are developmentally appropriate.

Developmental changes are continually occurring, so it is wise to expect that rules in family systems be always in a state of flux. Much of the time the rules evolve and change gradually without anyone paying attention to them, but in some situations it is helpful to consciously make adjustments and modifications.

Rule rigidity. Rule *rigidity* is when families do not have enough flexibility in rules or they are resistant to change. Sometimes rule rigidity occurs when rules are appropriate in some situations but not in others. The story in Box 7.2 is an example of this type of rule rigidity. The following incident is a different example.

The rule emerged, and it was necessary at a period of time. Later, it became obsolete, but it remained as an unexamined, submerged family rule. So are many of the rules families sustained. They have lost their purpose, but they continue on, as if breaking or changing them would be harmful. Sometimes families act as if changing a rule means destruction. In actual fact, to not change and adapt creates a better chance for destruction than holding to outdated and useless rules.

Example: The Apocryphal Story of the Roasting Pan.

The story is told of the young newlywed preparing Sunday dinner. He was preparing the roast when, to the surprise of his wife, he cut the end off the roast, wrapped it up, and put it in the refrigerator. His astounded wife asked him why. "I don't know," he replied, "that's the way my mom does it, I guess it's good to have a little left over." When the puzzled wife was visiting his mother, she asked her the same question, and got the same answer. Later, during a holiday, they all were at the grandmother's house, having roast, and to the wife's amazement, the grandmother cut off the end of the roast, wrapped it, and continued on with preparations. "Could you tell me why you just did that?" asked the wife. "Well," the grandmother said, "I bought this roasting pan many years ago, and as you can see it is quite small. There is hardly a roast I buy that fits."

Disabling rules. Another problem that occurs in some family systems is that some of the rules are disabling. This means that rules can cause family members to interact in unhealthy and damaging ways, and this interferes with families accomplishing their goals. Also, when rules are disabling, energy and a sense of direction dissipate.

Some examples of ineffective or disabling rules are those that result in abuse to system members. A family could have a rule legitimizing the hitting of family members by those who are bigger and stronger when someone violates a boundary. Another type of ineffective rule is one that labels individuals as having little value to the system. The rules may eliminate a person from important decisions, important conversation, and problem solving processes. Unfortunately, many times other family members may not realize that they have established simple rules at the expense of one of the system members. Unintended results can abound.

Some rules limit expression and keep family members from disagreeing openly, without reprisal (Satir, 1972). Such rules can limit freedom and squash individual growth and expression. They exclude individuals and make them feel like an outsider in their own family system.

One type of family rule that is destructive is to have rules that communicate mistrust (Lidz, 1963). In these situations a child may be taught to mistrust everything and everyone. Also rules may exist which prohibit family members from testing ideas in the outside world. The "facts" of the world are distorted to meet the needs of fam-

Discovering Rules and Patterns of Interaction

JOURNAL OF THOUGHTS 6.1: AT YOUR HOME

At your home, how did the following happen?

Was it ok to open anyone's mail? Explain.

Who controlled the remote control in the T.V. watching area? Explain.

Were there set places where people sat at mealtimes? Explain.

Were there specific meal times? Explain.

Did you have to put the toilet paper on the hanger in a certain way? Explain. (Are you wondering what in the world this issue is about? You will only have to ask 2–3 friends before you find out.)

ily members. Consequently, the children may not learn to test reality, but are trained to accept the particular brand of irrationality constructed by the family as reality.

Some ineffective family rules may suggest two rather powerful, yet contradictory, behaviors. For example, a family may have consciously selected a democratic parenting style encouraging individual expression and growth, but at the same time censure family members for seeking a life outside the family. They construct two competing rules: (1) We are an open and accepting family; (2) We accept only certain types of choices about really important life decisions. In an extreme case, the family may be filled with a myriad of inconsistencies and contradictions. The result may be people acting in inconsistent and unpredictable ways.

When families have rules that are disabling it is helpful to have enough adaptability and creativity that the old rules can be adjusted or new ones invented. In these situations honesty, openness, and willingness to compromise and try new ways of doing things can make the difference between a family being enabling and helpful in achieving personal and family goals or a system that is disabling and destructive. When there is adaptability, the rule part of families can serve as a generative mechanism that is capable of creating regularity out of chaos (Yerby & Buerkel-Rothfuss, 1982, p. 2).

IMPLICITNESS IS DESIRABLE

David Reiss (1981) developed an idea about what happens in families when they find attention is focused on the rules that are usually implicit. He reasoned that the first sign of a disorganizing family is the falling away of implicit regulation and coordination. In a smoothly running family, shared objectives, understandings, role allocations, and norms do not often have to be stated. Even when they are, limit-setting messages can be very brief and can often be conveyed gesturally. When a family finds it is engaged in laying out verbally explicit rules of itself, it is already in the midst of a stressful situation—although it may still be far from a full-blown crisis (Reiss, 1981, p. 179–180).

Apparently, when a family encounters a situation that is so unusual or stressful that their normal rules do not adequately deal with the situation, one effect this usually has is the family's attention is diverted to the rules it uses to manage. A typical consequence of this is that old rules are modified and/or new ones are invented. Many times these situations are handled without disrupting the normal operation of the family system, and the new version of family rules recedes into the implicit. However, when families are not able to devise a system of rules that cope with the new situation, a disorganizing cycle tends to occur.

The disorganizing cycle is that when greater attention is given to rules, more of them are made explicit, and the family becomes more disorganized. The disorganization apparently occurs for several reasons. As a family's attention is diverted to its rules its concentration on coping with other aspects of life decreases. This results in chores not getting done, missing work, meals being disrupted, etc. Also, the family realm has such complicated and yet intimate systems that they bog down when attempts are made to explicate very many rules. In the public spheres where relationships are more limited, rational, and efficiency oriented, it is helpful to bureaucratize and formalize laws, rules, and policies. But in the family realm, this strategy is the "kiss of death." Families can only operate when the majority of the beliefs they use to govern themselves are shared, implicit, and affectively comfortable.

Thus, Reiss' idea is that when families find it necessary to divert a substantial amount of their attention to explicating rules, it tends to disable them from doing other things, and these processes frequently become parts of a vicious cycle.

This idea is helpful in understanding many disabling cycles in families. For example, many American families have a difficult time adapting their implicit rule structure in a comfortable way during the teenage years. Many parents and teens try to deal with this by getting long lists of elaborate rules about what the teens can do and cannot do, and the rules become part of the problem. Also, when one member of a family begins to deviate from the behaviors that have traditionally been acceptable in a family, a typical response is to "lay down" rules about what is appropriate and acceptable, but the rules seldom help. It doesn't matter whether the "deviant" behavior is alcoholism, using prohibited drugs or a religious conversion, explicating rules tends to set up disabling cycles.

There are several stages of the family life cycle that may be exceptions to the generalization that families are functioning the best when rules are implicit. One exception is during the formative stage of a family. When couples are engaged or newly married they find it enjoyable and helpful to focus a great deal of their attention on defining their rules and beliefs. At this stage of family life it is enabling to focus on their values and rules as it helps them lay the foundations of their family system. Gradually, as they construct rules they can live with comfortably they move beyond this stage and the rule part of their system becomes implicit.

The same process may also occur somewhat when families encounter major transitions in the family life cycle. For example, when a new child is born, children reach adolescence, children start leaving home, retirement is near, or a death occurs, families seem to find it helpful to spend some time defining and redefining their rules. Usually, however, this occurs without the cycle escalating excessively, and the family is gradually able to let their new "understandings" recede into the realm of the implicit.

USE DIFFERENT LEVELS OF ABSTRACTION IN MANAGING RULES

When rules are explicit they are some of the ideas that make up the ideological part of family systems. Also, most rules are fairly specific beliefs about how behavior should and should not occur, so they are at Level I when we think about where they are with regard to levels of abstraction. This means that most of the time when families are managing the rule part of their life they are focusing on their Level I ideas about behavior.

JOURNAL OF THOUGHTS 6.2: IMPLICIT AND EXPLICIT RULES

1.   Define implicit rules.

2.   Look up explicit and implicit in the dictionary and write what you found.

3. Identify four implicit rules in your family of origin (for example, we don't blow our noses on the towels, but no one ever makes a big deal out of it because everyone just seems to know it isn't right.

4. What would you do differently in your families of procreation with regard to rules if you could?

Discovering Rules and Patterns of Interaction

Levels of abstraction. The specific level (Level I) of rules is illustrated by what happens when a family decides one of the members of the family is not behaving in accordance with the family "standards" and they need to clarify or change some of the family rules. For example, if a husband believes his wife does not show enough respect for his ideas and opinions he may be uncomfortable enough that he shares his feelings with his wife. The conversation that usually follows deals with fairly specific transformation processes. He would say things like, "You don't pay enough attention to my opinions." Or, if he has learned that I-statements create less defensiveness, he may say something like: "I'm uncomfortable with something. I don't think that my opinions are respected enough." This usually leads to a discussion about when incidents have occurred that didn't have enough respect, what the husband wants and feels, and what the wife wants and feels. Let's assume they then realize they both have had a number of unusual demands in their careers lately. She has responded to the situation by being caught up in her own demands, and he has responded by feeling inadequate and isolated. They may then decide that she ought to pay more attention to his ideas and he ought to be less sensitive. These are decisions to slightly adjust the rules their family rules.

This discussion did not involve Level II or Level III processes in their family system. It remained with fairly specific behaviors, feelings, and ideas that were part of the routine, daily transformation processes in the family.

Most of the time, families can remain at Level I and do everything they need to in managing the rule part of their family system. Also, most of the time when they are successful in adjusting or creating rules effectively they focus briefly on the rules and the rules then slip into the implicit parts of their system.

There are, however, some situations when families are not able to resolve their conflicts or concerns about rules when they only deal with the Level I processes. For example, when families begin to approach the adolescent stage of family development, the children often change some of their basic values more rapidly than the parents and the conflicts that result from these changes usually appear first as conflicts over family rules. The Level III changes in values are at the heart of the conflict over values, but it would be very unusual for the conflict to begin with the family members recognizing or talking about their Level III value conflicts. It almost invariably begins with conflicts about the Level I rules. Some of the specific ways these differences appear are the teenagers may want to stay out later, or they want more say about who their friends are. They may want more freedom to explore ways of behaving that are different from the ways they have behaved, or they may want to change their appearance, the way they dress, or the places they go for entertainment.

In these situations, the parents often find themselves being concerned about the judgment of the teens and they are cautious about changing the family rules. The teens, on the other hand, are eager to get more autonomy and freedom and explore new things, and they push for major changes. In these situations families who only

Chapter 6

focus on Level I processes usually encounter considerable difficulty in finding consensus about their family rules, and the conflicts escalate into pressure, arguments, defiance, attempts to enforce rules, and resistance.

When families find their "normal" ways of modifying and creating rules (staying at Level I) does not resolve their problems, there is a strategy that is often helpful. It is move to higher levels of abstraction and deal with the more fundamental parts of the family system such as values, family paradigms, goals, and the basic structure of the way the family operates. Family scientists have discovered three fairly different ways of moving to the more abstract parts of family systems. They are:

1. Focus on differences and similarities in Level III things such as the family's worldview, values, family paradigms, and long-term goals.
2. Deal with Level II aspects of rules. These are called metarules.
3. Deal with other Level II aspects of the family system such as the methods of making decisions, the changing patterns of authority, or the changing power in the family system.

Focus on Level III parts of the family system.   Family members tend to be fairly cautious, defensive, and rigid about family rules when they have concerns about whether there is agreement about the more fundamental beliefs such as values and family paradigms. And, on the other hand, when family members believe the other members of the family share the same fundamental philosophy of life and life-goals, this provides a certain type of security and confidence that allows people to be more flexible and adaptable.

What this means for managing family rules is that when a family is having difficulty managing their rules with the normal (Level I) procedures, it can be helpful to back off and check out how similar the more basic beliefs are. If there are fundamental differences or conflicts at the family paradigm level, these differences often make it impossible to come to consensus about Level I rules. When families understand this, they realize it is helpful to deal with the more fundamental beliefs first. If consensus can be reached at the philosophy of life level, this provides a foundation for then dealing with the more specific and concrete level of family rules. And, conversely, if agreements cannot be reached at Level III, this has important implications for what the family can and cannot do at the level of rules. When families have fundamental differences at Level III, the only way it is possible to have consensus and agreement at Level I is for the family members to be flexible, adaptable, and tolerate considerable diversity in the family rules.

Focus on metarules.   The word meta means about. Therefore, metarules are rules about rules. The metarules that family scientists focus most of their attention on are metarules about how to create new rules, how to eliminate old rules, or how to change rules. Laing was referring to metarules in his comment that sometimes "there are rules against seeing the rules, and hence against seeing all the issues that arise from complying with or breaking them" (1972, p. 106).

There are many examples of metarules. When families have young children it is common to have a metarule that it is parents and not children who make and change the family rules. An example of a metarule could be when the children want a rule changed, they can ask the parents, and even express their desires, but the parents decide. As the children in families mature, the metarules usually change. For example, a typical metarule when the children are teenagers could be that the ones who are the most upset by old rules and make the biggest scene determine the rules.

Hopefully, families have a metarule structure that assists them when rules no longer work. This issue is closely tied to the ideas of adaptability. As rules become obsolete, an adaptable family will have a viable metarule structure that allows them to replace, alter, and/or negotiate new rules that may be more appropriate for the situation. Some families do not have an adequate set of metarules about how to change their rules. When this occurs, families tend to become "stuck" in ways of doing things that were appropriate for earlier stages of development, and they have difficulty making the transitions into new stages of development.

One of the important ways family therapists help families is to help them develop metarules that help them change and grow. As Greenburg observed in his analysis of one of the main schools of thought in family therapy: It was postulated that a central function of the therapist entailed the facilitation and the development of rules for change (Greenberg, 1977, p. 396).

When families try to "back off" and think about their metarules, they find themselves having a fairly abstract conversation. For example, assume a young man is studying family science, and after he studies these ideas he realizes that he has been locked into a Level I struggle with his parents about rules. He realizes the struggle is a standoff and is not getting anywhere. He wants to have the freedom to decide what to study at the university, where to work, who to associate with, etc. His parents, however, want to have considerable say in his life. He now realizes he and his parents have been only dealing with Level I processes when they were putting pressure on each other and trying to talk the other into agreeing with them. He now wants to talk about the metarules to see if they can find a better way to change the family rules. He could initiate this type of conversation by saying things like:

"Mom and dad, I'd like to see us change some of the ways we do things (euphemism for family rules) in our family, but I don't know how to do it. What should one of us do if we want to make some changes? What would we say to get the others' attention, and how do we change things? What do you two do when one of you wants to make some changes, and how do you decide to make a change?"

When families or people who are trying to help families focus on Level II processes, it demands fairly sophisticated complicated ways of thinking. Most of the time people focus their attention on the specific and easy-to-think-about processes that occur at Level I, and most of the time that is all that is necessary. However, it is occasionally helpful to consciously think and converse about the meta level issues. Especially when the less abstract Level I ways of making decisions about rules is not adequate.

Manage Rule Sequences

When we focus on rule sequences as a strategy to understand family processes, it makes it easier to understand why Virginia Satir (1972) compared family life to an iceberg where the majority of what is happening is beneath the surface. Families are aware of some sequences, and most families try to deliberately manage a few of them. The totality of family life, however, is such a complex set of interlocking and complex sequences that most of them occur out of the consciousness of the participants.

Even though most feedback loops are submerged, families can become aware of some of them, and they can learn skills that help manage at least some of them. In fact, our experience suggests that even families that are not well educated and not very resourceful find it relatively easy to modify vicious cycles when they become aware of them. Therefore, the key is recognizing vicious cycles.

There are several skills that can help families become aware of rule sequences. One skill is to occasionally try to "think sequences" or "think cycles" rather than just "think individuals" when problems occur in a family. Another strategy that sometimes helps is to explore the possibility that the "problem" is a reasonable response to a vicious cycle the family hasn't noticed. As Haley has observed, it is difficult for people in families to recognize cycles that are more complicated than three steps, but it is possible. Also, only identifying two or three steps in a cycle frequently is enough to be helpful. Often when families recognize two or three steps, these insights lead to the discovery of other steps that aren't readily apparent.

Another skill that can help families recognize rule sequences is to ask people who are not in the middle of the situation if they see any vicious cycles operating. When we learn to "think" this way, members of the family who are not caught up in the vicious cycles can sometimes recognize what is happening and make suggestions that can help those who are involved recognize what is going on. The following situation illustrates how an undesirable rule sequence was repeated in a family many times before a family member that was not involved recognized it.

Step 1. The father's emotional distress would occasionally increase. Many incidents could be the ones to re-activate the cycle after a dormant period. For example, pressures at work, health frustrations, in-law troubles, a personal disappointment, etc. could activate his stress.

Step 2. The father would behave in less patient and more critical or obnoxious ways. The first and second steps were a mini-cycle called a positive feedback loop that would increase both conditions with father getting more emotionally distressed, less patient, and more critical around the home.

Discovering Rules and Patterns of Interaction

SPOTLIGHT ON RESEARCH 6.1: CHANGING RULES ABOUT WORK SCHEDULES

Hill, Hawkins, Ferris, & Weitzman (2001) published a research article that shows how family rules about work and home are changing. In a typical family, most of the men and many of the women would have gone out to work, possibly commuting to work, staying away from home. Hill, Hawkins, Ferris, and Weitzman interviewed over 6,000 employees who work for IBM. They found that family patterns interaction and rules (such as who goes to work, when they go, and what they do when they come home) is a feature of family life that can be changed. They found that when companies allowed flexible work hours, work from home, and the ability to re-structure the rules of family life, there were positive outcomes both at home, personally (for the workers), and for the business. People got more done at home, they enjoyed their work more, and they could work longer hours without it interfering with home life.

This type of change in lifestyle and family rule structure seems to decrease stress (like the stress in commuting). Workers could also live in different locations rather than the more expensive residences closer to work. These distant residences were probably in neighborhoods that were more inviting. Additionally, with flexible family schedules and rules about work, a family could share childcare and home responsibilities more easily. Also, these parents were better able to respond to unexpected situations such as a child becoming ill. One parent could alter the day's daily routine and pick up the hours in another way.

On the following page, comment how the adults (or adult) in your home decided who would work outside the home. Do you think "flex-time" applies to your own family? Explain.

Continue your response below:

Eventually he would become angry or obnoxious enough that Step 3 would occur.

Step 3. The teenage daughter's room was usually messy and when the father wasn't upset, he would usually ignore it. However, when he was upset and noticed the daughter's room was messy he would get after the daughter to clean her room.

Step 4. The daughter would clean her room according to her father's standards rather than her own.

Step 5. The father's pressure on the daughter would increase her emotional distress. Often this was because she would feel angry and resentful. (Sometimes the whole cycle would be re-activated with Step 5 too.)

Step 6. The daughter's behavior in some area of her life would be less desirable. This could take many forms. It could be she was more irritable or critical, didn't do well at school, or misbehaved.

Step 7. The father's emotional distress would increase, and he would be less patient, etc.

The cycle would repeat again and again until something occurred to disrupt it. The cycle also had several variations. For example, sometimes the mother would get involved instead of the father, and sometimes both parents would get upset before pressuring the daughter. During one of the family "scenes" an older brother happened to notice the connection between Steps 3 and 5. What he saw was 3 then 5 then 3 then 5 then 3 then 5 then 3 then 5, etc. He described what he thought he saw and it was enough for the family to eventually recognize they had a rule-bound vicious cycle. Once the cycle was in the consciousness of the family, they were able to see the other steps and devise several ways to disrupt it.

One strategy they devised was to work harder to find a compromise on the standards of cleanliness for the daughter's room. They realized that the on-going negative tension (remember the chapter on emotions) could be contributing to the cycle, and, if the father and daughter were more comfortable about the standards for the room, it might help disrupt the feedback loop.

A second strategy emerged from the belief that high levels of negative emotion were a key factor or at least a good barometer. A few strategies were then consciously devised to help each other find ways to reduce negative emotion when it was recognized. After that, the members of the family were a little more alert to their own moments of distress and the emotional distress in others, and they looked for ways to help each other calm down when upset.

This situation illustrates several important ideas. It illustrates that families can learn to manage at least some rule sequences that involve vicious cycles. It also illustrates several strategies that can be helpful in managing these sequences.

Chapter 6

SUMMARY

This chapter discussed two types of *rules* that operate in family systems. One of these types is *social norms*. These are beliefs that proscribe or prescribe behavior. Some norms are learned as part of the culture. Others are unique to a particular family, and they are passed from one generation to another. Another family creates other rules, and they are therefore unique to that family. These rules have many purposes. They regulate the way resources are managed, regulate emotional distance, clarify boundaries, control the implementation of decisions, clarify how to deal with exceptions and violation of rules, etc.

The second type of rules we discussed were family rules. Some family rules govern and maintain behaviors that are inconsistent with the normative beliefs. A family does not usually know these, but they can be inferred by watching the patterns in family behavior. Some family rules are simple rules that govern the way individuals behave. Sometimes these rules are connected into *rule sequences*. These are patterned ways of behaving that involve sequences of behavior of several individuals. Rules sequences usually have a cyclic or feedback loop aspect to them, and most families are not aware of them. These sequences can be healthy and enabling, or they can be disabling and help keep a family "stuck" in earlier developmental stages.

Problems sometimes occur in the *rule* part of family systems, and when this occurs families need to consciously manage this part of their systems. Family scientists have discovered several strategies that can be helpful in managing this part of family life. When rules become developmentally inappropriate, too rigid, or disabling, learning to be adaptable is a helpful strategy. Usually the more *implicit* rules are, the better. Therefore, when families find it necessary to deal explicitly with their rules, it is desir-

able to deal with them as little as possible and then let them "slide out of awareness." Most of the time the rule aspect of families can be managed by focusing on Level I processes. However, when conflicts about rules are not readily resolved, it can be helpful to move to Level II and Level III parts of family systems.

Chapter 6

STUDY QUESTIONS

1. Define what a rule is.

2. How are rules and social norms different?

3. What is a rule sequence? Give an example of one.

4. Name four different types of rules and how they could occur in family life.

5. Define social norm and give an example

6. What are some ways your text suggests to manage rule sequences in families?

KEY TERMS

Rules
Social norms
Rule sequences
Folkways
Distance regulation
Levels of family system

PART III

Expressive Family Processes

CHAPTER SEVEN

Communication in Family Life

Communication in Family Life

Main Points:

1. We, by definition, have to communicate with those around us, especially family members.

2. There are several important aspects of communication that we must attend to as we understand how families interact. These include the intent part of the message and the content part.

3. There are several kinds of competitive messages. These include small talk, control talk, non sequitur, correcting and lecturing, superlatives, sarcasm and cutting humor, distancing, martyring, and meta-communication.

4. There are several types of positive communication styles. These include straight talk, seeking clarification, reinforcing, seeking congruence, and appropriate self-disclosure.

5. Gender differences play a large role in understanding family communication.

6. There are specific strategies one can use to facilitate better family communication.

Communication in Family Life

I know you believe you understand what you think I said, but I am not sure you realize that what you heard is not what I meant. (Anonymous, from a poster)

INTRODUCTION

Communication is at the heart of expressive family processes. Remember that family processes are strategies that families use to achieve goals, maintain ideological focus, and cope with life's changes and turbulence. While some of those strategies are hidden from view, many goal-attaining strategies are more visible and expressive. How family members communicate, what they communicate about, and how they resolve differences are examples of these expressive family processes. In this chapter, we explore the power of family communication. In addition, we discuss several communication principles along with suggestions for making family communication stronger.

"We converse our way through life" (Berger, Kellner, & Hansfried, 1973). The most frequent activity you do with friends and family members is, most probably, talk. Communicating is a fundamental activity of life. We communicate about who we are, our dreams, our goals, what we think is good or bad, we critique those around us, we negotiate conflict, start fights, and try to find forgiveness. When we communicate, we reveal our weaknesses and strengths and explore our expectations, hopes, and disappointments (Duck, 1997).

Obviously, communication is more than just talking. Communication is the process by which meaning is created and managed (Krauss & Fussell, 1996). An early founder of the study of family communication once wrote, "We do not originate communication, we participate in it" (Watzlawick, Beavin, & Jackson, 1967). Watzlawick and his colleagues also described another important mantra of family communication: you cannot *not* communicate. In other words, it is impossible to avoid communicating with those in your world. Even if you decide you will never speak to someone again, that is still a type of communication. The point is that communication is a fundamental aspect of relationships; it is the way in which we discover each other, define relationships, and define who we are. We cannot avoid this important family process.

Communication begins when people meet and begin to establish a relationship. With each person in our world, we create a private and somewhat individualized message system (Tannen, 1986). As we become more involved and committed to a particular relationship, the rules and patterns of interaction take on a richer texture and fuller meaning.

We develop these special communication relationships from an early age. First, we watch and communicate with our parents and close family members. Then we branch out and watch the interaction of people on television and movies; we observe how our siblings solve problems and communicate with their friends; we continue to learn by watching our parents and other significant adults.

Each time a new friendship or relationship is formed, our ways of communicating and interacting change and adapt. The changes are not apparent and most of the time we do not talk about how we communicate to each other; the patterns just seem to unfold. Some have suggested that this unfolding is like peeling back the layers of an onion (and sometimes we cry).

In this chapter, the goal is for you to consider the power of communication in primary relationships. We will not spend much time on how one communicates and builds ties with friends or the intricacies of communicating in the workplace. Instead we will focus on the communication in families and other close relationships. Specifically, we explore the importance of communication in primary relationships, types of communication, communication styles that build stronger personal bonds, and the role of disclosure in important relationships. The problems inherent in relationship communication are covered only superficially. The next chapter is devoted to those issues. Additionally, a large section of this chapter deals with gender differences in communication: It has become apparent to researchers that men and women communicate differently in close relationships. It is important that we learn about these differences as we make decisions about how to build stronger bonds with family members. Finally, the latter part of this chapter focuses on several strategies for making partner and family communication more effective.

THE IMPORTANCE OF COMMUNICATION

The study of communication in families is like looking at a ray of light shining through a prism and projecting a rainbow pattern on the wall. The rainbow of information we see tells us about the hidden goals, deeply held beliefs, power differences, and expectations of daily life within families and close relationships. Communication is the process of making meaning: as we interact, the rainbow of feelings, dreams, and wants are exposed.

Most family scientists agree that effective communication is at the heart of understanding family strength. Conversely, when couples are experiencing relationship difficulty, it is often the communication style, content, and intent that one turns to for some understanding. Virginia Satir was an author and family therapist who wrote several books and articles about family communication. She showed us how communication is at the center for understanding family life "Once a human being has arrived on this earth, communication is the largest single factor determining what kinds of relationships he makes with others and what happens to him in the world" (Satir, 1972 p. 30).

As was mentioned above, when we enter into new relationships, a primary task in forming a new partnership is the development of an individualized, private message system (Tannen, 1986). As relationships are established, new rules and patterns of interaction take shape and emerge. In some ways, these emerging relational patterns are mysterious. That is, we do not sit and consciously plan them out; each conversational choice builds on the previous exchange.

The parts of communication. We form some type of idea about what messages we want to send to our partner, family members, or friends and we *encode* that message. By encode we mean that each person has to take the thought to be communicated and convert that thought into a message that can be sent. One way messages can be sent is through words or other observable modes of communication. We call these observable modes of communication *content* or *overt* messages (Watzlawick et al., 1967 p. 51). The word overt means obvious, explicit, observable, and visible. The content element of a message is the "report" part of the message. It is the explicit and obvious raw data of the message, often times sent in words.

Intent messages. However, the most powerful kinds of messages we send are the intent or covert messages. Intent messages are usually more concealed, not obvious, but implicit and hidden from view. The covert intent messages we send are much more subtle and harder to define than overt messages. But these powerful intentional messages have the potential to override the actual words being used. The intent messages are carried in our tone of voice and things like the small sighs that slip out and the way our eyebrows curl down and tell the receiver we disapprove, for example.

After watching the first 2000 presidential debate between Al Gore and George W. Bush, many people commented about Al Gore's nonverbal facial gesturing, sighs of apparent impatience, and aggressive body posture. People seemed to remember the covert, non-verbal tone far better than they did the words that were spoken. From these intent messages, regardless of what words he used, Al Gore seemed to some to be impatient, aggressive, and rather uncaring. Before the second debate he had gotten feedback about his (probably unintended) intent messages and in the debate he changed his style of communicating.

Noller (1984) has shown that the intent (nonverbal) element of communication can convey three important messages. First, intent messages can reveal our interpersonal attitudes toward the sender, toward the topic, or toward the situation. The intent messages provide small clues about assessment of the receiver. The receiver(s) naturally extrapolate from those clues and have to guess what we think of them. The receiver does not have much to go on, but will make a guess about our judgment of them based on those limited observations. Most people are fairly skilled at picking up tones and facial clues that reveal our attitude toward them.

Chapter 7

Second, intent messages tell the receiver how we feel about ourselves. Some of us have bad "poker faces." Whether we are having a miserable or great day seems to be written on our foreheads. Some people have the enviable skill of emotional constancy; even if they are having a rotten day, it is hard to tell. But for most of us our daily moods are frequently communicated in the message packages we send to those around us. Even if we don't intend on doing so, we tell people with our intent messages if we are depressed, confused, elated, excited, or bored. For most of us, those important intent messages about feelings seem to leak out and people collect the evidence and wonder if we are ill, what we are happy about, or why we are depressed. Especially in close relationships, partners and children read the mood messages that seem to be chained to the content messages.

The third aspect of intent messages is that they handle our interactions with others. We monitor the gaze and posture of others, looking for clues of when to end the conversion, when to let them have a turn, when to laugh, and when to not respond. As Noller (1984) wrote, "One would expect that married couples who communicate well with one another would get to know each other's conversational patterns, and as well, get to know each other's nonverbal cues" (Noller, 1984 p. 6).

Decoding is another important feature of this process. Decoding refers to the idea that the person to whom we are sending a message has to interpret the message. He or she has to translate the words (the overt part of the message) as well as the covert facial expressions, tone of voice, posture, and other contextual clues within the message and try to guess what message we are intending to send. As you have experienced, things can go wrong with this process as the person decodes a message from us in a way that we did not intend.

Some messages are sent and the receiver does not decode them in the same way we were hoping they would. At other times neither the sender nor the receiver are able to send or receive what they intended. Being clear in one's messages and accurately decoding messages from others takes a fair amount of practice and skill for most of us. Few things in life are more puzzling and even aggravating to people than when the messages they send are lost, misunderstood, or misjudged.

We can judge the quality of a relationship by listening to the style of communication revealed in close relationships. To an astute observer, how we think and feel about the other person (and ourselves) is exposed by the way we communicate and talk with them. If we are condescending and hurtful, we have one type of intentions; if we are kind and gentle, we have another type of intentions.

Types and Kinds

One way to begin to understand the various colors in the prism of communication is to explore other facets of the communication process. Thus far we have mentioned how the encoding/decoding process works, and we have mentioned the

ACTIVITY 7.1 - SCULPTURE OF FAMILY COMMUNICATION

A paper sculpture is an artistic presentation of your family. Feel free to be as unique, artistic, symbolic, and abstract as you would like. It is meant to represent the communication styles you find within your families of origin or pro-creation, either one.

1.   Decide what family you will make a picture of. It can be your family of origin or family of procreation. If you have more than one family for some reason, you may do either or both.

2.   Trace or cut out circles on a plain piece of paper, making enough for yourself and each person or set of persons or things you want to include. There are no restrictions on whom you include or how you symbolize them. (Parents, siblings, neighbors, pets, your father's golf game—whoever or whatever has a significant effect on the family) If you wish you may vary size, shape, or color of the units to express yourself more fully. Remember you are describing the communication styles symbolically with this picture.

3.   Label each circle. A single circle may have only one name or more than one if you see those people/things as a unit.

4.   Arrange the pieces on a colored 8 1/2" x 11" piece of paper so they express the relationships you feel in your family. When you feel comfortable with the total arrangement, firmly glue them in place.

5.   Draw any boundary or connecting lines you feel complete the picture.

6.   Attach a page or two explaining what you have done. Explain who the components are (age, sex, relationship to you, why included), why you arranged them as you did, the meaning of any connecting or boundary lines, and any special uses of size, shape, or color.

6.   List any people you left out that you might logically have included and explain why you left them out.

7. Conclude with a paragraph explaining what you learned by doing this project.

This activity is adapted from Nancy V. Wedemeyer and Harold D. Grotevant, 1982. "Mapping the Family System: A Technique for Teaching Family Systems Theory Concepts", Family Relations, Vol 31, pages 185-194.

idea that communication contains an explicit report element and an implicit intent element. With those ideas in mind, let's turn to other features of the communication rainbow.

What do we talk about? Have you ever kept a diary of what you talk about with your friends? Experiment with writing down several conversations. What are the topics you spend the most time with? Who leads in choosing the topics? Who seems to decide when the topic should change?

A few years ago two researchers asked the same questions of married couples (Dickson-Markman & Markman, 1988). They asked couples whom they had conversations with and how much time they spent on a variety of topics. Not surprisingly, most couples spent far more time with their spouses than they did others (even friends or other family members). On average, couples had about 1.24 interactions per day that lasted long enough to be considered a conversational exchange. Those exchanges lasted an average of about two hours. The most frequent topics of discussion were work, home maintenance, children and other family members, conversations they had during the day with other people, and food. Notice what is missing from this list. These researchers found that couples rarely spend time talking about their own relationship. When they did talk about their relationship, it usually occurred after a sexual encounter or during an escalating conflict.

Another view of couples' interaction came from a study by Noller and Feeny (1998). These researchers found that couples reported an average of 22 conversations per week (about three per day) with each being about 20–30 minutes long. Of course, the length of time spent conversing with our partners is influenced by work schedules, numbers of children in the home, and the age/stage of family members. In another interesting study, Kirchler (1989) found that couples who reported higher levels of marital satisfaction spent more time together at home and more time talking about personal topics. Of course, the question arises: "Does good communication add to their feelings of couple satisfaction or do couples who like each other already stay home and talk more?" No one has tackled that research yet.

KINDS OF MESSAGES

Another way to explore the kinds of messages we send to our partners has been illuminated by Miller, Nunnally, Wackman, and Miller (1988). These family scientists suggested that communication in close relationships could be organized into four types. We have reworded and updated their categories and call them: small talk, competition/control talk, meta communication, and cooperative/straight talk (Miller et al., 1988).

Small talk. When we encounter a friend, stranger, or family member, we often just want to chat. Small talk topics usually focus on news items, the recent rainstorm, daily routines, something silly a child said, or what's on for dinner. The purpose of this type of conversation is to build trust and establish bonds of connection. People who are not skilled at making small talk are sometimes seen as intrusive when they skip it and move immediately to requests, lectures, or inquiries. Conversely, if one only knows how to engage in small talk, then it is difficult to build lasting relationships with others.

Shop talk. Another type of small talk is what Miller and associates labeled shop talk. Shop talk is really small talk that happens at or about the workplace. Often when we meet with friends or colleagues who work with us, we talk about office politics, work-related issues, and events related to employment. This type of small talk can become divisive or boring. Many people do not want to carry work into home life or recreational settings.

Competitive/control talk. Frequently, we try to influence others. Control talk is about influence and change. When we praise, lecture, direct, request, or suggest things to family members we are using control talk. Parents often supervise their children, monitor their activities by asking where they have been, and teach them about while the children are doing homework. All of these activities are control related.

As can be easily imagined, too much control talk can lead to trouble. Sometimes when we push too hard, expect too much, and demand multiple requirements of family members, they understandably fight back. *Fight talk* is usually in response to someone pushing us to do or believe something when we don't want to. Both Gottman (1994; 1999) and Miller et al. (1988) found that when one partner provokes or pushes too hard to get something done or changed that about 80% of time the other partner fights back. Most family scientists agree that using force to affect change in someone is ineffective. This idea is captured in the *Communication and Change Principle* found below.

PRINCIPLE 7.1: COMMUNICATION AND CHANGE

The strategies we use to change someone or something a person is doing often make the situation worse and decrease the chance that desired change will occur.

The above principle tells us that the strategies we employ to get something done or change something or someone (even if the goal of the change is a worthy one) often make the situation worse and decrease the chance the desired change will occur. When we are aggressive, competitive, and punitive with others, they don't usually change; they just build up resentment toward us.

Any time we resort to compulsion, attempts to control someone, or try to dominate the situation with what we want to do, the generous spirit of cooperation

leaves us. The following is a list of some kinds of destructive, competitive fight talk strategies that people often use that usually don't work and usually have the effect of making family life destructive.

Interrupting. Often when we are impatient and controlling, we interrupt the other person and try to redirect the conversation to go in the direction we want. Sometimes we become so unaware that we interrupt one another that it seems like the natural thing to do in conversation.

Kennedy and Camden (1993) showed that not all interruptions are a sign of dominating and controlling communication, only some kinds are. First, they found that women are far more likely to interrupt than are men. But more important, they found that most of the interruptions that occurred in their study were *confirmation interruptions*. Confirmation interruptions occur when one seeks clarification, agrees with what is being said, or supports what is being discussed. Some interruptions, however, are not supportive. They are meant to change the subject, disagree, and disconfirm what is being discussed. Couples who have communication styles that build relationships make fewer combative, competitive, and dominating interruptions.

Non sequitur. The *non sequitur* is another competitive fighting tool used effectively by partners who are trying to dominate others. The term *non sequitur* is a logical term indicating that one idea does not follow from the next. One partner may be talking about work or dinner; the other (maybe even in mid-sentence) interrupts the flow of the conversation and interjects a thought seemingly unconnected to the conversation. Again, such controlling and dominating communication strategies destroy relationship integrity.

Correcting and lecturing. "If I've told you once, I've told you a million times—" Most of us have been at the receiving end of controlling fight language that begins with sentences like the one above. Giving unsolicited advice, over-rehearsing a topic, and attempting to change someone through sermonizing usually creates no positive advantage. Like most competitive communication, lecturing creates resistance and resentment. This is particularly true in parent-child relationships when accompanied by harsh discipline (Swinford et al., 2000). Swinford et al. have shown that using harsh forms of correction can have serious unintended effects. Children who grow up where there is frequent competitive, controlling, and dominating correction are much more likely to use violent behavior with their own intimate partners when they become adults. The unintended results of using harsh correction and lecturing can be increased resentment, hostility, and revenge by the recipient.

Superlatives. Another type of competitive fight talk is the use of superlatives. Superlatives are usually adverbs we throw into the conversation to exaggerate the point. These exaggerations and word-enhancing helpers are used to magnify our comment. Some examples are using never, always, "Ever since I've known you, you constantly . . . ," and "You are a total idiot." Here are some more examples of superlatives: *completely, continually, incessantly, utterly, absolutely, entirely, perfectly, thoroughly*, and *extremely*. In actuality, there are few times in which the words *never, completely*, or *continually* are accurate; *always* is a long time and hasn't occurred yet. We use superlatives in our language to assert control, exaggerate a point, and dominate the conversation. The usual effect is that we push people to fight back. As with other competitive fight talk strategies, the use of superlatives is ineffective in changing someone's behavior or communicating a need or want. For the next few days, count how many times you use or hear someone use superlatives; you may be surprised at the number of times they slip into your conversations. As you count how many times people use them when communicating to you, you may also be surprised.

Sarcasm and cutting humor. Another common strategy for gaining control and domination in a relationship is using sarcasm and cutting humor to put others down. In current usage, the term *dissing* is popular. *Dis* is a short form of *disrespect* and means to make someone look foolish or unworthy. It also means to use wisecracks or make fun of what someone says or does. Current Western-American culture seems to thrive on the comedic repartee of dissing: This type of demeaning humor is frequently seen on sit-com and talk shows. Again, when we use sarcasm and cutting

JOURNAL OF THOUGHTS 7.1: LISTENING FOR SUPERLATIVES AND OTHER FORMS OF COMPETITIVE COMMUNICATION

Review the forms of competitive communication below. List each of the types found in your text and others you may have thought of.

Note below over a two-day period how many times you hear these types of communication patterns from others. List the times and person. Also, try to tell if their intent was to control, manipulate, or change those around them.

Now, how about you? Over another two-day time period, take note below how many times and in what situations you use competitive communication in your everyday interactions.

humor in an attempt to better ourselves and make others look foolish, we are chasing away the spirit of harmony and unity in close relationships. It destroys trust and creates resentments that may be difficult to reconcile.

Distancing. When we give up on the other person, decide we have had enough, and disengage we are distancing. Rather than battle with someone, we choose to retreat and build barriers.

Martyring. Closely tied to distancing is martyring. The martyr seeks control through a particular type of distancing strategy. He or she will say, "OK—I see you don't care what I think at all; I'll just go into the kitchen where I belong and make dinner. I guess I'll leave the big decisions to you." The intent is clearly manipulative and controlling. It is designed to get the other partner to say, "Oh, honey, come on. That's not what I meant. No, please stay. Come on, what do you think?"

Interrupting, use of non sequiturs, correcting and lecturing, sarcasm and cutting humor, distancing, playing the martyr, and overuse or inaccurate use of superlatives are communication strategies that are likely to backfire. Anytime we use overt or intent messages to manipulate and elicit responses from those around us, we are slipping into some form of competitive communication style.

Meta-communication/Search talk. Miller et al. (1988) also list *search talk* as an important type of relationship communication. When we talk about how we talk about things, we call this *search talk* or *meta-communication*. Meta-communication is important because it allows us to put the normal flow of decision-making, problem solving, and conflict resolution on hold. Then we step aside and ask deeper questions like, "Why do we argue that way?" We may express appreciation for the kind tone in a partner's voice or find ways of adjusting how we interact. A good metaphor for meta communication is the racetrack example used in Chapter 2. Most of the time the racecar is zooming around the track. In terms of communication, we would be solving problems, scheduling our lives, making decisions, and attempting to understand the needs and wants of those around us. But occasionally we must pull into the pit stop area and examine the process itself. We look under the hood, so to speak, change a tire, and refuel. We don't need to do that often, but it does need to happen.

If done effectively, meta-communication can be useful in building stronger relationships. However, if done too often or not frequently enough, it can be less than helpful. As new relationships are formed, one would expect the individuals to spend more time exploring how they do things in their relationships. As relationships mature, only infrequent "pit stops" are needed and couples spend the bulk of their time doing their relationship tasks instead of talking about how they do them. Spending too much time talking about how we talk irritates most people. In addition, if meta communication is rare, opportunities are lost to build stronger, more effective communication bonds.

Cooperative/Straight talk.   Learning to take the "barbed wire and buckshot" out of our intimate communications with others is a lifelong effort for most people. Most of us are a bit competitive, controlling, and dominate others too frequently. The following is a list of communication patterns that come straight from the heart, are non-competitive in their intent message, and tend to build relationship strength.

Seeking meaning.   One way to send non-defensive, non-combative, non-competitive intent and content messages to those close to us is to seek meaning. When we seek meaning, we listen carefully, non-judgmentally, and without thinking about what we want to say next. Listening with the intent of seeking meaning means we are studying and learning from the sender. We ask the other person to expand his or her thoughts, explore ideas, and express opinions. There is no hidden agenda; there is no impatience as we wait for a place to break into the other person's story so we can give our lecture, tell a better story, or make a joke of what is being said.

Instead, we look into the sender's eyes with affection, concern, and caring; we only want to hear what he or she has to tell us. For many people, this is surprisingly difficult. You may be surprised, however, that when you practice this skill, your appreciation for the other person is greatly enhanced. Additionally, we learn far more in these situations than when we are impatiently waiting for a spot to jump in and tell our stories. Satir (1967) suggested that the way we *frame* (or interpret) what others are saying tells a lot about us. For example, if we are jumping in, being competitive, or listening for only negative elements in someone's story or comments, it may mean that we have a lower sense of self worth. Confident and mature listeners have little need to best someone's story, make fun, be sarcastic, or interrupt.

Seeking clarification. When we seek clarification we go beyond seeking the meaning of the interaction. In this situation, we are listening closely and find some aspect of the message unclear to us. Good counselors are experts at knowing how to seek clarification. They gently encourage the sender to expand an idea or give examples of what they mean, or they will connect what is being said to some other part of the sender's message. When we do this, we encourage the sender and build trust. The sender cannot help but see that you really care and what to know what he or she feels or needs.

Reinforcing. As the sender is explaining an important message to us, it is important that we tell him or her (using both intent and content messages) that we appreciate the story or concern. We reinforce or reward the disclosure by saying simple things like, "uh-huh," "sure," "I see," or "really?" Remember that it is the intent part of the message that carries the relationship communication. When we encourage or reinforce people for telling us their story or expressing a need or want, we tell them that we want to be trusted, that what they want is important to us, and that we will take their story/request/need seriously. Trust and connection are lost when we are uncaring or even lazy in developing these skills. Each new encounter during a day starts the relationship over (even if we have been married for 20 years). We define how we care for our partners each time we greet them, listen to their stories, respond to a request, or simply take note of the difficult day they are having. If we become lazy in these daily encounters, our close family and friends will begin to think we take that relationship for granted.

Seeking congruence. According to Jacob (1987), *congruency* of messages leads to greater relationship satisfaction. Congruency occurs when we take the time to make sure that the intent and content aspects of messages are similar, or congruent. If one partner says, "I love you" with the content message, but the intent message is one of distance and coolness, then the messages are not congruent and the chances for building relationship strength decrease. On the other hand, if one's nonverbal (intent) language confirms that the partner does, indeed, love the other, the message package (both content and intent) builds the relationship. When congruence is missing, relationship confusion and anxiety are created.

When messages are congruent, family members are more likely to receive and send messages with greater clarity. Conversely, when there is less congruence (Satir, 1967; Sieburg, 1985; Wynne, 1984), family members may have problems with relationship ambiguity. The message confusion creates relationship ambiguity and can affect how we feel about ourselves. A child can experience doubt about what parents really think about him or her if the parents' messages are not authentic. When messages are congruent, authentic, and not confused, children (and spouses) are not left to wonder about how those important to them really feel about them.

Further, message congruence seems to have a significant effect on those within a relationship dyad (Sieburg, 1985; Wynne, 1984). These researchers suggest that when congruence is low it is more likely that family members would have poorer self-perceptions. It seems that message confusion creates relationship ambiguity and personal weakness. Additionally, when we are more confident of our own inner self, we are more likely to communicate with greater congruence. Apparently, this is one reason why clear, direct, involved, and open communication is associated with more functional marriages (Jacob, 1987).

Appropriate self-disclosure.   One of the more powerful types of cooperative communication is the use of appropriate self-disclosure. This occurs when an individual reveals to one or more people some personal information they would not otherwise learn. We acquire information through daily interactions. As we become more confident in the reliability of those close to us, we reveal more and more about who we are, what our needs are, and what we need from others.

Waring and Chelune (1983) found that self-disclosure accounts for more than half the variation in intimacy among couples. That is, while there are many factors that contribute to a feeling of intimacy with another, those feelings of closeness are tied to our ability to share special and private information about our inner lives. So when researchers ask couples about how much they share with one another, the result is that the more a spouse engages in appropriate self-disclosure, the more likely both partners are to be satisfied with the relationship (Bograd & Spilka, 1996; Hansen & Schuldt, 1982; Rosenfeld & Bowen, 1991).

There is an important message in the self-disclosure research for men. Bell, Daly, and Gonzalez (1987) found that wives whose husbands self-disclose more (e.g., sensitivity, spirituality, physical affection, self-inclusion, and honesty) also reported much higher levels of marital satisfaction. They also found that what was disclosed to spouses was important. They wanted to know if secrecy was something that damaged marriages. They found that when men were able to disclose more about the relationship (with the partner), that was more important than whether or not he kept some secrets about his personal life. They and others suggest that sometimes it is better to leave some things unsaid. A popular phase captures this idea: *Which hill are you willing to die for?* One must know the difference between being honest and open about relationship issues that really matter and keeping silent about those topics that will only makes things worse. Sometimes it is better to just let a topic drift away, unexplored and undiscussed.

For most of us, it takes concentration and practice to know when to comment and when to let go of a topic or issue. Baxter and Wilmont (1985) found that relationships could be strengthened when those in close relationships held back and did not "tell all." Sometimes partners' overdisclosures create a relationship threat and have the opposite of the intended effect. The intended message of the disclosure may have been to confide, build closeness, and connect. Instead, the message received is one of threat and confrontation.

On the other side of this coin, one should not keep secrets from partners as a way to deceive and manipulate. Vangelisti (1994) and Caughlin and Vangelisti (1999) found that the relationship between family secrets and family satisfaction depended on

JOURNAL OF THOUGHTS 7.2: COMMUNICATION IN YOUR FAMILY OF ORIGIN

What was the communication like in your family of origin? There are two ways to approach this assignment. First, you could visit your home (if you do not live there) for two days or so and carefully listen for the list of competitive and non-competitive communication items found in the text. Write a two-page report here that describes those interactions and how you think they contribute or detract from the climate in your home. Second, if you cannot or don't want to visit home, simply reflect back and do the same assignment, except from memory.

the reasons why the secrets were kept. If partners were keeping secretes to avoid evaluation or to keep from getting in trouble, these messages were perceived as divisive. However, when family members kept secrets to protect people, this strategy was seen as a sign of relationship strength.

Learning the art of appropriate disclosure and secrecy are key elements of a good relationships. Timing is everything in building strong relationships. Over time, we learn when to disclose, when to hold back, and when to let the topic drop permanently. Learning when and how to employ these communication strategies takes higher levels of emotional maturity and years to perfect.

GENDER IN COMMUNICATION

Much has been said about how men and women communicate differently in close relationships. Certainly, gender differences with respect to communication are an important topic for study. Men, generally, are socialized to communicate differently than women. They see the world of relationships with a slightly different hue. So, to learn how to strengthen relationship ties between men and women, one must attend to those differences. For example, Beck (1988) re-substantiated the idea that men don't talk about personal things as much as women do. He found that women think their marriages are stronger and working better when there is plenty of dialogue and exchange about the relationship. On the other hand, the men in this study generally felt the opposite: when communication turned to topics of relationships and marital evaluation, they felt the relationship was much more likely to be in trouble.

Similarly, Mackey and O'Brien (1995) found that a frequent source of tension between marital partners was husbands' discomfort with talking about their inner thoughts and feelings. These husbands were not only uncomfortable talking about feelings, they also judged feeling-connected relationship messages as negative and harmful. Other researchers found that husbands actively try to control the amount of communication about feelings and personal topics. These researchers found that husbands are uncomfortable participating in what we labeled "search talk" above. Correspondingly, their wives were unhappy with the lack of these relationship messages between them and their partners (Ball, Cowan, & Cowan, 1995).

In a popular book about this topic, Deborah Tannen (1990) emphasized that men approach life as a contest in which each party is striving to "preserve independence and avoid failure" (Tannen 1990, p. 25) Women, on the other hand, approach life as a community affair in which the goal is to connect, maintain intimacy, and avoid isolation. Men try to get out of relationships; women try to stay connected.

Similarly, several researchers have commented on the notion that men view relationships as a backdrop for attaining, maintaining, and evaluating status. When men interact, they are more likely to compare themselves to the other person, rating the position and social rank of the other, and protecting information about themselves that would diminish their status ranking with the other. Conversely, women, in general, are more likely to engage in relationships for connection and association.

In the same vein, when problems arise, women usually respond with more understanding; men tend to give advice and try to solve the problems (Tannen, 1990). This can result in relationship problems: in times of distress, what may be needed are supportive, encouraging, and nurturing responses. Men may be slower to realize those needs and, instead, be quicker to give a lecture, provide solutions, and sermonize. Some have suggested that this is because men see the world as more hierarchical; women see the world as cooperative and focus on connectivity (Olson & DeFrain, 1994).

As Tannen (1990, p. 25) suggests, men spend more time thinking in terms of hierarchy; they are attuned to the process of evaluating. Men frequently evaluate to determine whether they are a notch up or a notch down vis-à-vis the other. Men like to keep score and tally how many bouts they lost and how many they won. A male colleague recently described a bad day by saying, "Some days you eat the bear; some days the bear eats you."

According to Tannen, a primary goal for women in relationships is to design their communication style so that it helps them avoid isolation. Therefore, women are the networkers of the world. They are fonder of association with others than they are of keeping score. And they are more likely to seek out friends and community members who will provide that expanded associative role.

Topical differences. Bischoping (1993) found that men and women communicate about different topics in casual conversation. The primary small-talk topics that both men and women seem to discuss are money and work. However, men more frequently speak about leisure. This includes sports, personal fitness, movies, etc. On the other hand, while women do talk some about leisure, they also talk about men more than men talk about women. In fact, in this study the women were four times more likely to talk about men than men were to talk about women.

Message clarity. Another feature of gendered communication is that wives send clearer messages to husbands (Noller & Fitzpatrick, 1993:Thompson & Walker, 1989). These researchers also noted that husbands tend to give more neutral messages. A neutral message has an unclear or absent emotional/affective tone attached. Wives send more messages with some affective or emotional tone.

Additionally, wives set the emotional tone of arguments. They are more likely to escalate conflicts and use emotional appeals and threats.

Married couples who love each other tell each other a thousand things without talking. — *Chinese proverb*

Interruptions.   Interrupting was once considered a sign of dominance in relationships. Therefore, it was assumed that men would interrupt women more often since they are typically in a more dominant position relative to women. As our understanding of this important family process has become more sophisticated, it has become clear that not all interruptions are the same (see the discussion above). Sometimes we interrupt to show support, to seek clarification, show concern, and even to voice agreement (Aries, 1996). Of course, interruptions can also be used to commandeer the relational space between communicating partners. Interruptions can also be used to demonstrate dominance and power. Again, the intent message in the interruption has to be gauged. The research in this area continues to grow but has several problems. First, we know little about couple interruptions in natural settings. Most of the research has been done with college students in laboratory settings measuring short periods of conversation (usually about 10—15 minutes). An important exception is John Gottman's (1994) research. For the last 20 years he has been observing the same couples in a controlled setting as they resolve problems and conflict. Some of his findings are mentioned in the next section.

Most researchers agree (cf. Aries, 1996) that there is actually far less interrupting than family scientists once thought. Therefore, it is difficult to determine an accurate sense of what interruptions really mean to relationships when the research is based on short conversations between non-family members.

In addition, as Aries (1996) notes, the idea that men would dominate conversations and interrupt more than women has been discounted. In fact, James and Clarke (1993) concluded that most of the research indicates that men and women interrupt at about the same rates. However, when the couples are observed participating in personal casual conversation, women interrupt men more than men interrupt women. Again, most of that interruption is supportive and connective rather than competitive and aggressive.

Directness.   One gender difference in communication style is how direct men and women are in conversation. Women usually approach conflict indirectly. This means they will try to solve the situation and possibly take some type of conflict-reducing measures that their partners do not recognize.

When men are faced with confrontation, conflict, and disagreements they use direct approaches such as bargaining and negotiation. Note that the root word in bargain is gain. Men spend more time positioning themselves to secure gain. Women drop hints, suggest, mention, propose, and defer. Men ask, demand, seek closure, and stipulate (Noller & Fitzpatrick, 1990).

In like manner, men expect compliance, especially when talking to a woman. Women begin message exchanges expecting non-compliance (Falbo & Peplau, 1980). Another way that we see differences in directness is that women approach difficult situations in ways that involve and engage participants. Men approach similar situations expecting to promote, suggest, and even demand resolutions that feature autonomy and authority (Tannen, 1990). To that end, women are more accommodating, supportive, and socially responsive. Men, instead, provide suggestions and solutions to problems, as well as opinions and information (Aries, 1982).

An interesting window into the above differences can be found in the language structure women use to communicate. Women are more tentative in their language and use tag phrases such as "isn't it?" Men state things in ways that do not invite contradiction (Noller & Fitzpatrick, 1993).

In sum, the approach men and women use in conversation and relationship connection is gendered. This means that men and women use different relationship strategies. This, of course implies that men and women may have different goals in relationships. Men typically see relationships as a feature of life necessary to attain other goals such as being a notch up at work, getting a better job, winning an argument, or closing a deal. Women are more likely to see the relationship as an end in itself. There is no secondary goal.

It is important to note that this section was written rather gingerly and carefully. The research on men and women's communication styles is still emerging and it is frequently changing in findings and emphasis. Certainly our notion about men and women's roles and strategies in close relationships is a fertile area for research.

MAKING RELATIONSHIPS STRONGER THROUGH MORE EFFECTIVE COMMUNICATION STRATEGIES

First, you have to want to change. All of the information in this chapter (or book) is relatively useless if you, the reader, do not want to change. Second, only reading this information will do little to assist you in developing stronger, more effective relationships with those you care about. Not only does one have to be highly motivated to change something as long lasting as a relationship pattern, but also one has to put principles into action and make a serious effort.

Third, you can only change yourself. As we learned in Chapter 6, efforts to change others only end in frustration and disaster. It is difficult to change yourself if your partner is unwilling to participate and change as well.

THE FOUR HORSEMEN OF THE APOCALYPSE AND OTHER THINGS THAT PLAGUE GOOD RELATIONSHIPS

John Gottman (1999) has been observing the same couples while they interact in a controlled laboratory setting for more than 20 years. During that time, as each couple returned for a weekend in the lab-apartment, he has videotaped, recorded, and analyzed their interactions. The following ideas come from two of his books: *Why Marriages Succeed or Fail* (1994) and *The Seven Principles for Making Marriage Work* (1999).

In these books, he affirms that one of the primary keys to understanding why some couples remain together and others do not is the amount of conflict they exhibit in their daily interactions.

"If there is one lesson I have learned from my years of research it is that a lasting marriage results from a couple's ability to resolve the conflicts that are inevitable . . ." (Gottman, 1999, p. 28). He goes on to assert that many couples mistakenly believe that by simply reducing the struggles in marriage and tolerating low-level conflicts, they will be happy. He believes, instead, that having differences is normal and expected. The real test is whether couples can resolve their differences. He has found that there are at least three types of conflict resolution in marriage. The first is a *validating* style. In this type of marriage, the couples are quick to find ways of compromising and soothing each other. In addition, the validating couples help each other and find compromise a daily feature of their relationship.

The second kind of conflict-resolving relationships are what Gottman calls *conflict-avoiding* marriages (Gottman, 1999, p. 28). These couples run from conflict and rarely struggle together with the daily challenges of life. Since they rarely lock horns, they rarely explore the grievances that arise in daily family life. The final type of relationship is labeled the *volatile marriage.* For these couples, arguing and fighting are frequent, everyday events. They thrash about, resist the will of the other, and their communication often erupts into a fiery, passionate clash. Which type do you think is less likely to get a divorce? Surprisingly, Gottman found that all three styles are about equally stable and likely to end in divorce or not.

The 5 to 1 ratio. More important, Gottman found that the ratio of competitive/control talk to cooperative/straight talk (to use the language of our chapter) was much more important in predicting marital breakup than was the overall style of the communication. In fact, he found that marriages that survived for many years contained partners who could maintain at least a five-to-one ratio of positives to negatives (Gottman, 1999, p. 29). Look back at the list of negative, competitive/control expressions listed earlier. At the top of this inventory are inappropriate interrupting, lecturing, scolding, using the *non sequitur*, being a martyr, and the use of sarcasm. Now look at the positive list of straight-talk communication forms. These include seeking meaning and clarification, communication congruence, and appropriate disclosure.

Harsh startup. Gottman indicates that one of the most severe problems in communication styles is when we use competitive control communication to begin our exchanges with our partners. Let's label this idea the *Harsh Startup Principle.*

Look back at the list of controlling/competitive forms of communication. This principle tells us that not only are these strategies destructive but their destructiveness is amplified when one of them is the first thing out of our mouths. Imagine a scene in which the wife walks in the door from work. The husband barely says hello, but then launches into a lecture, "I thought you said you were going to be home at

> PRINCIPLE 7.2: HARSH STARTUP
>
> *The tone and intent of the way we begin conversations is a sign of relationship strength. When we lead out with harsh, negative, and biting comments it is a sign our relationship is weaker. Conversely, if we lead out with a calm, generous, gentle, and civil intent, it is a sign we care more about our partner and that the relationship is stronger.*

5:30. Did you remember that we are supposed to be at the Frogman's by 7:00? What were you thinking?" Gottman's (1999) research shows us that about 96% of the time when a conversation begins with a harsh startup from the control/competitive communication styles listed above, it will end with a negative tone. And it does not seem to matter if you try to make it up. "Oh . . . okay, I am sorry, that was too blunt. Let me start over." Actually, you can't start over. The damage for that encounter cannot be recalled.

Remember each contact with our partners is a "new encounter" (Ehrlich, 2000). We sometimes believe that our encounters with our close family members are continuous. Actually, they are not. Each time we meet and greet is a new scene in the relationship play. That does not mean it is a new play, but it is a new scene. Our partners read our intent tones, gather information about how we feel toward them, reflect on what information they want to disclose, and prepare messages to send to us. If we ignore this important rule and assume that context of the new encounter is not important, we are missing an important principle of life. As Ehrlich states:

> *"Many of the defining moments of our lives can be traced to the impact of first encounters . . . . There is magic in the power in the first encounter . . . [his assertion is that] all human communication encounters are first encounters."* (Ehrlich, 2000, p. 5)

Our job in close relationships is to realize that each new day, each new encounter is manageable. We can and must manage those repeated first impressions. But most of us get lazy and act as if the repeated first encounters don't matter much. So, we simply blast away with what is on our mind. And, if what is on our minds get encoded into a nasty, controlling demand or lecture, it is almost certain that that segment of the relationship exchange will end on a negative tone and maybe even in a full-fledged fight. Most people when challenged or pushed with a message that is confrontational, threatening, or demanding, do not repeatedly return the confrontation with generosity and openness. Instead, we will eventually (or quickly) become resistant, combative, and even hostile.

Communication in Family Life

Therefore, one place to start in building stronger relationship patterns with those you love is to plan more carefully how you express concerns, wants, wishes, requests, desires, and needs. Open the encounters with small talk that is at least neutral and, if possible, positive. Timing is crucial. Waiting for the right moment to express a need or want can make all the difference in the outcomes.

The Four Horsemen. Gottman expands our list of competitive communication styles and includes four specific types of negative communication patterns he calls the "Four Horseman of the Apocalypse." His reference is to the Biblical vision of the end of the world in which four horsemen usher in the final demise of the world. His assertion is that when we participate in these four deadly kinds of competitive interactions, our own world of marriage and family may come tumbling down on us. These four strategies of marital doom are criticism, contempt, defensiveness, and withdrawal. As you will note, they are similar to types of control language listed above.

As you read about these four deadly communication styles, keep in mind they are presented with the idea that learning about them and how to avoid the use of them is an important way of building strong communication patterns in marriage.

Criticism. As a conversation begins to unfold after a harsh startup has occurred, what type of competitive or cooperative language happens next? Gottman (1999) claims that, after a harsh startup, it is likely that more control/competitive language will follow. Specifically, he indicates that there are four types of competitive lan-

guage that are damning to close relationships. The first is criticism. Criticism has many elements of destructive communication. This type of communication sends the messages of disapproval, condemnation, denigration, and denunciation. It is sometimes like a heated ping-pong match...hitting the comments right back at the partner which as much force as possible.

We cannot go through life living with our partners without, at some time, being annoyed at something they do: it is a fact of life. The trick is deciding what type of message to send, how to encode it and make sure it does not damage the relationship. Having a complaint is normal, natural, and predictable. Using criticism in response to an irritation does not help the situation; it makes things worse. It is one thing to say, "The way you talked to my mother last night concerns me. You seem to be annoyed with her lately."

It is another thing to take the annoyance or concern to another level of attack and make our words more global and general. "You are a socially clumsy oaf—every time you get around my mother, you blow her off and make her feel like a moron." Once we become less specific and more general, we begin using more superlatives, personal attack, lectures, and sarcasm. We are much less likely to use message clarity, seek meaning, and find congruence in our communication exchanges. Gottman (1999 p. 28) indicates that harsh startups are often disguises for impending criticism. We slam someone quickly with a complaint (but it is not couched in the language of seeking meaning and congruence) and then move rapidly to the general, non-specific criticism. The following is a true example of how this works. On a rainy Saturday night, a family decided that all of them (Mom, Dad, and 18-year-old Jacob) would go to a movie. Jacob had been up all the previous night watching movies with friends, waiting to go early in the morning to a ticket office to stand in line for tickets to a concert. After the ticket adventure, he and his friends played basketball for much of the day. Consequently, he was tired and fell asleep during the afternoon. But he still wanted to go to the movie. Mom and dad had some shopping to do before the movie. Jacob did not want to go shopping, but instead would meet Mom and Dad at the show at 7:30 p.m. The pre-purchased ticket was left on the kitchen counter with a note to meet us at the movie.

Mom and Dad saved a seat for him; the movie began, but no Jacob. After the movie they returned home to find him with a sour face in the kitchen. Dad said, "So, what happened? You didn't wake up in time for the movie?" (It was a bit of a harsh startup, a little sarcastic, and tiny bit critical.) Jacob took the bait and responded with a harsh startup of his own. "Well, if you guys would ever tell me what is going on, maybe I could figure out what to do." That took Dad by surprise. He thought the evening plans were quite clear. His startup with a critical intent inevitably led to a confrontation. Dad assumed Jacob simply did not get up in time and had wasted the $7.50 for the ticket. Jacob was annoyed because Dad had made a mistake and Jacob did not know what to do. You see, Dad had purchased the tickets in the afternoon. Apparently, the ticket seller did not hear him correctly and had sold Dad three tickets for the afternoon matinee. Printed on the ticket was a 4:30 time for the movie. Jacob assumed that Mom and Dad had told him the wrong time, the movie was over when he awoke from his nap, and the theater would not let him in with an afternoon ticket. He was mad at Dad because of his mistake. Dad was mad at Jacob because he was being irresponsible.

All of the relationship trouble could have been avoided. If both Jacob and Dad had not blasted a harsh startup in the new encounter after the movie, several minutes of negative, relationship-destroying conversation could have been avoided. All Dad would have had to say was, "Gee, we missed you what happened?"

Here are some other examples of complaints compared to criticisms:

Example of Complaint: Looks like there is no milk this morning for cereal. I thought you were going shopping yesterday; did something come up?

Example of Criticism: You never follow through with plans; you spend all day watching golf on TV then complain when there is no milk in the fridge.

Example of Complaint: I just finished balancing the checkbook. I was kind of annoyed that you spent that extra $100 on buying more CDs. We could have made an extra payment on the credit card.

Example of Criticism: We have got to sit down and talk about money. Every plan we make gets destroyed by this obsession you have buying more and more CDs. Your financial irresponsibility is killing us. I can't believe you don't care enough about our relationship to pay attention to our finances.

Contempt. Often, the conversation boils over even more. Sometimes couples don't stop at criticism; they take it a notch higher and resort to words and intent messages that convey contempt (Gottman, 1999). Contempt can be defined as content and intent messages that convey disdain, scorn, and censure. When we see couples elevating a conflict to this level, there is a sneering and sniping tone to their voices. It often involves name-calling, eye-rolling, mockery, and sneering (Gottman, 1999). It often conveys more than just a competition but goes one step further and sends a message of disgust. This type of demeaning conversation destroys trust, alienates us from our partners, and sends a message that we have no respect for the person. As Gottman indicates, a common response to contemptuous comments is belligerence and increased aggressive anger toward our partners.

Defensiveness. Both criticism and contempt result in sharp increases in defensive responses. Unfortunately, the use of defensiveness does not work well. Resistance and self-protection often bring more attack rather than resolution. Attacking spouses are more likely to press on for resolution than they are to back down. Think for a minute. When was the last time someone criticized you and you respond with a defense ("I was not; I was only 20 minutes late"), and the attacking person said, "Oh, gee, that's right, I was wrong, sorry for bringing it up"? If you are like most people, that rarely happens. Defensiveness spawns more competitive exchanges and escalates conflicts. These Three Horsemen of the Apocalypse work together, pushing us to attack, denounce, and defend.

Stonewalling. Rather than continue the confrontation, sometimes a partner will tune out. "Okay, that's it for me. Do what ever you want. I could not care less." Think back to our list of competitive/controlling communication patterns. Among them you will find distancing and martyring. Both of these are captured in Gottman's (1999) fourth deadly Horseman. Stonewalling, distancing, and using the martyr strategy usually come later in relationships. Years of head-butting and competitive exchanges have conveyed the message that no change occurs in most of the relationship struggles that have occurred. So, one might conclude, what's the point of struggling? Gottman (1999) tells us that 85% of the time it is the husband who retreats and resorts to stonewalling. He decides that the aggravation is not worth the effort.

USEFUL STRATEGIES

So, what can we do to avoid the deadly effects of competitive/controlling communication in our close relationships? Below are a few suggestions. Most of them revolve around a few simple ideas that stem from research conducted by Burr et al. (1995). In Burr's research, he discovered that couples who were successful in attaining their goals were more likely to use kindness and generosity in their daily interactions. In fact, kindness seemed to be more important than being an "effective" communicator. Couples who were more clumsy, more forgetful, and ineffective in communicating what they wanted in a relationship were able to meet their goals better (despite communication problems) when they were kinder and more generous. Couples who were good communicators (i.e., clear messages, precise directions, and accurate expectations) were not as successful with their family's goals if kindness was absent. Therefore, to strengthen the chances of a family being able to meet their goals, members must realize how important the role of kindness and generosity is in family life.

Second, as we think in terms of kindness rather than competition and control, we can begin to remove the criticism, contempt, defensiveness, and stonewalling from our response menus during the daily contact we have with family members. Learning and identifying these patterns is an important step in being able to stop them. Most of us know little about the communication strategies we use to try and get people to do things we want them to do.

Third, as we learned in Chapter 2, the more we try to change people, the more likely we will end by hurting close relationships. One of the more ironic scenes we have experienced in years of teaching this material involved a couple in a class. They were having one of their worst fights in months about a simple topic. She was insisting that he stop being so competitive and controlling. Her strategy to get him to consider changing was to use criticism, contempt, whining, and martyrdom-filled barrages of messages. Of course, as can be predicted, he started to fight back, realized the futility of defending himself, and withdrew to far corner of their relationship from which he was unwilling to emerge.

If you are reading this text and thinking, "I must take this home and make my partner see the light," you are already in trouble. The only person you can try to change is yourself. That is difficult if your partner is a died-in-the-wool competitive communicator. You might try the approach of suggesting that you wish to try strengthening your relationship based on some material you have been reading. Suggest that he or she read it also. Then, come together (meta communication) and

SPOTLIGHT ON RESEARCH 7.1: PREDICTING MARITAL HAPPINESS AND STABILITY IN NEWLYWED INTERACTIONS

Gottman, Coan, Carrere, and Swanson (1998) conducted a study of 130 newlywed couples. The primary point of the study was to see if the researchers could tell over time if they way they interacted with each other initially predicted if they would stay married by the end of the study. The participants were initially screened and observed in a laboratory setting in which they resided for several days. The observers recorded what they said and did. In an important part of this study, the experimenter asked the couples (during the first interview shortly after marriage) to choose several topics to discuss that they rated as problematic. The couples discussed the chosen topics for 15 minutes and then viewed a recording of what had happened. Each individual rated the tapes as to the feelings they were having during the conversations.

An interesting finding in this and several other research studies conducted by Gottman is that anger is not very telling as a measure of marital problems. Instead, with these newlyweds, high levels of contempt, belligerence, and defensiveness were strong predictors of marital troubles later. These couples were asked to return to the lab each year for six years. Each time, it was confirmed that the power of contemptuous, belligerent, and defensive behavior has a major impact on the ability of the couple to meet their goals in a relationship.

Also of interest is the direct finding that active listening seems to be of little importance in building strong relationships. For many years, family life educators have tried to get couples to paraphrase what the other couple says as a way to get them focus on the problem and show care. Gottman and his associates have repeatedly shown that this strategy has little effect on whether a couple is together years later.

This study also showed that a common Level II (see Chapter 5) pattern of interaction that seems to lead to divorce is when the wife uses some form of harsh startup. She says something like, "Why did you spend that money, we were saving it for our trip next summer. Are you a dope or what?" That is followed by the husband's refusal to be influenced by his wife. This pattern continues with pouting (low intensity negativity) by the wife and no attempt by the husband to defuse the situation. The couple stews about issues for days at a time.

It was also clear that there were few if any relationships that did not have struggles. What seem to separate the group that was to be divorced from those who stay together was how much positive feeling happened during conflict. While conflict was unavoidable, the intent message of ultimately caring for the other person is critical. Also, those who can de-escalate a conflict were also more likely to stay together. Someone would step forward and change the topic, tell a joke, or somehow break-the-ice. The couples who had the most trouble were those who could not let it go.

Your response:

Can you think of a recent situation in which there was a harsh start-up and you responded negatively? Describe what happened.

ACTIVITY 7.2 - FIND A MOVIE WITH INTERACTION

Find a movie of your choosing that has a couple interacting about some difficult issue. The couple doesn't have to be married, but the assignment will be more effective if you find a couple that is married, living together, or is otherwise committed. Choose a 3-10 min. (approx.) segment in which this couple is having an intense exchange. It does not have to be a negative battle, but one in which they are clearly concerned about solving some issue or problem.

Record the dialogue below.

Continue recording the dialogue here.

Now go back to the dialogue, do an analysis of the script you have created and tell how each of the comments, gestures, verbal and non-verbal remarks fit the lists of communication elements described in your chapter. Summarize what you learn about this couple.

JOURNAL OF THOUGHT 7.3: WHAT CAN YOU DO?

In the following two pages, build a strategy for enhancing the relations you are in now or ones you think you will have in the future. This can be with family members of your original family, future family, or current relationships. What do you need to do to make it better? There are many good ideas in the chapter to use as starting points. What do you specifically want to begin doing or stop doing? How will you do that? Devise a specific plan.

Chapter 7

talk about how you talk about things. If that is unsuccessful, you may want to find a counselor who can guide you through ways of strengthening your communication strategies. Change is possible, but only if both partners are sincerely committed to change.

Alternatively, you may wish to purchase Gottman's book cited above: *The Seven Principles for Making Marriage Work* (1999). There are several exercises in the book that help partners work on changing how they communicate.

Ultimately, change comes down to you. Teaching yourself another way of communicating can dramatically change your life. Take careful note about how many messages of kindness and generosity you send vis-à-vis how many negative, competitive, controlling messages. Take note of what sends you into retreat. What do you do when attacked, when you are impatient with another, or when you want something changed in another person? Also, if you're annoyed with your partner, how is your timing for sharing your irritation? Timing is important. Make sure that each new encounter with a partner begins with sincere kindness, care, and loving connection. Then, use carefully chosen words to express a complaint and avoid slipping into the minefield of superlatives, attacks, overgeneralizations, and sarcasm. If possible, try to avoid mimicking the clever repartee you see on television and in movies. While possibly humorous in that medium, the sarcastic, demeaning humor portrayed in the media will not build strong relationships.

Remember that the style of communication you adopt with your partner will spill over into the type of messages sent to your children. In turn, they will pass those patterns of interaction along to their children and spouses.

Chapter 7

STUDY QUESTIONS:

1. What is meant when we use the term intent messages?

2. What is a *non sequitur*?

3. Why do family scientists make the claim that 'you cannot not communicate'?

4. What does 'decoding' refer to?

5. What is 'meta-communication'?

6. Name four ideas that reinforce the notion that it is critical to understand gender in the study of family communication.

7. Describe the Harsh Startup Principle and tell how this idea can be used in families.

KEY TERMS

Meta-communication
Decoding
Intent messages
Content messages
Types of communication (e.g., dissing, straight talk, control talk, etc.)
Harsh Startup

CHAPTER
EIGHT

Regulating Distance

Regulating Distance

Main Points:

1. A key to understanding family processes is to know about the emotional climate in a family.

2. Sometimes a family's emotional climate can create a situation in which family members become overly connected to the family system.

3. If a family member is over-connected to his family, he/she may have a difficult time separating their emotions from their thinking selves.

4. There are at least two ways that a family's emotional climate can produce family members who feel over-connected. Both of these ways are examples of families who have a low tolerance for intimacy: chronic anxiety and emotional triangling.

5. Chronic anxiety refers to long-term negative emotion in the family emotional system. All families encounter important negative emotions such as despair, futility, and serious disappointment. Family emotional systems can be wisely managed by dealing with these negative emotions so they do not become chronic.

6. Emotional triangles or triangling occurs when a family member has some anxiety about a family relationship and draws a third person into the problem as a strategy to solve the problem. Triangling is usually destructive in a family system.

7. There are four ways listed here that one could cope with a high level of over-connectedness. These are using a genogram, understanding invisible loyalties, the benign assumption, and avoiding emotional cutoff.

8. The ideas about family emotional systems have several implications for families and those who try to help families.

Regulating Distance

Your family did not suddenly appear one day. Instead, who we are as families evolved from ongoing, developmental, and historical processes. For example, from my family of origin, I brought certain emotional and value oriented ties. My wife, Larri-Lea also brought with her an orientation about how one should (or could) feel about another person or group of people within a family. One of the more important aspects of how our family system functions or fails to thrive is how Larri-Lea and I manage the emotional relationships between us and between each of our five children. Families, who are better able to meet goals, maintain longer and more fulfilling relationships, and meet crisis are those families who have a capacity for tolerating intimacy and tolerating individuality (Farley, 1979; Sabatelli & Anderson, 1991; Gavazzi, Anderson, & Sabatelli, 1993). An important aspect of understanding family processes is an awareness of how to balance these two ideas. In this chapter, we focus primarily on the idea of learning to balance closeness in family life. Generally, family theorists and therapists refer to this topic as differentiation in families. Differentiation, or the ability to maintain appropriate emotional distance from other family members, is a key skill in successful family life. To differentiate means to appropriately separate, segment, and make different. When differentiation in families is problematic, families are either so emotionally close that there is little difference among the family members, or they are so emotionally separate that bonding, support, and connection are faint and removed.

DIFFERENTIATION

When we speak of tolerating individuality, we often refer to the idea that a major task of families is to regulate distance. By that, we mean that families have to learn how to effectively let go of their children as they get older. That is, they have to teach them how to be independent thinkers and allow them the freedom to make choices and a sense of individuality. Family researchers and therapists have long taught that it is a sign of family strength when families create a climate of increasing independence in their children. The opposite situation is where families have little or no tolerance for individuality and instead demand conformity and compliance at any cost. Usually, to achieve this domination in children, over-connected parents create a climate of chronic anxiety, animosity, distrust, and conflict.

This type of family climate has the potential to create deep emotional problems for children who are raised with this type of parenting strategy. One early writer and originator of this concept was Murray Bowen (1976). He authored several important research papers that describe how destructive unhealthy over-connection is in family life. At its most negative point, he suggested that occasionally family members become so connected to the family emotional system that this connection interferes with their ability to manage the other aspects of their lives.

According to several family researchers (Bowen, 1976; Gavazzi & Sabatelli, 1990, Gavazzi, 1993; Green & Werner, 1996), our experience with family connectedness begins early in our lives. One of the jobs of a child is to resolve the inevitable strong connections between him/her and his/her parents. We all are strongly connected to what happens in our families in early life, but the climate or tone of the family environment predicts whether or not we can build our own identity separate and apart from that of our parents and early family members. As we pass into early adulthood, one of the most important psychological tasks we approach is the search for independence, identity, or individuation. All of those terms mean essentially the same thing and refer to a person's need to separate from his/her family of origin and become a unique individual.

A term used by these family scholars to describe how connectedness and intimacy works in families is *differentiation*. The root of this term is "different." In other words, to differentiate is to separate and become unique. This term is also used in biology and the idea is similar. A primary difference between cancer cells and healthy cells is that healthy cells are differentiated. That means they know how to specialize and some cells become hair, others heart tissue, and still others know to become skin. Cancer cells, however, have forgotten who they are and are undifferentiated. Instead of becoming something specific and purposeful, they just grow and consume. So a mass of undifferentiated cells is worthless to the body and even destructive. Researchers suggest that differentiation levels have been linked to the family's ability to prepare and successfully launch its offspring (Carter & McGoldrick, 1989; Farley, 1979; Kerr & Bowen, 1988; Gavazzi, 1994).

When the goal of a family is to create a mass of undifferentiated members who have forgotten or never knew a special purpose that resides outside of their families of origin, the children who then try to make their way in the world do not seem to do as well. When we are young, no one really expects us to differentiate and become unique. But as we get older it is essential for the health of both the individual and the family that each family member feels a sense of uniqueness, special-ness, and individuality.

As we get older it is, of course important to remain a part of one's family. However, a major task of life is to create one's own world of choices and decisions. Some individuals never really move beyond being emotionally connected to their parents. It is as if they have a very long emotional umbilical cord still attached to their mother and/or father.

JOURNAL OF THOUGHTS 8.1: DEFINE THE EMOTIONS

1. What do we mean by fusion in this chapter?

2. What is a family "emotional field" or climate?

3. How differentiated was your family? Explain what this means and how it relates to your family.

Families who know how to build differentiation allow individuals to express individuality and are still intimately connected to the other family members (Gavazzi, 1993) As the child ages, the families are less intrusive, more supportive.

Poorly differentiated families express a lower tolerance of the uniqueness of the individual family members. Think back to the chapter on ideologies. Families who are more closed and have rigid boundaries with regard to the outside world are much more likely to be chronically anxious about making sure family members do not break any rules. However, inside the family walls, the boundaries are usually very blurred. That is, because they are so intrusive they may insist on opening everyone's mail, not letting children play behind closed doors, and forcing family members to participate in all family activities.

It is also the case that in poorly differentiated families there is a low tolerance for intimacy. The conflict that arises from intrusive attempts to maintain control and domination may completely squelch any kindness, generosity, or feelings of love. The overall result is a young person who is very unsure of his/her place in the world. The prevailing message is one of doubt, unresolved emotions, and a perpetual seeking for validation.

Fusion. According to some researchers (Reiss, 1981), all infants and young children are fused (extremely connected) with an emotional "field," "atmosphere," or "climate" in their parental family. This means infants and children are naturally and involuntarily caught up in the emotional processes of their parents and siblings.

This higher level of connection has at least two possible outcomes. First, when the emotional climate in a family is more positive and there are higher levels of trust, concern, confidence, and appreciation, the children sense these emotions and respond to them positively. Within this supportive and more open climate, teenagers are more able to establish a clear and separate identity from their families of origin (Anderson & Fleming, 1986).

However, for some families there is a negative side. When the climate in a home has an atmosphere of high levels of tension, animosity, resentment, and bitterness, there is a different result. Instead of children learning how to construct positive identities that exist independent of the family, they are captured by the hostile emotional family climate. According to Bowen, the result is that as the child gets older he/she finds it much more difficult to escape the effects of this negative home atmosphere.

It is as if these young emerging adults do not have the ability to separate their emotions from their intellect. While most children mature and try to form a self or identity that has unique qualities and attributes, children from over-connected families have great difficulty with this task. It may be that some will spend most, if not all, of their adult lives trying to free themselves from the family influence of the past.

Thus, differentiation/fusion is an emotional process that refers to how much people are able to separate from the emotional climate that occurred in their families while they were young. Families with higher levels of negativity, hostility, and animosity are more likely to generate unhealthy levels of connectedness (fusion) in family life. This spirit of contention and control in families keeps children from developing a strong inner identity and, instead, their primary identity remains connected or fused to their families of origin.

Results. When a person grows up in a negative climate as described above and is fused to his/her family's emotional field, it is thought that these children have a more difficult time with certain problem solving and other life skills. For example, one researcher (Papero, 1983) found that a negative home climate created a situation in which the person in such a fused state has trouble controlling the feeling part of his/her life. In other words, the emotions created by coming from a more fused family system seem to override a person's thinking system.

Likewise, he found that in families where the climate was more positive and, consequently, there was less fusion, the family members were much more likely to be able to separate their thinking selves from their emotional selves. When people are more highly differentiated, they seem to be able to maintain more objectivity and to think carefully for longer periods of time in spite of the emotional arousal (Papero, 1983, p. 140).

Sauer (1982) listed several characteristics of families who are more intrusive, enmeshed, or fused. Check this list found in Activity 8.1 and see if any of those questions fit how your family relates to one another.

Other researchers concur with similar findings. For example, appropriate levels of differentiation in a family are more likely to produce teenagers who can build stronger relationships with other people (Sabatelli & Cecil-Pigo, 1985), have fewer problems with alcohol abuse (Bartle & Sabatelli, 1989); have higher levels of psychomaturity (Gavazzi, Anderson, & Sabatelli, 1993) and were much less likely to have general problems at school, difficulty with peers, participation in illegal activities, and fewer problems with their families of origin (Gavazzi, 1993).

One reason fusion seems to be so powerful in predicting problems is that children from highly connected families usually grow up in a very conflicted, dominating, demanding world. One result of being raised in that type of climate is that children who live in a highly conflicted world have a difficult time separating their thinking selves from their feeling worlds (Nichols & Schwartz, 1995, p. 371). As Bowen said, a "poorly differentiated person is trapped within a feeling world….A more differentiated person can participate freely in the emotional sphere without the fear of becoming too fused with others. He is also free to shift to calm, logical reasoning for decisions that govern his life" (Bowen, 1976, p. 67).

> *At the fusion end of the spectrum, the intellect is so flooded by emotionality that the total life course is determined by the emotional process and by what "feels right" rather than by beliefs or opinions. The intellect exists as an appendage of the feeling system. (Bowen, 1976, p. 66)*

Regulating Distance

SPOTLIGHT ON RESEARCH 8.1: WELL BEING IN KOREAN YOUTH AND FAMILY
DIFFERENTIATION

Chun and MacDermid (1997) surveyed 170 Korean teens and their families to try and discover how family differentiation contributes to individuation. In is commonly believed by researchers that adolescents do better at making the transition into adulthood if they have a stronger sense of self and are more individuated from their parents. Families in which differentiation is low should therefore produce children who are low individuation. The more distance regulation problems they report, the more likely the teens are to have unresolved emotional ties to their family.

According to Chun and MacDermid, in Korean families it seems only to be the case in the relationship between the teen and his father. For girls, the differentiation between daughter and mother is key. Unlike teens in the U.S. the total family differentiation score did not matter as much. Also, Chun and MacDermid were surprised to find out that the more individuated the Koreans teens felt, the lower their self-esteem scores were. For these teens closeness (even extreme closeness by U.S. standards) increased self-esteem and seemed to have the opposite effect from that found by researchers analyzing U.S. families.

This study shows us that we need to be very careful in overgeneralizing about family processes. What may seem like a useful and appropriate strategy in one culture may have the opposite effect in another.

Your response:
Think of 8-10 questions you would ask a family to determine how enmeshed/fused they are.

Regulating Distance

ACTIVITY 8.1 - CHARACTERISTICS OF ENMESHED FAMILIES. (SAUER, 1982)

The following list of family interaction styles was developed by Sauer (1982). Read each of the items below and score your family. There is no known published research about how families in general score on these items. Therefore, simply write a short description about your family in the space provided. Informally, if you find yourself commenting in agreement with each item, your family may be more on the enmeshed side of the ledger.

1. Think to a time when you are with your family of origin and there are others present who are not family members. Highly enmeshed families often speak for other family members and monitor what they say, interpret what a family members says, and even answers questions for them. Does this happen in your family? How much? How does it make you feel?

2. Parents in enmeshed families tend to "over monitor." In fact, their over-attention may be intrusive and overbearing. They want to know everything about your friends, school activities, TV watching, and even what you think. It is, of course wonderful when parents are involved, but enmeshment goes beyond that into intrusive behavior. In your family, do you feel cared for, left alone, over-monitored, or is there a better word to describe how your parents watched over you when you were growing up?

3. In enmeshed families, they often control the movements of older children by creating danger myths. That is, even when it is appropriate and even helpful to have children do things on their own, they won't let their children out of sight for "fear" of something bad happening. That is not to say that parents should in anyway be casual about what their children do. However, when it is age appropriate, did your parents allow you explore, visit, and extend your world beyond their control? Explain.

4. Highly enmeshed families do "everything" together, or so it would seem. If there is a movie to go to, all must go. If one person cannot go or does not like the choice, then the event will probably be called off. How was this for your family? Where children allowed to not go sometimes, when appropriate?

5. Enmeshed families generally have a "communal" family ideology. With toys, clothes, and food "what belongs to one belongs to all." Were you allowed to have your own clothes, toys, and snacks that did not have to be shared? Did all your clothes come from hand-me-downs and/or were shared with other siblings. Keep in mind that this is not an economic issue,

necessarily. Sometimes families have to share because there is no other way. But in enmeshed families, the amount of resources available does not matter as much with regard to this issue.

6. Privacy in enmeshed families is a rare thing. In more enmeshed families, individual mail is opened, phone calls monitored and listened to, and secrets are forbidden. In many such families, even closed doors are not allowed. The parents feel they must be in touch at all times, knowing and monitoring what is going on.

7. In enmeshed families, important discussions are rarely held between only two people. So, if there is an important topic to cover, a third person will have to be present and is drawn into the dialogue. For example, I know a family in which the eldest son is frequently brought into the conversation of the parents. They will wait for weeks to solve a problem until they visit him. Then all big decisions are made with the third person in attendance. Does this happen in your family? Even while you are at school, you may get phone calls with others on the line, making decisions to bring you "up-to-date." Again, be careful not to confuse caring and loving behaviors with intrusive, enmeshed ones.

After you have answered the questions above, write a short (one page) summary of how the idea of enmeshment relates to your family. For some of you, each of the items will sound odd and unbelievable. The assignment will be simple and short. For others, you will find many examples of each question. What do you make of that? What can you do about it? How would you design your future family differently? If you come from a family that has a low score on the above items, tell how you know your family cares. What do they do to watch over you and help you?

Regulating Distance

Another family researcher, Kerr (1981), conducted several studies in which he found that calm people think more fairly, clearly, and objectively. However, when highly connected/fused individuals were placed in emotionally charged situations they responded less calmly and, instead, more irrationally and sought approval from others, placing blame on others, tried to dominate others in the situation (Kerr, 1981, p. 237).

Therefore, one application of this principle is that when family climates have less conflict, family members develop a greater sense of differentiation or personal individuality and, consequently, they do much better at solving life's difficult problems. When a highly stressful event occurs, they are much more likely to be able to think clearly about their options and generate effective solutions. When a person comes from a home climate that creates fusion, he/she is more likely to make less effective choices under stress because they are more apt to live in a feeling, emotionally charged world in which their feelings overflow with each new stressful event.

An anxious family elevates a facet of a problem to the cause of the problem. (Kerr & Bowen, 1988, p. 61)

CHRONIC FAMILY ANXIETY

There are at least two facets of inner family life that help us understand how over-connectedness operates. Remember that families in which there is a low tolerance for intimacy and individuality are usually characterized by higher levels of conflict, animosity, and anxiety. Researchers realized this many years ago and labeled this phenomena chronic family anxiety. This idea describes the seemingly perpetual bickering, nattering, intrusive control attempts that characterize over-connected families.

The second idea explored later is triangulation. This idea suggests that often in over connected families troubled family members try to coop or recruit another family member to solve some problem they are having with a third family member.

Anxiety can be defined as a negative emotion that includes distress or uneasiness of mind caused by apprehension of danger or misfortune. Acute anxiety is different from chronic anxiety. Acute anxiety is usually a short-term response to a stressful situation, and most of the time it is a rational response to a real (rather than imagined) problem. For example, when a couple is told by a doctor their child has a serious disease, the natural emotional response is to have acute anxiety or feelings of "distress or uneasiness of mind caused by apprehension of danger or misfortune." Acute anxiety tends to leave after a person learns to cope with the stressful situation or the danger leaves. For example, the anxiety leaves a couple when they learn how to cope with the illness or if the diagnosis is not accurate.

Chapter 8

All individuals and families encounter situations that create acute anxiety. It occurs whenever there are serious problems to be dealt with and whenever negative emotions such as despair, futility, inadequacy, inferiority, lack of fulfillment, discouragement, emotional hurt, or serious disappointments occur. One of the challenges all families face is to find ways to deal with these problems and their negative emotions so that they do not lead to chronic anxiety.

Chronic anxiety is when uneasiness, distress, or apprehension endures for long periods of time. Usually the sources of chronic anxiety are difficult to identify, as are the original causes, and it is an underlying condition that persists and colors many different situations.

There are some types of chronic anxiety that usually are not important in family systems. For example, people can have psychic fears or apprehensions that are related to their work, their education, or their friendships, and these forms or types of chronic anxiety sometimes have little impact of family life. Also, people can have chronic anxiety about many other things that have little to do with family systems. They can have chronic anxiety about being in an elevator or being in dark places, and many of these chronic anxieties only occur outside the home and have little impact on family systems.

Bowen studied one type of chronic anxiety that is very important in family systems. It is long-term tension or resentment. This occurs when family members feel others in their family have been unjust to them in important ways. Emotional undercurrents can occur when family members love deeply, with close bonds, and then feel betrayed, abandoned, deceived, or ignored.

The solution is for families to find ways to deal with negative emotions such as resentment and disappointment so they do not lead to chronic ills in their system. The healing balm of such things as forgiveness, patience, and the willingness to let ourselves and others be frail and inadequate, are strategies that can help families keep chronic anxiety low enough that it doesn't invisibly erode the basic structures of the family system.

Chronic family anxiety is significant because it can lead to destructive emotional climates such as general feelings of animosity, malice, rancor, enmity, and hatred. Emotions such as these create seriously disabling processes in most families because they interfere with the most positive emotions that people seek (such as love, compassion, care, and nurturance).

Another reason this type of chronic anxiety is usually disabling is because it keeps family members "on edge," and even minor problems can be enough to create intense emotional reactions of anger, aggression, violence, and abuse. It is similar to having a pot of water simmering, where a slight increase in temperature is enough to make it boil.

When families do not have chronic anxiety in their emotional system they do not over-respond to minor problems, and they can marshal their resources to cope with the problems effectively. But, when they have ongoing tension, they have less ability to cope with even minor problems. The principle that Bowen developed can be called the chronic anxiety principle.

PRINCIPLE 8.1: CHRONIC ANXIETY PRINCIPLE

The higher the level of chronic anxiety in a family (or other relationship) the less likely they will be able to attain their goals or be adaptive.

EMOTIONAL TRIANGLES

The second indicator strategy used by highly connected families is triangling. Emotional triangles (or triangling) are a common occurrence in families who are over-connected and in which there are high levels of fusion. Triangling occurs when two parts of a family system have an ongoing conflict and they focus on something else ("triangle in") as a way of gaining control over the situation or stabilizing their problem. There are many things that can be triangled in. Sometimes it is another member of the family or someone outside the family. (Often this is what is happening in unhealthy generational alliances, and it is often what happens when someone has an extramarital affair.) People can also triangle in other things such as an issue, an organization, a hobby, or their career.

Emotional triangles have a number of rules that govern how they operate. And family scientists are beginning to isolate and describe these rules. Having a knowledge of these rules can help us understand the emotional processes that are always swirling around in triangles, and it also can help us keep from becoming fused ourselves or being triangled into situations in undesirable ways. This latter idea is reflected in an insightful observation made by Edwin Friedman (1985):

Chapter 8

It has been said, "What Peter says about Paul tells you more about Peter than it does about Paul." In the concept of an emotional triangle, "What Peter says to you about his relationship with Paul has to do with his relationship with you." (p. 36)

Friedman (1988) has developed several "laws" about emotional triangles that help us understand what they are and how they operate in families (p. 36–39). His ideas have been edited and changed to include the language of family in them, but they were originally meant to reflect the relationships found in any group.

Often, one family member keeps the relationship of two other family members in balance. In other words, many times a family member will feel it is her (or his) responsibility to make sure that a child (for example) has a good relationship with his father. Or a child may feel a need to get two parents closer or stop high levels of conflict. (For the sake of explanation, I have chosen to use a hypothetical situation in which a mother is trying to resolve conflict between a teen son and the father. However, keep in mind that these ideas refer to any combination of people in a relationship system.)

When Mary (the mother in our example) tries to change the relationship between Juan (the son) and Michael (the father) she may see some change but rarely for more than a few days. It is almost always the case that a relationship that is changed in this way (by the mother trying to make the son and father closer) will revert to the way it was before.

When Mary tries to make Juan and Michael get along better, her attempts almost always result in a worse relationship between Juan and Michael. The harder she tries to change their relationship (even though this is a good and wonderful goal) it has the opposite result from what she wanted.

The more Mary tries to get Juan and Michael to have a better relationship, not only is it less likely to get better but Mary is more likely to feel worse about their relationship and take on the stress of them not being close to one another.

The only hope that Mary has of building stronger family relationships is for her to build strong connections with Juan and Michael individually. She has to realize that the connection between Juan and Michael is their responsibility and her intervention will most likely only make things worse (Friedman, 1985, p. 36–39).

The root of triangulation is ongoing, long-term anxiety (negative emotion) that is not resolved. The best alternative is to find ways to resolve the roots to the problem by finding ways to resolve the negative affect. The next best alternative is to find ways to manage the negative emotions so they do not disrupt healthy individual development, healthy family development, and attaining goals. (Friedman, 1985)

Regulating Distance

There are a number of practical implications of these ideas. One of the most obvious implications is that families can avoid emotional triangles or eliminate them if they can find ways to avoid long-term negative emotions such as resentment, tension, animosity, anger, fear, apprehension, and anxiety. Many families pay a great deal of attention to such overt and visible things as the behavior of members of the family, getting good grades in school, athletic accomplishments, efficiency in handling money, and the reputation of the family, but they ignore the emotional processes in the family. These families would be more effective if they were to also pay attention to what is happening in their emotional system and try to find ways to resolve the ongoing, long-term negative feelings.

Additionally, whenever we try to help families cope with family "problems" it is advisable to pay attention to the triangles in the system. Observing the triangles can provide useful clues about unresolved tension that may be interfering with the family's ability to cope with their problems.

A third implication is to try to be aware of how we might be part of triangles. Often when someone solicits advice or help for a relationship problem, it is an attempt to triangle us into the problem situation. Being aware of the triangulation processes can provide useful ideas about how to help and how to avoid making the problem worse.

In summary, some helpful guidelines whenever we try to deal with emotional triangles are: Avoid being fused when trying to think about a triangle. This means to wait until you can find a situation where your own functional level of fusion is within comfortable limits.

Try to align with both other corners. If this is not possible, be on guard about being triangled in. Try to resolve the underlying negative emotion, because it is at the heart of the triangle. Questions that sometimes help are: Is there some unfinished business in the past that needs to be taken care of? Can the family rules be changed to help alleviate the chronic anxiety? Does someone need to adapt to development that has been occurring? Is it possible to reframe the situation so it can be seen in a different way? If the underlying negative emotions can be eliminated, try to identify some ways to live with the situation so it is not disabling.

COPING WITH FUSION

Family scientists suggest three ways of coping with emotional distress in families: (1) it is useful to learn how to use and analyze a genogram and deal with insights it provides, (2) to resolve invisible loyalties, (3) generate a benign assumption in family life, and (4) avoid a strategy many people try and is usually unsuccessful—emotional cutoff.

Using a genogram. Genograms can provide insights about the amount of differentiation occurring in families. One reason they are helpful is that patterns of fusion and differentiation are often carried from one generation to another. Usually in each generation there are some children who tend to have a little more differentiation, and there are some children who tend to have a little less, but many children repeat the patterns of the earlier generations.

Using a genogram chart, first examine and evaluate the differentiation-fusion patterns that have existed over several generations in a family. This usually provides insights about how some people have been more fused than others, and it can provide clues about a particular individual's fusion. It also helps people think about their differentiation as part of a larger pattern.

Examining your own differentiation in the context of a genogram can make you become more aware of strategies you can use to become more differentiated. For example, it may help you realize you are an autonomous individual who needs to "stand on your own two feet."

In Chapter 4 it was suggested that transitional characters are people who can change the direction of a family. Learning about these important principles means that you have the groundwork for step one of any change process: You have the knowledge. However, having the knowledge does not mean that the knowing will, by itself, change you. There are millions of people who know that smoking cigarettes will kill them and that there are 400 known cancer-causing agents in tobacco. Yet, the knowledge without a daily resolve to change means that they continue living their lives as they always have, using a product that probably will kill them. The same is true for those of us who eat too much. Change is difficult and only those who practice fighting the momentum of the past can really become a transitional character.

It also may help to realize that some feelings were appropriate when you were a child, but not as an adult. It also may help you realize how some of the family patterns which keep you "fused" to your family system were petty sibling rivalries you have now outgrown. It may help you be able to relate to your parents as individuals who also struggle with their limitations and circumstances.

Dealing with invisible loyalties. Ivan Boszormenyi-Nagy and his colleagues have developed another strategy for resolving undesirable emotional connections in family systems. Their first book was entitled Invisible Loyalties (Boszormenyi-Nagy & Sparks, 1973), and in it they described how families accumulate multigenerational patterns of obligations and rights. Some examples of positive things received are existence, love, nurturance, identity, heritage, values, bonds, and understanding.

Part of these patterns are obligations that are deeply felt emotional ties. These include such things as indebtedness, basic duties, and a sense of ethical responsibility. Boszormenyi-Nagy calls these deeply felt connections invisible loyalties, and they involve such processes as giving and taking, helping and hindering, injustices and healing, teaching and receiving, and various combinations of hurting and acts of caring.

Boszormenyi-Nagy and Sparks suggested that it is helpful to use the concept of a family ledger to think about these family processes. The ledger is a balance sheet

JOURNAL OF THOUGHTS 8.2: WHAT THOUGHTS CAME TO MIND

1. What thoughts came to mind when you read this chapter with regard to emotions in families?

2. Is the description of a highly fused family like your family or not? Tell why or why not.

3.   What would be the effects of living in a highly fused family?

JOURNAL OF THOUGHTS 8.3: TRIANGLES

1.   Summarize the laws of triangles here.

2.   Are you currently in a triangled relationship with anyone? Explain how. (If you are not…congratulations, you may be one of the three people on earth who are not.) Seriously, if you can't think of one, you may know someone else who is, write about them.

3. What can one do to get out of triangle situations? Be as specific as you can, refer to any situation you may be in or have experienced recently.

of obligations and rights, debts and credits that accumulate over time. In more effective families, family members tend to balance the ledger with justice in the exchange of debts and obligations. Sometimes, however, the justice comes too slowly, or it is insufficient and there is too great an accumulation of injustices.

In other situations some individuals perceive the pattern has been unjust, and this is deeply troubling. When these inequities occur, it creates chronic anxiety, resentments, and animosities that are disruptive to family members individually and collectively.

One of Boszormenyi-Nagy and Sparks' examples of this process is a mother who is angry at being rejected by her mother, and she tries to correct this injustice by offering total devotion to her own daughter. However, in the language of balance of payments, the mother assumes the daughter should reestablish family justice by being appreciative and giving to her the acceptance and understanding her own mother did not give her. In this type of situation, the mother is often excessively devoted to her daughter, creating resentment rather than appreciation. This can lead to the daughter's having unexplained negative feelings toward the "loving" mother. Confusion and emotional disruption prevail between the mother and daughter. Improvement results when either the mother or daughter realize how the mother is trying to "balance the payments" or "make up" for her own deprivation. An understanding of this principle can free the mother and the daughter from the destructive, invisible, emotional processes.

Fusion can be created when the emotionally based resentments are captivating and consuming. When this occurs the individuals are unable to differentiate from the emotional network. Then family members can examine the family ledger to see if patterns of emotional obligations, injustices, unresolved problems, misunderstandings, or debts are keeping some members of the family "fused" to the family emotional system. Often, according to Boszormenyi-Nagy and Sparks, the main difficulty is the invisibility of these patterns of "unfinished business." Therefore, when the patterns are discovered it is many times relatively easy to talk them through and resolve the emotional obligations.

The benign assumption. Family theorists and therapists suggest that one way to combat the potential effects of negativity and chronic anxiety in families is to develop an emotional climate that has a benign tone (Beavers, 1985). Beavers and his associates have suggested that an important aspect of stronger families is when they build a climate that is devoid of malignant attitude. An example would probably best help to define how this works.

In families where there is a malignant or highly contentious tone, each daily event that annoys or even has the potential to annoy someone is responded to with far more negative response than the event should warrant. Suppose someone spills milk at the table. In a malignant climate the parent might say something like, "See, that is another example of how you always try to make my life miserable. You are a brat and deserve to be punished." Families in which there is a benign assumption would probably respond with something that is far less dramatic, histrionic, animated, and nasty. Instead, the parent does not assume that each time something happens (like the milk spilling, or the lost shoe) that it is a "federal case" (as my mom would say). Instead, they may even give a little laugh and say, "Oops, run and get a rag before it gets all over."

When there is no benign assumption, it is more common that daily events are interpreted as threatening and as an attack. It is as if the glass of life is always full of stress and accusation to overflowing and each new event creates a spill, so to speak. The application is, of course, to somehow break through the habitual over-reactivity that too many families develop. They seem to be awash in a malignant assumptive world, filled with threat, anxiety, and unresolved anger. While you may not be able to do much about your family of origin, you certainly can begin to work on your family of procreation. Literally nothing good comes of high levels of contention and a climate of the malignant assumption in family life. These two doses of strife only increase the distance between family members and decrease the levels of intimacy.

Emotional cutoff—An undesirable method. The fourth way one can cope with highly charged emotions in families is to face the problems in families head-on and not use emotional cutoff a method of trying to deal with fusion that is generally ineffective. Emotional cutoff refers to attempts to deny fusion rather than resolve it. The result is that people may stop interacting with their family, or they may move away from their family, but they are still emotionally fused. In these situations the fusion still has the same effects, even though the parental family may be thousands of miles away.

According to Bowen (1976), emotional cutoff is determined by the way people handle their unresolved emotional attachments to their parents. He claims that all people have some degree of unresolved emotional attachment to their parents, and furthermore the lower the level of differentiation, the more intense the unresolved attachment. How the individual approaches the idea of cutoff will greatly influence the way "people separate themselves from the past in order to start their lives in the present generation" (p.83).

Bowen put much thought into the selection of a term to best describe this process. For example, he considered using such terms as separation, isolation, withdrawal, running away, or denying the importance of the parental family. "However much cutoff may sound like informal slang, I could find no other term as accurate for describing the process" (p. 83).

He further states "the degree of unresolved emotional attachment to the parents is equivalent to the degree of undifferentiation that must somehow be handled in the person's own life and in future generations. The unresolved attachment is handled by the intrapsychic process of denial and isolation of self while living close to the parents; or by physically running away; or by a combination of emotional isolation and physical distance: (p. 84). He is also convinced that the more intense cutoff is, the more

ACTIVITY 8.2 – RESOLVING UNRESOLVED FAMILY EMOTIONS

This activity is to try to change a part of the family emotional system in your family. There are many different things you could do. For example, you could write a letter of appreciation to someone, do something special for someone, help solve a problem or misunderstanding that has not been resolved, express your feelings of love for someone you feel deeply about, etc.

Chapter 8

likely his own children to do a more forceful cutoff with him in the next generation. There are many variations in the intensity of this basic process and in the way the cutoff is handled. The person who runs away from his family of origin is in serious need of emotional closeness, but at the same time, they are allergic to it" (p. 84).

Thus, emotional cutoff is always a less desirable solution than working through or resolving the emotional problems in a way that will promote healthy differentiation. In some situations, however, it may not be possible to differentiate; then emotional cutoff becomes one of the options to be considered. On several occasions students and professionals have challenged the tone of this paragraph. I have heard from several who say that if there is abuse of any kind (i.e., sexual, physical, or emotional) leaving and not looking back may be the best thing and usually a prime option to be explored.

LIMITATIONS OF THE CONCEPT OF FUSION

The concept of fusion has several limitations. First, Bowen's descriptions of fusion are sometimes gender biased. Feminist scholars have pointed out that Bowen overemphasized intellectual control and ignored many healthy forms of emotional attachment and priority to relationship maintenance (Goodrich, Rampage, Ellman & Halstead, 1988, p. 147).

While many of Bowen's early writings and comments about the fusion principle can be interpreted as gender biased, the principle that excessive fusion has harmful effects is not a gender-biased principle. Most of Bowen's writings occurred in the 1960s and the early 1970s, when scholars were not as sensitive to gender issues as they could have been. For example, if a person is raised in a hostile family and more fusion results, that is seen as unhealthy and a negative outcome. Further, if those people are more likely to live in a "feeling world," some would point out that a positive characteristic of women is that they are characterized as being more attuned to important feelings and emotions than men are. However, the principle remains important because it speaks directly to the point that emotions are necessarily "bad." But, it detrimental to the individual as he/she tries to attain life goals to be less able to keep destructive emotions from surfacing at the expense of one's ability to problem solve, make effective decisions, and generate solutions.

A second limitation of the concept of fusion is that people sometimes think that if someone were differentiated they would live their life in a fairly intellectual, sterile, or unemotional way. Again, if we define fusion precisely and as described above, this is not true. Differentiated people can be as involved with the emotional aspect of their life as they want. Again, the key is that when people are differentiated they can do what they want rather than what the emotion dictates. Fused family members are not as free to choose what they want because the emotional part of their life controls them.

279

Chapter 8

IMPLICATIONS FOR FAMILIES

The ideas presented in this chapter have several important implications for families and those who try to help families. One of these implications is that the emotional part of family life is much more important than most social scientists have realized, and we should emphasize it more than we usually do. As Bowen (1976) has observed, emotional forces govern far more of life than we once thought. This suggests that family scientists ought to give high priority to the emotional aspects of family systems whenever we try to understand family processes or try to help families. Ironically, though, most families and most social scientists tend to give much more emphasis to the rational parts of family processes than the emotional parts.

Family decision making. When we try to understand problem solving or decision-making in families, we tend to judge the quality of the decision-making by how rational, sensible, or efficient the people or the decisions are (Klien & Hill, 1979). Scholars, parents, and spouses say things like:

"That wouldn't be smart."
"Calm down, and be reasonable."
"Let's think this through carefully."
"But that's not even logical."
"Let's be sensible about this."

If we were more sensitive to the emotional processes in the family realm, we would find ourselves making different kinds of statements. We'd say things like:

"How would it feel if…?"
"I'm getting upset about…"
"It's not logical, but it feels good to…"
"Down deep inside, it seems that…"
"I have a funny feeling that…"

Think about the decision making you have seen in your own family and in other families when you've been on the "inside." What is the ratio of the two kinds of statements? Do about half deal with what Bowen calls the intellectual system and half deal with the emotional system? We don't have any research about this, but our guess is that at least 90% of the attention in most American families is on the intellectual part. And, even when we use words like feel, most of the time we are referring to how we think rather than to an emotional state

Most of the time the important aspects of decision making in the family realm are, first, how do the individuals feel in the decision making process and, secondarily, how do they feel about the decision. This means that the most important aspect is not

---

JOURNAL OF THOUGHTS 8.4 : WHAT TO DO?

1. According to the text and your experience what are the best and worst ways of coping with highly fused relationships?

2.   What is the best way to disengage from destructive triangled relationships?

ACTIVITY 8.3 - UNFINISHED BUSINESS

Many of us have *unfinished business* in our families. Unfinished business refers to situations where the "ledger" of family obligations, responsibilities, and loyalties is out of balance. Some situations that can lead to unfinished business are when resentments occur but they aren't resolved, or when someone has had hurt feelings they haven't dealt with adequately. Many times the unfinished business involves things that happen between the members of two different generations. For example, a parent may have dealt with a child or several children unfairly, or a parent may have been abusive, intolerant, or inappropriate in other ways. Or, it may be that while someone was a child or teenager they did not realize some of the noble and helpful things their parents or grandparents did and they haven't shown the appreciation, gratitude, or respect they should. What usually happens in these situations is that some members of the family system carry around "chronic" negative emotion, and their negative feelings influence the emotional atmosphere or emotional climate in the whole family system. These underlying emotional patterns have a great influence on what happens inside individuals, in the relationships between people, and day to day rhythms and routines of family life.

This activity is for people who are involved in some unfinished business in their family system and they'd like to improve the situation. Those who do not have any unfinished business should skip this activity.

Step #1: Describe on a piece of paper what the *unfinished business* is in your family system. Sometimes a quarter of a page is enough, but if you need more space use it. (Sometimes we think we understand it clearly without writing it down, and sometimes we do, but often it helps us clarify what is going on when we put it on paper.)

Step #2: Try to think of several things you might be able to do that might help "take care of" the unfinished business. Brainstorm a bit to try to think of more things than you'd actually be able to do. Write them down. You also might benefit from consulting with some others about what you might do.

Step #3: Decide on a plan and implement it. Describe what happened.

Step #4: After you've completed this activity, what did you learn from it?

how wise or effective a decision is but how the couple or family feels about what is going on.

On a more modest scale, these ideas help us understand why a "consensus-seeking" method of decision-making is so helpful in families. A consensus-seeking method of decision-making is one in which a family keeps working until they find a decision that is emotionally acceptable to everyone. The issue is not whether it is acceptable intellectually. To be a satisfactory decision, it must be acceptable emotionally. The key to the process is for families to "shift gears" or change their method of making decisions so they can get solutions that everyone will feel good about. When this happens, it transforms the emotional atmosphere in most families in a way that is often almost magical.

The consensus-seeking method of decision-making is different from using authority or power, and it is different for democratic methods where the majority wins. When decision-making is based on authority, the powerful people in the family (usually the males or the parents) determine the decisions. Even when those who have the authority or the power are benevolent, and they consult with those who have less power, this authoritarian method has several limitations. It places the responsibility on those who have the power rather than helping those who have less power, such as the children, to learn how to assume and manage responsibility. When those who have little power are mature adults, there is almost certain to be negative emotional response to the family members who have assumed control.

SUMMARY

This chapter discussed two aspects of the family emotional differentiation/fusion and chronic anxiety where problems frequently occur, and suggested strategies for helping families deal effectively with them. Fusion occurs when family members are excessively tied to the emotional system in their parental family. It is a condition where family members become victims of the emotionality in their lives, and when fusion occurs it interferes with the ability people have to use their intellect. Fusion can occur in an emotionally charged situation, and it can come and go in a matter of a few minutes. Sometimes functional fusion is desirable and wholesome. One can imagine examples of this process: Think of times when people get "carried away emotionally" in athletic contests, symphonies, or during sexual intercourse. Many times, however, functional fusion leads to undesirable consequences, where people say and do things they are sorry for later.

Chronic anxiety comes about when feelings of resentment, apprehension, and rancor exist for long periods of time as part of the emotional climate (emotional field) in a family. Triangling and problems with health are two disabling processes in families that grow out of chronic anxiety. The chapter concludes with a discussion of several implications these ideas have for people who try to understand and help families.

Chapter 8

STUDY QUESTIONS:

1. Define what is meant by the term differentiation in family life.

2. Give several examples of poor differentiation in families.

3. "What Peter says about Paul tells you more about Peter than it does Paul." Explain what this means within the context it was presented.

4. Define emotional triangle and give an example of how one might work in a family.

5. Is fusion different than differentiation? How, if it is?

6. Tell what is meant by the term chronic anxiety and give examples of how it works in family life.

7. Tell why emotional cutoff is a poor strategy for coping with family emotions.

KEY TERMS

Differentiation
Connectedness
Fusion
Emotional Triangles
Emotional Cutoff
The Benign Assumption

CHAPTER NINE

Building and Maintaining
Effective Rituals

Building and Maintaining Effective Rituals

Main Points:

1. Family rituals and routines are similar in the following four ways:
   a. They both always involve more than one member of a family.
   b. They both have overt or visible behavior or action. Thus, just thinking about something is not ritual or routine.
   c. There is repetition in the form and in the content of what is done.
   d. There is morphostasis and morphogenesis in all of them.

2. Rituals are different from routines in at least four ways:
   a. Rituals tend to have more emotion.
   b. Rituals tend to have more symbolism.
   c. Rituals tend to have more "staged" or unusual behavior.
   d. The three stages of preparation, enactment, and return to normal are more elaborate and pronounced in rituals.

3. When rituals are wisely managed they can help families attain important goals such as: unity, closeness, intimacy, meaning, membership changes, etc.

4. Families can be wise or unwise in the ways they manage rituals and routines.

5. Families can be creative in making new rituals and changing old ones.

Building and Maintaining
Effective Family Rituals

INTRODUCTION

We are all familiar with family rituals. Some of them occur on holidays such as Christmas, Thanksgiving, the 4th of July, Passover, or the Latin American Three Kings Day. On these special days families do a number of things in ways that are different from the ordinary. They trim trees, wrap and open presents, bake turkeys in a special way, color eggs, have religious ceremonies, go to parades, watch football games, etc.

Some family rituals do not occur on holidays. They are more ordinary, and some of them are repeated on a daily basis. For example, we give each other kisses and hugs in special ways and wave goodbye as we leave for work and school. We "tuck" small children in bed, tell bedtime stories, eat certain meals at certain times and in certain ways, and have special places to sit and read.

Even though we're all familiar with family rituals, when we try to study this part of the family realm we discover that the terms we use are fairly vague and elusive, and it is also complicated. For example, are rituals the same as routines, traditions, customs and habits? Are they the same as family rules, or are they different? And, if they are different, what are the differences? Thus, a good place to begin this chapter is to define some of these terms.

WHAT ARE RITUALS AND ROUTINES?

The term *ritual* is "an elusive concept, on the one hand transparent and conspicuous in its enactment, on the other, subtle and mysterious in its boundaries and effects on participants" (Wolin & Bennett, 1984, p. 401). Also, scholars in many fields study rituals and routines. For example, anthropology, sociology, psychology, and family science all have a body of literature about them. Since the scholars in each of these disciplines have differing perspectives, they study different aspects of rituals, and do not agree on how to define the terms (Gillis, 1996).

To illustrate these differences, Boyce et al., (1983) says, it is not useful to try to distinguish between rituals, celebrations, and traditions, and they suggest we use the term routines for all of them. Curran (1983) and Meredith (1985) argue that all of the routine and ritualized parts of family life should be called family traditions. Wise (1986) and Gillis (1996) prefer to divide them into routines and rituals, and a recent group of scholars suggests we use the term ritual to refer to all of these events because "while these terms—rituals, celebrations, and traditions—may have subtle differences, they all appear to refer to the same general collection of family-oriented activities" (Meredith et al., 1989, p. 76).

A useful solution to this confusion of terms is to think about the difference between family rituals and routines. These two terms can be defined by describing how they are similar to each other in some ways and different in other ways. They are similar in the following four ways:

1. Rituals and routines both always involve more than one member of a family.
2. They both have overt or visible behavior or action. Thus, just thinking about something is not ritual or routine.
3. There is repetition in the form and in the content of what is done. The form refers to how something is done and the content refers to what is done. Some rituals are repeated many times by the same family members, and some are just experienced once in the lifetime of a family member, but other individuals repeat them.
4. There is morphostasis and morphogenesis in all of them. This means they all have some continuity over time, but they also all evolve and change over time as individuals and families develop and as the external environment of families changes.

In addition to these common characteristics, rituals are different from routines in at least four ways. First, they differ in the amount of emotion that is involved. There is a great deal of emotion during weddings, funerals, children leaving home to go to school, the birth of a new child, a Bar Mitzvah, and celebrations of important holidays such as Christmas and Thanksgiving. When these traditions involve important emotionality they become ritualized, and the best term for them is family rituals. There is relatively little emotion in the more ordinary events such as kissing each other hello when returning home each day, talking about the events of the day, vacuuming the carpet once a week, doing dishes, and helping children with their homework. There is routine in these traditions, but there is little ritualization, so they are called family routines.

A second way rituals and routines are different is in the amount of symbolism. Some traditions tend to have a large number of symbols. Weddings, for example, symbolize leaving the old households, being "given away," making important commitments and covenants, maturity, being a rite of passage from being single to being married, etc. Many other events such as a funeral, wake, Christmas, Bar Mitzvah, and a christening have several different levels of symbolic meaning, and the symbolism in these events makes them rituals. When family events have less symbolism, they become more ordinary and are called family routines.

Some family scholars in recent years have used the term metaphor (Imber-Black & Roberts, 1992) to try to describe the symbolic aspect of family rituals. A metaphor in this context refers to an abstract set of ideas or beliefs that is understood and shared but difficult to put into words. Rituals can provide a somewhat tangible representation of the more abstract idea in the metaphor, and thereby have a symbolism that provides meaning, purpose, and a sense of completeness and integration that is difficult to acquire in more rational ways of behaving or conversing.

The symbolism in the Thanksgiving holiday illustrates the metaphorical aspects of a typical American ritual (Pleck, 2000). The unity of the family huddled together over a table of food is a metaphor for the unity of the family wherever they are in the world. They "give thanks" for the bounty before them as a symbol of the end of the harvest.

Some metaphors in family rituals are less desirable and less healthy. One family, for example, celebrated most holidays with alcohol as a prominent guest. Almost always harsh words were eventually spoken, tempers would flare and the celebrations would turn into a living hell. Unintentionally, this reoccurring ritual was a mini-version act of their entire life. The family was chaotic, and had unresolved conflicts that had gone on for several generations, but they were never brought into the open and dealt with. The family retreated into distance, anger, and hostility, and the dependency on the alcohol was an escape. All of the attempts to end the alcohol problem ended in disappointment. It was not until Bob, one of the sons, insisted on the abstinence of alcohol at holiday celebrations (even if it meant the absence of his drinking father), that the family was able to begin to have the healing effects of warm, peaceful holidays and a greater harmony and peace in general.

A third way rituals and routines are different is in how ordinary versus extraordinary their behaviors are. When traditions are part of the usual ways of behaving they are not special or "staged," and the term routine is a good term to describe them. Rituals tend to have behavior that is relatively unique, unusual, or extraordinary (Pleck, 2000).

For example, when a family bows their head, is quiet, and says a prayer in a reverent manner before eating a meal, these are "special" behaviors. Even if these special behaviors occur fairly frequently in the family they still have a certain "uniqueness" or lack of "routineness" in them. When families get dressed up to celebrate New Year and they have a special meal these are fairly unusual ways of behaving and they are therefore rituals. Routines involve more ordinary ways of doing things. For example, English families tend to use a knife and fork to eat vegetables, and American families just use a fork, and these patterns are part of the routines for family life. Getting up in the morning rather than the evening, eating three fairly sizable meals rather than ten small meals, and turning the lights out before going to bed are routines.

Some rituals are so unusual and out-of-the-ordinary that they are sacred or highly dramatic, and it is easy to tell them from routines. Other rituals are just barely unusual. For example, using the special china for certain meals, cleaning the house extra nice when company is coming, and getting ready for a special date may be unusual enough that they become family rituals. Even events such as reading the daily newspaper or watching certain television programs can evolve from routine to ritual if they become unusual enough. For example, if family members like to get a certain combination of refreshments, lighting, seating, and emotional involvement while watching certain television programs, these become family rituals.

The fourth way rituals and routines are different is in the preparation for the event and the follow-up activities. "Ritual is not just the ceremony or actual performance, but the whole process of preparing for it, experiencing it, and reintegration back into everyday life" (Roberts, 1988, p. 8). Even rituals that are fairly frequent have a preparation phase and a back-to-normal phase, and these phases are important parts of the ritual. Routines do not have the same three phases because they are such a normal part of everyday life.

An example of these phases is the preparation for the ritual of Thanksgiving dinner. Many American families put a great deal of time into inviting relatives and preparing the food and the home. Many schedules take a temporary change as miles and miles are traveled in preparation for the Thanksgiving feast and get-together. If someone does not think these processes are important, witness the lack of students at college campuses during such holidays. When students can't go to their own home, it is painful to stay alone, and hence many homes "adopt" these not-able-to-return-home students into their own family rituals.

Wolin and Bennett describe the preparation phase of rituals as a transformation. In their words:

> *The phenomenon of transformation begins as the family readies the house and its participants for the subsequent performance. Children and guests may arrive from out of town and take up temporary quarters in unused bedrooms. Food is purchased and often prepared several days in advance. Special clothing comes from the closets or the cleaners. The house is at the same time organized and chaotic, with a general air of anticipatory excitement. On Thanksgiving morning, children may crowd around the television set for the Macy's parade or take some regular outing to occupy their time. Cooking begins in earnest. These important preparatory events constitute a transitional period, a passage from nonritual to ritual.* (Wolin & Bennett, 1984, p. 408)

Building and Maintaining Effective Rituals

ACTIVITY 9.1 - A HISTORY OF YOUR FAMILY RITUALS

The purpose of this activity is to: (a) help you see how family stories of family rituals can influence you and your family and (b) strengthen generational bonds. There are three different kinds of family stories that influence us in different ways:

Common, Everyday Stories: These stories relate everyday experiences of our ancestors, such as describing life at home or at a job. They give us a glimpse into how people lived their everyday lives and can give us some details into who our ancestors were and what they were like.

Ritual Stories: These stories are more meaningful to us because they deal with things that we can relate with or they are stories that deal with more life changing events, such as a tragedy or a great success. They often deal with stories of love and courtship, and also with kind or noble acts. These stories involve more life-changing events or include details about common, everyday life that we can closely relate with.

Deeply Meaningful Stories: These stories deal with more inward changes in our ancestors such as spiritual conversion or miracles. They deal with things like reconciliation between family members or stories of sacrifice and giving. They concern breakthroughs in personal progress and growth and tend to give us more information about how these important events affected our ancestors. These usually are very special to those who hear them and have a powerful effect helping us feel closer to our ancestors.

Your assignment is to collect one story from each of these categories: one that is a common everyday story (a routine), one that is meaningful (containing a ritual or tradition) and one that is deeply meaningful to you. One of these must be a story that you did not know before this assignment was given. These stories ought to deal with things that happened before your parents were born, and it is best if they happened in the life of your great grandparents or someone before them.

There are several ways you can do this research. You can write letters to your grandparents, parents, aunts or uncles indicating to them that you are trying to do research into your "family history" and tell them you are trying to learn about events that were interesting, unusual, inspiring, or that would help you better understand the "heritage" your ancestors left you. You can describe the three categories to them and see if they have any stories that would fit them. You can also talk on the telephone to older relatives, or if your family is having a reunion during the course you can attend it and talk to people. It is also possible that someone in your family has compiled some family histories that you have not seen and you can get copies of them and read them.

Write down these stories so that they are part of your family history. After each story, please include a couple of paragraphs that describe why the story is important to you and how it has affected and will affect you and your family. This is an important part of the assignment and will help you articulate the impact of these stories on your life. Please be honest in describing the impact and share your true feelings concerning these stories.

After you have completed the first two steps, take a few minutes to think about what happened during this activity and describe how this activity brought you closer to your ancestors or changed you in other ways.

JOURNAL OF THOUGHTS 9.1: WHAT IS THE DIFFERENCE?

1.   Comment on the basic difference between rituals and routines.

2.   What is your favorite ritual in family life? Why? Take some time and think about what makes it special.

3. What ritual event in your family is the worst for you? Why?

Building and Maintaining Effective Rituals

In summary, rituals and routines both involve more than one individual, behavior rather than just thinking, repetition, morphogenesis, and morphostasis. Rituals are different from routines in that they tend to involve more emotion, symbolism, and stylized or staged behavior; and they have the three stages of preparing, experiencing, and shifting back into the ordinary.

Even though many rituals tend to be quite different from many routines, it is important to also realize that there are some situations where there is overlap and the differences are not clear.

Rituals and routines are different from family rules because rules are the "understandings" about how all kinds of things are done. Rules deal with such things as using dishes and utensils when we eat rather than putting the food on a table and eating with our hands. Rules define how we should do millions of daily things such as closing doors when it is cold and knocking on a door or ringing a doorbell rather than walking directly into a family's house. Rules are not rituals because they don't have several of the components of rituals. They have little, if any, symbolic meaning, and they aren't emotional—even though emotion occurs when some rules are broken. Thus, rituals and routines are events and rules are the beliefs that govern how these events are to be carried out in a family.

HOW ARE RITUALS AND ROUTINES CREATED?

Bossard and Boll (1950) discovered that rituals originate in two ways in families. Some rituals are part of cultural traditions, and they are handed down from one generation to the next. Many of these "traditional" rituals involve holiday celebrations and religious activities such as having a Thanksgiving dinner, attending church, and sending Christmas cards.

The second way family rituals originate is for families to create or invent their own. These rituals arise out of immediate family interaction in a specific situation, such as going to bed, getting up, eating meals, doing household chores, relaxing over weekends, and vacationing in summertime. Whereas the traditional rites were usually rich pageants, the spontaneous ones were relatively simple. They were, however, more numerous, more frequently practiced, and were related to a stricter utilitarian purpose. For this reason, they were often more quickly subject to change (Bossard & Boll, 1950; Pleck, 2000).

Developmental processes.   There are developmental processes in the way rituals are created and evolve over time in families. When a new family begins with the union of two or more people, they pull from their past to develop unique family rituals. Also, during the formative stage of the family life cycle there tends to be a searching for events that can be ritualized. For example, when a man and women start going together, they usually create rituals around events that would otherwise be minor things. For example, they may pick out a song that is "their song" and whenever they hear it they enact their own special ritual of hugging, smiling, and commenting on it being something special to them. Or, they may have anniversary celebrations of things

such as the day they met, their first date, the day they got engaged, the day they decided to live together, etc. Other possibilities are they may develop rituals about certain places that had an unusual importance to them, such as the place where they decided to get married.

As families continue to acquire new rituals, some of the rituals they created in the formative stage of the family development fade away and are not remembered. Also, the way rituals are emphasized changes at different stages of the family life cycle. When families have children between two and about 12 years old they find themselves creating and experiencing bathing rituals, bedtime rituals, eating rituals, and rituals as they visit certain friends and relatives. Also, during this child-rearing stage of family development many families find they emphasize some of the traditional holidays such as Easter and Christmas in elaborate ways that center around the children.

As families move into the stages where they have teenage children and are launching children, their rituals usually evolve. The young adults prefer lively rituals that involve friends, music, and action; and the parents usually find themselves preferring more sedentary and symbolic rituals.

Rituals and routines continue to evolve and change as families move into the post-childrearing stages of the family cycle. Grand-parenting brings rituals such as small children to parks and zoos, reminiscing, and telling stories about how things "used to be." Often the younger generations patiently, and sometimes not so patiently, listen over and over again to stories that become parts of the family folk-lore. The routines and rituals of aging couples become even less energetic, but they remain an important part of the emotional and symbolic fabric of the family life of the elderly.

Building and Maintaining Effective Rituals

As clinical researchers, we have also found family rituals to serve as a window into a family's underlying shared identity, providing special access to the behavioral and emotional tenor characterizing each family. (Wolin & Bennett, 1984, p. 401).

Ritual is a statement in metaphoric terms about the paradoxes of human existence. (Crocker, 1973, p. 47).

The main principle about rituals and routines can be summarized in the following way:

PRINCIPLE 9.1: RITUALS AND ROUTINES

Family rituals and routines are valuable resources, and when they are wisely used they can help families attain important goals such as: unity, closeness, intimacy, meaning, membership changes, etc.

Rituals tend to deal with the more cheerful and optimistic aspects of life providing positive emotional bonds. Rituals also provide a reservoir of such things as good will, feelings of we-can-do-it, we're together, and trust; and this helps families cope with the tragic and challenging aspects of life. They also can help provide a sense of "home" and a feeling that the world is, at least in some ways, a good place, and a comfortable place. In addition, since they tend to help families deal with paradoxes and ambiguities and have guiding metaphors, they tend to help family members acquire meaning and purpose, explanation and coherence, and a sense of being in some control of life, or having life be somewhat predictable. They also provide memories that lead to the often-told stories and myths that create a mythology helpful to the sense of family. They help with life cycle transitions by providing rites of passage. They also include many soft, tender, and affectionate moments, thereby helping family members learn that emotionality is appropriate and desirable.

Family scientists have identified seven specific goals that rituals and routines can help with. They are (1) creating healthy emotional ties, (2) membership changes, (3) healing, (4) identity definition and redefinition, (5) belief expression and negotiation, (6) celebration, and (7) help deal with paradoxes, and ambiguities.

Creating healthy emotional ties. Several studies of family processes have found that rituals tend to help families create continuity, solidarity, integration, and bonds (Schvaneveldt & Lee, 1983; Meredith, 1985; Meredith, Abbott, Lamanna, & Sanders, 1989). There are many reasons rituals help families accomplish these goals. Meredith and Abbott summarize some of these reasons in the following way:

> *Family rituals, first and foremost, encourage contact between family members, usually in a relaxed, enjoyable setting. Family conflicts and problems are temporarily set aside...Rituals may help to bridge the intergenerational gaps that separate family members by providing activity between parents and children and extended family members. A major theme of most family rituals is appreciation of one another and the enjoyment of life together; therefore commitment to the family may be renewed by the regular observance of family rituals. Family values and beliefs may be learned and perpetuated through rituals fostering a sense of unity and oneness. In sum, rituals may be family strengthening for many reasons.* (Meredith, Abbott, Lamanna, & Sanders, 1989, p. 77)

Membership changes. Families deal with membership changes in many ways. Some changes are major events such as births, deaths, marriages, and divorces; and most cultures and families have rather elaborate rituals that help them deal with these major transitions (Gillis, 1996). For example, weddings help individuals, families, and friends make the adjustment of two families of origin coming together and a new family unit being created. Announcements, christenings and other baby naming rituals help new members be assimilated, and funerals and wakes help families cope with death. Bar Mitzvah redefines membership in families and in the Jewish commu-

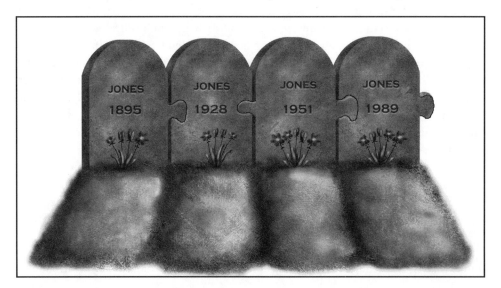

nity, and graduation ceremonies help families redefine the relationship of parents and children and their involvement with school systems.

There are some major changes in membership where families have few rituals that help them make the symbolic and emotional adjustments that are necessary. For example, there are few rituals associated with divorce and adoption. There are none when couples begin living together or stop living together, and there are none for beginning or ending homosexual relationships. Even though the number of stepfamilies has increased dramatically in recent years, there are few ways to ritualize the formation of a stepfamily. Weddings are used to create the marital part of stepfamilies, but the children have a peripheral role in the wedding, and sometimes they are even excluded. One consequence is that often the marital part of the new stepfamily is formed symbolically and emotionally, but the family system isn't usually formed as gracefully and effectively.

An extreme example of this may be seen in a stepfamily that came for therapy due to stepparent–stepchild conflict that was rapidly leading to the extrusion of a child. This couple's wedding was celebrated with extended family and friends, but their five children from their prior marriages, ages six to twelve, were barred from attending. The wedding ritual had publicly affirmed the new couple, but not the new stepfamily (Imber-Black & Roberts, 1992).

Healing. All individuals and families encounter situations where healing is needed. Healing is needed after periods of conflict, when there is pain and grief, when there is reconciliation, when there is death, and when major changes occur such as retirement, disabilities, and mid-life crises. Rituals provide a vehicle that can help healing.

Identity definition and redefinition. Rituals and routines can help individuals and families create, maintain, and change identities. Weddings, for example, do more than just redefine memberships. They transform identities by some members of the family becoming a spouse and others becoming in-laws. Rituals such as birthday celebrations, daily goodbyes and greetings, and goodnight kisses reaffirm who the individuals are, their importance to the family, and they cement the emotional connections that maintain identity and create enduring intimacy.

Many of the religious, ethnic, and cultural rituals that families participate in have important implications for identity creation, change, and maintenance. In them specific foods, dress and ceremonies may serve to symbolize the identity theme. Such celebrations define an individual's identity as part of a larger cultural group. In the multi-ethnic society of the United States, participation in such rituals as the Chinese New Year or Greek Orthodox Easter allow even highly assimilated persons to stay connected to their ethnic and religious identity. Cultural rituals, such as Veteran's Day, Mother's Day, and Father's Day, all involve the identity theme, as these mark and celebrate particular aspects of people's identities. (Imber-Black & Roberts, 1992)

Rites of passage. Some rituals provide the vehicle for rites of passage that facilitate growth and change. There are few rites of passage during adolescence in the American culture, but some cultural groups such as Judaism and several Indian cultures have a number of rituals that help families and individuals mark the transitions from childhood to adulthood.

Rituals have the power to be therapeutic. For example, the ritual in funerals helps the participants move from one stage of life, through grief, and on to another stage of life. Doty (1986) explains that rituals have the power to transform. This is part of the wonderment and power of rituals. When transitions, catastrophes and unexpected events occur in a family, rituals have a healing power that allows, encourages, and facilitates changes.

Meaning and purpose. Doty (1986) also suggests that rituals help families deal with the deepest levels of shared meanings and values. Not only is it shared meaning of what things are now, but how things ought to be and can be. There are many abstract and ultimate concerns that are important to people that are difficult to understand and clear answers are elusive. For example, questions about the origins of life, the purposes of even existing, the nature of reality, the role of birth and death, the role of the sacred, and the possibility of life after death are challenging concerns. They are challenging intellectually and emotionally because many of them are ultimate and profound, and it is difficult for individuals and families to come to terms with these concerns.

Rituals provide a vehicle that helps families find and maintain solutions to these complicated and ultimate concerns. The symbolism in rituals such as christening, baptism, celebrating the beginning of a new year, Thanksgiving, and Easter each help provide a sense of meaning and purpose that would be elusive and difficult to have without these or similar rituals.

Rituals also help with another aspect of meaning and purpose. Life has many forms of injustice and inequity. There also are many aspects of life where there is little sense of control, and there are many contradictions and paradoxes. Rituals can help families deal with these complexities. As Roberts has observed:

> *Ritual can hold both sides of a contradiction at the same time. We all live with the ultimate paradoxes of life/death, connection/distance, ideal/real, and good/evil. Ritual can incorporate both sides of contradictions so that they can be managed simultaneously. For instance, a wedding ceremony has within it both loss and mourning and joy and celebration. People say, "You're not losing a daughter, you're gaining a son-in-law." Parents give their child away at the same time as they welcome a new member to their extended family.* (Roberts, 1988, p. 16)

302

JOURNAL OF THOUGHTS 9.2: STAGING

1. One of the things that make rituals so special is the staging. To help you remember this idea, write a description of what staging means.

2. Now, describe a ritual at your house and use the ideas about staging to show how that ritual works.

3. Were there any surprises in your description? Did you feel any emotion or did any daydreaming happen? If so what?

Building and Maintaining Effective Rituals

Order and predictability. Families also can use rituals and routines to help create a sense of order and predictability in life. They help create a sense of "home." For example, routines such as preparing and eating meals, leaving and returning home, dressing and undressing, preparing one's self to be dressed and groomed in an acceptable way, and having a favorite chair to relax in at the end of a day provide a sense of continuity, comfort, and peace that is an important part of life (Gillis, 1996).

It is likely that rituals and routines contribute in different ways to this goal. Rituals probably provide a sense of order and predictability about the more important issues, questions, and paradoxes of life, and routines seem to contribute in a different way. They help provide a sense of order in the daily rhythms and cycles, and contribute to a sense of comfort. The daily routines probably contribute to homes being a haven or place of refuge, a place where people can let their hair down, be "off stage" and escape from the competitiveness and aggression of the marketplace or school.

MANAGING RITUALS

Rituals and routines are not inherently healthy and facilitating. They can be unhealthy and destructive if families are not wise in the way they create them and carry them out. Research and clinical experience have identified four ideas that can help families be wise and effective. These ideas are: (1) it is enabling to have an adequate amount of ritualization—not too little or too much, (2) it is helpful to have distinctiveness in the rituals when there are problems that could be passed on to future generations, (3) families ought to have developmentally appropriate morphostasis and morphogenesis, and (4) they should avoid the inappropriate use of rituals and routines.

Have moderate ritualization. Research suggests a moderate amount of ritualization is helpful to families, and it is disruptive to have too much or too little emphasis on them (Bossard & Boll, 1950; Meredith, Abbott, Lamanna, & Sanders, 1989).

There is considerable variability in how many rituals families have and in the type of rituals they have, but being involved in rituals and being committed to them is helpful (Wolin & Bennett, 1984, p. 406).

This idea is consistent with The Golden Mean Principle. The Golden Mean suggests that moderation is wise in all types of family processes that involve time, effort, and energy, and that includes rituals and routines. Family scientists refer to the extremes in this area as underritualization or overritualization.

Underritualization. Underritualization occurs when families have few or no rituals. Our fast-paced society that emphasizes economic, occupational, and materialistic parts of life creates a hustle-bustle attitude in which many families have little time with the whole family or even a majority of the family together at any time. Also, the emphasis in many families on passive entertainment such as watching television and listening to music with headphones can lead to little attention to family rituals. The result of this is a loss of family and individual identity, loss of structure and stability, and little cohesiveness.

Seccombe (1999) found that in the disadvantaged families of the slums, most of them were disorganized, lacking in set patterns of behavior, schedules, and norms, and made few claims to particular spaces and possessions. Apparently, the families had become prey to the discrimination and oppression, lack of opportunity, and no hope for anything but poverty; as a consequence, the disorganization of the family, with few rituals and the loss of family identity, resulted. An example is a family with an alcoholic father who stopped all holiday ritualization so drinking would not be there to pull him back down.

There are many important events where rituals could help families cope and we do not have adequate ritualization. For example, there are few or no rituals to help families deal with events such as miscarriages, stillborns, rape, life-course transitions such as when one moves from childhood to adolescence and adolescence to adulthood (Quinn, Newfield, & Protinsky, 1985). Rituals could help unite people, provide support, provide containment of emotions, and move participants on to acceptance and on to positive growth in these situations, but there tends to be an underritualization (Quinn et al., 1985; Laird, 1988).

Another example of how underritualization can be disabling is what happened when there was a stillborn birth in a family. The family had an unwritten rule that no one was to talk about the death. The body of the baby was taken from the mother soon after the caesarian section. The mortuary flew the baby inside a casket, while the family drove in a car, from one state to a distant, desired state of burial. The casket was taken from the airport to the burial plot in the back of a station wagon, while the family rode in their separate car. The father declined to carry the casket from the car to the graveside, previous to a very short memorial service. Few visits were made to the cemetery and talk about the little child was almost non-existent.

What a change could have taken place if rituals had been used along the way, even one-time rituals. If only the family had been aware of the importance of touching and looking at the dead baby to help work through feelings of loss. If only they had realized the importance of talking about the grief and crushed expectations. There are many rituals that can help families work through the paradoxes, complexities, and ambiguities in these situations.

For example, if someone were in charge of transporting the casket and baby, it could help. If they had a more elaborate funeral or graveside ceremony that ritual would allow people to express consolation, support and understanding it would help. It would help if the funeral were followed by a luncheon, dinner, or time to visit where family and friends could gather to help contain emotions and move in a forward direction. This would provide opportunities for the parents and children to express their deep-felt emotions, and allow for acceptance and moving on in the lives of this entrapped family. Rituals are one of the few ways we have to incorporate both sides of the contradictions involving living and dying, and rituals not only allow the participants to see both sides, but also understand, experience, and cope with both sides.

Many difficult and tragic events are not well ritualized in our modern society. Incidents such as health changes that make it necessary to retire early, divorce, rape, and coping with physical abuse or incest are cases where rituals could be used. Rituals in these areas could acknowledge the destructive aspects of these experiences and help create new structures for the future. They could help celebrate the survival of the participants, rather than leave them as victims, and this could help open communication about the events, use more of the family and community resources, and create cohesion rather than fragmentation in the families.

Overritualization. Overritualization can occur when families try to incorporate too much input from people or organizations outside the family. It can be too overwhelming if young couples try to incorporate all of the rituals from both parental families, and also try to include the rituals that are encouraged by various cultural, civic, religious, and fraternal groups. Couples need to selectively adopt and include rituals in their new family.

Overritualization also can occur when families never give up rituals that have lost their usefulness. For example, many families who have young children find it meaningful to have a large number of rituals around Christmas time. Later, however, as the children mature, some of the rituals are less relevant and important, and if some of the members of the family try to continue them it can lead to being overwhelmed by the rituals.

People and families also differ in the amount of ritualization that is desirable. Some families find it helpful to have a relatively large number of rituals and others find it effective to invest less of their time and energy in rituals. There is some evidence that the parent and grandparent generations like more family rituals than teenagers and young adults (Meredith, Abbott, Lamanna, & Sanders, 1989). It is possible that teenagers and young adults have so many other demands, challenges, activities, and developmental tasks they are trying to manage that this is a period of life when it is effective to be less involved in family rituals. Being less involved in family rituals may actually help young adults disengage from their parental family and create their own family. Then, as they create their own new family they may find it enabling to selectively get re-involved in some of the rituals in their larger family and create their own for their new family.

Distinctiveness of rituals. A group of researchers at George Washington University have discovered an idea that can help families be wise in the way they manage their rituals. The idea has to do with the *distinctiveness* of family rituals.

They have found that when families have an undesirable characteristic such as alcoholism it is helpful to keep the rituals distinctive from or separated from the problem. Apparently, if family rituals can be separated from the family problems there tends to be less generational transmission of the problems. For example, if families are able to keep the alcohol problems separated from their holiday celebrations it decreases the likelihood the alcoholism will be passed on to future generations. If families are able to still have a pleasant dinnertime together, even though they have an alcohol problem in the family, it helps decrease the likelihood that the alcohol problem will be passed on.

This idea probably works with other kinds of family problems too. For example, if families have problems such as physical abuse, fighting, closeness avoidance, aggressiveness, excessive competitiveness, or lack of intimacy, it is probably true that the more they can separate these problems from their family rituals the greater the likelihood the problems will not be passed on to future generations.

A practical implication of this is to try to agree to "not fight," "not drink," "be nice," or "be home" during family rituals—such as at Thanksgiving or birthdays.

Balance in stability and change.   One of the paradoxes of rituals is they are stable and change at the same time. They need to have some stability and be repeated over and over again to be rituals, but at the same time, individuals and families are continually developing and changing, and rituals need to adapt to these changes.

Healthy flexibility is seen when the way Christmas is celebrated is different when there are small children in a home and when there are just older people in a home. It also is illustrated when families with teenagers find themselves doing many of their rituals without the teenage children. Parents of small children and school-age children enjoy such rituals as family picnics and family reunions, but adolescents are in the middle of individuating and forcing the teens to attend may have more undesirable effects than desirable.

Healthy flexibility occurs when the type of birthday parties given to children changes as they grow older. Young children enjoy small family parties with games, cakes and singing, but teens are different. They tend to want more friends over, or go out somewhere to a movie, activity, or video arcade. Rituals must be flexible enough to change over time so they are meaningful to the participants and carry the power that is potentially available in them. It is wise to "include" members of a family in rituals to promote the shared aspect of them, but this too should not be overdone.

Too much stability occurs when families get "stuck" in certain developmental stages and try to maintain rituals after they have outlived their usefulness. Some families maintain rituals in rigid, repressive, and degrading ways to preserve the status quo. These rigid patterns appear sometimes when families experience serious problems such as incestuous behavior, and they try to have rigid rituals to keep their secrets from getting out.

SPOTLIGHT ON RESEARCH 9.1: TRANSITION TO PARENTHOOD IN MEXICAN-AMERICAN FAMILIES

Niska, Kathleen, Snyder, Mariah, and Lia-Hoagberg, Betty
Public Health Nursing, (1998). Family ritual facilitates adaptation to parenthood. P. 329-337.

In this study, 25 Mexican-American first-time young mothers and fathers were interviewed to find out what assisted them in making a smoother transition to parenthood. Interviews with these mothers and fathers and with other extended family members indicated that the presence of an intergenerational family ritual facilitated adaptation to parenthood in 24 of the 25 families. For example, in many Mexican American families new parents practice a ritual called *La cuarentena*. In this family ritual the patterns and living arrangements for mothers are very orchestrated for 40 days before the birth of the child. Among the changes required in this ritual are cultural prescriptions for types of food the mother can eat and the clothing she can wear. Also, during this time, fathers take much more charge at home and cook meals and care for other children. One of the purposes of La cuarentena is that it instills parental responsibility and incorporates individuals into the family. It also has the function of integrating and connecting the family members during this special family critical life-event.

Chapter 9

Your response:
What are ritualistic events surrounding the birth of a child in your family?

Another form of rigidity can occur when substance abuse such as alcoholism dominates rituals too much. When all of a family's activities end up with heavy drinking it can dominate what is done so much that new ways of doing things can't emerge.

Family reunions also illustrate the need for balance in stability and variety. If the only activity in a family reunion ritual is to sit around and talk about ancestors not known to the young people, and the young people are forced to listen for hours, it soon becomes drudgery. Compare that to reunions in which food is part of the ritual, different activities are available such as short programs, games and activities, prizes, treats, hiking, swimming, etc. Which would attract the future attendance at a family reunion?

Avoid inappropriate use of rituals. There are many ways rituals can be abused. For example, parents can use rituals to try to control children long after the children should be in control of their own lives. Also, rituals can be used to perpetuate pseudomutality, skeletons, cross generational alliances, avoiding letting children go, avoiding independence, etc., and they are enormously powerful because they tap into a set of dimensions that are hard to identify, define, articulate, understand because they deal with deep emotions that are dealt with implicitly and symbolically rather than with simple, overt, cognitive processes, and attempts to defy it can be defined as disloyalty.

Another way rituals can be abused is to adapt them to certain family members while ignoring others. For example, one wife emphasized her traditions and demanded that the husband's be eliminated. They visited her extended family, to the exclusion of the husband's, and her past family's rituals became the present family's rituals. Not only was the husband's wealth of experiences and memories lost, but also a number of new problems were created by the lack of balance.

GUIDELINES WHEN CREATING OR CHANGING RITUALS

Family scientists have discovered that deliberately trying to create new rituals can help families accomplish their developmental tasks and cope with difficulties. One couple, for example, was struggling with past incidents of anger, mistrust, hurt, and lack of understanding. Extramarital affairs were present as well as verbal declarations of wanting something different than what they had. A second wedding and honeymoon and a burning and burying of symbolic items from the dark past helped them create a new start. They ritualized the end of the past ways of doing things and creatively used new rituals to make things better and different, and the couple was able to change. It was a powerful way of getting "permission" to start over, while cutting off the old way.

Family scientists began in the 1970s to try to help families create new rituals as a strategy for dealing with problems and difficulties. This approach to helping families began when a group of Italian scholars started to prescribe rituals as a part of their family therapy (Palazzoli, 1974; Palazzoli et al., 1978). Gradually, as more and more family therapists and family life educators gained experience in helping families with rituals, a few guidelines have been developed that are helpful in trying to create or modify rituals (van der Hart, 1983; Whiting, 1988).

The guidelines that have been developed in the field are mostly for how to design rituals as a part of family therapy or psychotherapy. However, I think if we generalize the guidelines a little bit they can be adapted so other family professionals can use them. And, we also believe families can use them without any professional assistance to find new ways to create and modify their family rituals.

There are at least three concerns when trying to deliberately create or modify rituals. These concerns are with: (1) the *goals*, which are the purposes or objectives, (2) the *form*, which refers to how the rituals are carried out, and (3) the *content*, which refers to what is symbolized and what the behaviors are.

Goals. When someone wants to design or modify a family ritual, it seems helpful to have at least a vague idea about what it is they want to accomplish. Imber-Black & Roberts (1992) refers to this part of rituals as the "ritual theme." A large number of scholars refer to this part of rituals as the functions of the rituals (Doty, 1986). The term in ecosystems theory that describes this part of rituals is the term *goal*. Seven goals were described earlier in this chapter, but that list of goals is illustrative rather than exhaustive. There can be many other goals. Some additional examples are celebration, adventure, dealing with paradoxes and ambiguities, and preserving memories.

Most of the time when people want to design or change rituals they are dealing with more than one goal. Also, most of the time some of the goals are fairly vague and difficult to describe precisely, so it is helpful to not worry too much about getting a clear statement of the goals, how the goals will be quantified, or measured. Rituals are so "right brain" oriented that vague impressions, images, metaphors, and similes are sometimes enough.

Form. Both form and content gradually evolve in a "chicken and egg" manner as ideas about what to do influence ideas about how to do it. Eventually, however, it is helpful to think through the form of the ritual. Whiting (1988) calls this part of designing rituals the "design elements." It refers to issues such as how much the rituals will be open versus closed, how time and space will be used, and how much repetition will occur.

The open versus closed aspect of rituals refers to how much the ritual is rigid versus flexible. In rituals that are quite closed, there is little room for innovation or variation and there are understandings or rules that define fairly clearly what is to be done. There must, of course, be some closed or structured aspects. In rituals that are more open, there are fewer rules and more flexibility for innovation, creativity, and individual differences. Apparently, there can be wide variation in how closed versus

312

open rituals are, and they should be tailored to different situations and to the family's personal preferences, values, and lifestyle.

Researchers have learned that timing and placement of our family rituals is critical. Of course, this implies that one has to plan and organize these events and take care to choose timing and place with attention to the goals we have chosen. (Whiting, 1988, p. 89.)

Repetition. A third aspect of the form of rituals that must be dealt with is the amount of repetition. Many rituals are repeated frequently in families. For example, a prayer or period of silence before eating a meal and kissing each other hello and good-bye are two rituals that are performed daily in many families. Other rituals, however, are just performed only once for the people involved. Giving a person a name and having a funeral for them are two examples. Also, a family may want to create a ritual that will just occur once to help them deal with a unique situation.

An example of this type of ritual is a healing ritual that could be designed to help a family find a way to let go of a former relationship. These one-time rituals could be created for many situations such as finding ways to accept a family member back into the family after the person has been excluded or finding ways to cope with a personal or financial failure.

Content. In many ways this is the most important aspect to consider when designing or modifying rituals because it gets to the heart of what rituals are about. The content deals with at least three different parts of rituals: (1) the behaviors that are performed, (2) the symbolism in what is done, and (3) the emotional aspects of the ritual.

THE BEHAVIORS

Whiting (1988) has identified several ritual techniques or symbolic actions that help us understand the kinds of behavior or action that can be used in designing rituals. One of the categories he has identified is *letting go*.

A *second* category of behaviors Whiting has identified is *giving and receiving*. The exchanging of food, gifts, verbal expressions, and cards are the hallmarks of some rituals.

For example, when a teenager is ready to begin driving, the parents could give the child a set of keys to the family automobile to symbolize the new status in an important step toward adulthood. When young adults are ready to leave home to attend college, families can use giving and receiving behaviors in rituals to help them accomplish this transition. The parents could give the student a computer that could symbolize, "You're in charge of your life, and you can do it." I heard a story about one young adult who, upon leaving home gave his parents an apron to use during family Bar-B-Q's. He had an extra string sewn on that was broken. He wanted to remind his dad that family life would go on even though he was moving away.

Documenting.   A *third* category of behavior in Whiting's model is documenting. This is the process of writing something in an "official" way to document something such as an event, a change, or a transition. Sending thank you cards is a simple example. Getting a marriage license and writing a will are other documenting processes that have enormous symbolism in them and can be used as rituals.

Love letters document commitment, care, concern, and interest. Many families have a ritual of sending notes of appreciation and love. Even something as subtle and minor as knowing that family members will place a long-distance telephone call to let others know they have arrived at a destination is a form of documentation, and when it is ritualized in a family it can have many positive effects.

Documenting rituals can be used to help family members remember pleasant experiences. For example, putting the pictures from a family vacation into a special album and making a place for it among other precious belongings documents and cements the positive aspects of the experience. Having a picture blown-up so a larger copy can be framed and hung in a special place in the home documents membership, importance, unity, and special events.

During times when a family is having conflict, it can sometimes be helpful to write agreements on paper, have the family members involved sign them, and put them on a bulletin board. This can serve as a reminder and focus attention on the areas of agreement.

The symbolism.   The second part of the content is the symbolism, and it is one of the most important parts of rituals. As Turner argued, "the symbol is the smallest unit of ritual" (Turner, 1967, p. 19).

Symbols are tangible or observable things that represent something else. Many different things can be symbols. For example, they can be a tangible object, emblem, token, word, phrase, image, figure, or sign. The symbol derives its meaning from the object, idea, or other part of reality that it represents.

Families and individuals differ in the kinds of symbols that are important and can be important to them. Some families find symbols of the past, both of the current generation and of previous generations, are important. Other families studiously avoid symbols of the past. Some families find religious symbols meaningful, and others find them empty and uncomfortable.

One way to try to understand the symbolism in a family is to try to identify the family paradigms that guide the family's thinking, images, and beliefs about what is important. Since family paradigms are highly abstract ideas, it is sometimes helpful to look at more specific parts of families to get clues about their paradigmatic beliefs. An examination of a family's main goals can provide helpful clues about these abstract ideals and beliefs. Also, clues can be acquired observing the tangible objects families put on their walls, the way they dress, the way they decorate their home, and the way they relate to their community.

A helpful clue about what is symbolized in a family is to identify the events or things that evoke strong emotion. When the parts of life that bring out strong emotions can be identified, an understanding of the family's symbols and things that are symbolized is close.

The emotion. There are few ideas that all family scientists can agree on, but an idea where there is widespread agreement is that the emotional aspects of the family realm are extremely important. As a result, family theorists, family researchers, family therapists, and family life educators all pay great attention to the emotional processes as they try to understand and help families. This makes it doubly ironic that the literature in the field about rituals almost ignores the emotional aspects of rituals. All of the scholars who have studied rituals highlight the cognitive aspects: the symbolism, the meanings, the metaphors, and perceptions. They also pay a great deal of attention to the repetition, the staging, the functions, and the therapeutic and developmental value of rituals.

Unfortunately, however, the role of the emotional aspects of rituals is almost ignored in the literature about family rituals. Therapists and educators who use rituals to help families include the emotional aspects, but when they write books and papers to describe what they are doing and what rituals are, the emotional aspects are hardly ever mentioned. I suggest that this is an unfortunate omission. I am convinced that it is the combination of the symbolism and emotionality that makes rituals such a rich and helpful part of the family realm.

I believe it is helpful to think about the emotional aspects of rituals whenever we try to help families develop or change rituals. Also, when families want to change or invent rituals they would be well advised to pay as much attention to the emotional aspects as any of the other aspects of rituals.Emotional aspects deal with how people feel, as they are involved with rituals. Are they attracted or repulsed? Do they experience feelings such as warmth, closeness, integrity, peace, or fulfillment? Or, are the feelings generally negative? For example, is a graduation experience an inconvenience or a fulfillment? Is a wedding and reception or open house viewed as a charade and superficially irrelevant experience? Are family celebrations on holidays an ordeal that is annoying or a fulfilling emotional experience?

Most family rituals involve some degree of emotional involvement, and some of them are extremely intense. One of the issues that is either overtly or covertly dealt with when designing and changing rituals is what type of emotion is expected and tolerated. How much intensity is desirable? At funerals, for example, the individuals in the immediate family often get carried away with their emotions and exhibit crying, wailing, and other forms of emotional distress. At weddings there are almost always tears.

Chapter 9

The analog messages and the relationship messages that are sent with rituals help define what is appropriate emotionally, and occasionally it may be wise to turn these nonverbal communication processes into verbal communication. For example, when a family is designing a healing ritual to cope with a loss or serious problem, it may be helpful to observe that this is a time when it may be acceptable, even desirable, to experience some deeply felt emotions.

The neglect of the emotional aspect of rituals by family scholars means that thus far we have few ideas about how or when to deal with the emotional aspects of family rituals. I hope this deficiency will be corrected in the coming years.

SUMMARY

Family rituals and routines are valuable resources, and when they are wisely used they can help families attain important goals such as: unity, closeness, intimacy, meaning, membership changes, etc. Seven family goals rituals and routines can help with are: creating healthy emotional ties, making changes in family membership, healing, forming and redefining the identities of individuals and families, providing rites of passage that help families and individuals make developmental transitions, helping families create a sense of meaning and purpose, and creating an adequate sense of order and predictability.

Rituals and routines can be enabling or disabling in families. Therefore, families should be wise in how they create and enact them. Four ideas that can help families be wise are to have moderate ritualization, distinctiveness when there are problems a family does not want to pass on to future generations, a balance of stability and change, and avoid using rituals in inappropriate ways.

Building and Maintaining Effective Rituals

STUDY QUESTIONS

1. What is a ritual?

2. Define the term routine.

3. Name three ways rituals and routines are different.

4. What is meant by overritualization?

5. How does staging make rituals important?

6. Why do rituals play an important roles in building family strength?

KEY TERMS

Ritual
Rules
Routines
Healthy emotional ties and rituals
Rites of passage
Overritualization
Underritualization
Distinctive rituals
Symbolism

PART IV

Change, Turbulence,
and Strength

CHAPTER
TEN

Changing During the Life Course

Changing During the Life course

Main Points:

1. *Family change* is a fundamental family process.

2. Some events (like births and weddings) trigger long-term and complex changes. Other events (like illnesses and relatives moving in) create short-term and simple change processes.

3. Many changes in family life are not predictable changes. For example, divorce, remarriage, and a family member becoming handicapped are not routine changes.

4. There is some predictability in family life, and there also is great variability.

5. *Morphogenesis* is change in the "form" or structure of families.

6. *Morphostasis* (sometimes called homeostasis) is the tendency in families to resist morphogenesis.

7. Ambivalence is universal and inevitable in families.

8. The *Epigenesis Principle* helps us understand family changes.

9. Several principles can help families accomplish transitions in family life.

Changing During the Life Course

You can never step in the same river twice. —Heraclitus

INTRODUCTION

In the next two chapters we examine two important aspects of family life: life events that occur during the normal or usual course of family life and events that are less expected and are more severe or traumatic.

In this chapter, I will also discuss general change in family life. An important element of family life is the element of change. Sometimes the changes that occur are expected, but sometimes they are a surprise. Sometimes the changes take family members away from us, and sometimes we gain new members. A key element of change in families is that much of the change seems to be routine or patterned. While the sequence is not always predictable, much of the time it is. Moreover, these changes occur both to the individuals in families and to the family itself.

WHAT IS FAMILY CHANGE?

The concept of family change is an important part of family science. The process of family change results from: (a) events that help unfold the fairly predictable and typical processes that make up the family life cycle or (b) other events that trigger unpredictable events that can result in turbulence and even crisis.

These events center on the idea that change is inevitable and inescapable. When we speak of family change and crisis we refer to processes that alter, convert, or modify what is happening in families. Much of family life involves change, transformations, evolution, instability, or an unfolding of potentials.

It is also important to remember that change in families is a more of a process rather than a single event. For example, if you ask someone when they divorced, they may tell you the day the judge decreed the divorce, the time period when the relationship began to fall apart, or they may choose to refer to the day they moved out of the house. Divorce, like many of the changes we will explore in this chapter, is filled with so many segments, pieces, and processes that it is difficult to tag one specific day or one particular time that "the divorce occurred."

While some events trigger change, most change in families is usually a longer process that occurs gradually over a period of time. Thus the routine part of family life takes into account time, and it involves a series of sequence of what is happening.

Third, changes in families include both dramatic changes in families but also some small or minor changes. Some of the more dramatic we experience are births, marriages, and deaths. These types of changes usually have long-term and complicated implications.

There also are many aspects of family life in which there are minor changes in the form or structure. For example, when children start going to school, this event usually creates adjustments that are usually easy to handle. When a new sibling is born into a family it is difficult but often manageable. Birth creates a series of changes as the various family members adjust and accommodate to the new member.

Another example of change that could be either dramatic or simpler is when a relative or friend comes to live with a family; it creates a different set of short-term change processes as the new member is assimilated into the family. When a family member starts to become very old and unable to help him or herself, when someone breaks a leg, or develops a serious illness, these events each create their own unique series of outcomes.

A couple in their mid-thirties was experiencing the long-awaited birth of their child. Shortly after the baby was born, the husband was looking through the window of the nursery, waiting for the infant to arrive, and the doctor asked if he could talk with him. In a few minutes they had the following dialogue:

> Bob: Is it really that bad? (long pause) Well, how can you tell? I mean...(fear and panic show on his face and in the way he talks) he's just hours old. How can you tell?
>
> Dr: It is the classical characteristics. He has the slanted eyes, the Simeon crease in the palm, the floppy muscle tone. . . and there's more. But it all adds up, and the hard fact is, Bob, your son has Down's Syndrome.
>
> Bob: Well, . . . uh, there's got to be some mistake. Joanna and I. . . we're good people. We're healthy people. And we don't fool around. We don't do drugs. We don't drink! I can't believe this. (Bob looks out the window as his eyes swell with tears.)
>
> Dr: You ought to think about institutionalizing the baby right away, before Joanna and you are bonded with it.
>
> Bob: (Outraged) A bond. The bond doesn't start today! That bond started the minute that baby was conceived! . . . Even before. . . He's been in our dreams, our hopes for years.
>
> Dr: This is not the child you've been waiting for. This is a child who will never learn to read or write or lead a normal life . . . or allow you to.
>
> Bob: This is going to break Joanna's heart. It just can't happen. It just can't.

Dr: Look, Joanna is a teacher, an intellectual. The child will never in a million years understand all the things that mean so much to her. Bob, you have a son by your first marriage. Do you want to saddle him with a half brother that he can't even relate to? What do you want to do, load your older son with a lifetime responsibility?

Bob: (In disbelief) So what are we to do with this baby? Do we just throw him away . . . pretend he doesn't even exist. He's a part of us. He's ours. Even if . . . Oh my . . . What are we going to do?

Dr: It's a hard fact to face. The best thing might be to make a clean break. We could handle all the details. We could have him put in a nice clean place. If you want, you can even tell your friends and your family that the baby died in child-birth. Then you'll never need to know if he's alive or dead.

FAMILY CHANGE IS DIFFERENT FROM INDIVIDUAL CHANGE

The individual life cycle takes place within the family life cycle, which is the primary context of human development. We think this perspective is crucial to understanding the emotional problems that people develop as they move together through life. (Carter & McGoldrick, 1989, p. 4)

The study of changes in families is different from human development. Human development refers to the systematic changes in individuals that occur between their conception and death (Shaffer, 1989, p. 6).

The study of human development focuses on patterned changes that occur because of maturation and learning, and it focuses on the cognitive, social, physical, and emotional development of individuals. It helps us understand that children and adults go through "stages" in their development. For example, most children go through a stage of negativism when they are about two years old. They say "no" frequently when they are asked to do something, and they are so negative that many parents in this stage of development think their child never says yes. No doesn't mean the same thing to them that it means to an adult because they say it about things they like to do, and often they say no about something and are still willing to do it. The negativism is a stage that is part of their cognitive and social development.

Later, when children are about eight years old they go through a moralistic stage where they are concerned with things being done according to the rules. If their parent is driving three miles over the speed limit, they're likely to point it out. During this stage, children pay a lot of attention to following the "right" rules of games and activities.

Chapter 10

Family change is different in that it refers to the patterned changes that occur in families rather than changes in individuals. For example, newly formed families begin with a formative period. In some cultures this first stage begins with courtship. In other cultures it begins when the parents negotiate a marriage, and in other cultures it starts when couples begin to live together. During the formative stage a family becomes more complex, more differentiated or separated from other family members, and, the goal is for them to become increasingly more competent. This initial stage is a creative period because many new family rules or "understandings" are constructed.

DIFFERENT KINDS OF CHANGE

Some changes in family life mean that people and families become more complex, more differentiated, and more able to cope with their life situation. This is especially the case when families are in the formative stage of the family life cycle. For example, when children start to arrive, the families usually become much more complex and differentiated and a number of other predictable changes occur.

All changes, however, do not lead to greater ability and complexity, and they are not all desirable. There are natural cycles for everything that is living, and these life spans all have ends as well as beginnings. When an older person's body starts wearing out this too is a part of the course of life. For example, most athletic skills "peak out" when the athletes are in their late twenties, or, for the more durable ones, in their early thirties. After that the legs, coordination, and endurance are just not the same. Athletes are not very thrilled about being "over the hill" when they are 29, but it is a part of the natural development of the human body.

There are also undesirable aspects to family changes. For example, every family is eventually decreased in size by the death of family members. When death occurs it leads to painful changes in bonds, feelings of love, and closeness. Also, it is a difficult time for most families when the needs of teenagers conflict with the needs of their middle-aged parents.

Many of the processes in family life have a bittersweet quality to them. Weddings, for example, are often a time of joy, but also a time of tears. The launching of children is a time of excitement and also loss. The coming of children is rewarding but also limiting and constraining. The natural movement from the excitement and euphoria of new love during engagement and the early months of marriage is both a loss and a relief to most couples.

Many different types of changes can occur. For example, the cycles of life in human development include mental, physical, and emotional changes. People increase in their mental ability as they move from infancy to adulthood. Later, as they approach old age their memory and other mental processes start to slip. Newborn infants do not see well, but their eyesight improves rapidly during the first month of life. Later, in their mid-forties, they'll need bi-focals. Tri-focals come in the fifties, and for some a

326

ACTIVITY 10.1 – THINKING ABOUT YOUR FAMILY LIFE COURSE

This activity is an experience in anticipating and evaluating your future family development. Begin the activity by getting a piece of 8 1/2" x 11" paper and making a vertical line about 8" or 9" long on the left side of the paper. This line represents time, and you will use it to describe some of the major developmental changes that will occur in your family.

If you were born in 1980 and started school in 1986, the bottom part of your line should look something like the following:

1986   6   I started school.

1980   0   I was born

Next, add the events you think will probably occur in your family life cycle. Events you may want to include are the probable or likely times when each of the following events will or may occur:

1.   Include the year when you were born at the bottom.
2.   Include the year when you will die at the top. The average life span for women in the U.S. today is about 75 years. The average lifespan for men is 69 years. If you are healthy, exercise, don't smoke, live on a farm, have a low stress job, don't drink, and have no family history of diabetes, cancer, high blood pressure, etc., you can add an appropriate number of years. If any of the opposites exist, subtract an appropriate number of years.
3.   The year when you will leave home or did leave home.
4.   Age when you will be financially independent of your parents.
5.   Age when you will or did marry.
6.   Age when first child born.
7.   Age when last child born.
8.   Age when first child leaves home.
9.   Age when last child leaves home.
10. Age when first of your parents dies.
11. Age when second parent dies.
12. Age when you will experience retirement.
13. Age when you will finish your formal schooling.
14. Age when your spouse will die.
15. Age when you will die.

Next, some developmental patterns in our families can be anticipated because they are fairly predictable. People leave home when they are young adults, and most people plan to die when they are old. However, there are many events that do not follow the typical and predictable patterns. Some of them are desirable and some are not desirable. Some of these unanticipated events happen to each of us, and they change the developmental patterns in our life. To determine which unpredictable events will (for this activity) happen to you, think of four numbers between 1 and 30. Write your numbers here:

Be sure to respond to all items before you read the next page!!!

Changing During the Life Course

Look at the following list to discover which unpredictable events are going to happen in your life. If one of the events you chose is not possible, go to the next one on the list. For example, if you picked an event that says your spouse will die at 30 and 75 both of these aren't possible, and you should go the next event.

Make a different developmental line on a new sheet of paper.

Unpredictable Events That can Change a "Normal" Family Life Course

1. Divorce at age 25 and remarry at 32 to a person who has three children.
2. Second child is severely handicapped.
3. First child divorces and returns to live with you.
4. Third child doesn't marry and leave home.
5. Your spouse dies when you are 30.
6. You have triplets when you are 30.
7. Divorce when you are 40 and never remarry.
8. Your second child contracts AIDS when she is 17 and lives seven more years.
9. You are never able to have children or adopt.
10. Your spouse dies when you are 60.
11. Divorce when you are 34, remarry at 36 to a person with 4 children. New spouse dies at 40.
12. Your business goes bankrupt when you are 35 and your income is less than half of what you wanted it to be for the rest of your life.
13. You have another child when you are 46.
14. You have two children die in an auto accident.
15. Your child is in an accident when he is 12 and will live the rest of his life in a wheelchair.
16. You divorce at 48 and never remarry.
17. Your brother and his wife die in an airline crash and you have agreed to raise their 4 children.
18. Your mother become senile and you need to move her into your home to take care of her when you are 45.
19. Your second child runs away permanently at 14.
20. You have a child that is mentally retarded—not enough to institutionalize, but enough that he will never be able to live independently.
21. Your spouse's father becomes senile when you are 55 and you need to move him into your home or spend a great deal of time caring for him.
22. You have a child so rebellious you need to make "alternative" living arrangements when she is 14.
23. You are not able to have or adopt children.
24. You win a lottery that is worth 10 million.
25. You die when you are 40.
26. You have a niece move in to live with your family when you are 42.

27. Your mother dies when you are 46 and your father dies when you are 51.
28. You have a son that dies of leukemia when he is 4.
29. Your spouse is in an automobile accident and is paralyzed from the waist down at age 35.
30. You become blind when you are 27.

After completing this activity this far, bring it with you to the class session. Do not complete the last question until later.

The last part of this activity is summarize the new insights you have acquired by doing this activity and studying family development for several days. Wait until after the sessions on development to write this last part. This part ought to be typed. If you didn't gain new insights, write a page or so summarizing what you could do to learn more about family developmental processes.

magnifying glass a little later. Young people are fairly adaptable, but older people usually don't have the same level of adaptability, and all these changes are parts of normal family life.

Families change in the size, sex composition, complexity of interrelationships, expectations, help patterns, and the patterns of emotional distance and closeness. The generational alignments evolve in several predictable ways, and the ways the family system copes with the environment changes.

PREDICTABILITY AND VARIABILITY IN FAMILY LIFE

When family scientists began to study family life in the 1950s (Duvall, 1955), they assumed most families moved through a very predictable series of stages. They developed the term family life cycle to describe this predictable pattern. One version of this cycle that has been widely used in recent years is the one suggested by Carter and McGoldrick (1989, p. 15). It has the following stages:

Stage 1 - Leaving home: Single young adults.
Stage 2 - The joining of families through marriage: The new couple.
Stage 3 - Families with young children.
Stage 4 - Families with adolescents.
Stage 5 - Launching children and moving on.
Stage 6 - Families in later life

Gradually, however, family scientists discovered most families do not proceed in an orderly way through this series of stages. This orientation focuses so much on children that it does not reflect the change sequence that many people actually go through. In fact, it is only a small minority of families who experience this cycle without any interruptions or without an unusual arrangement of the stages.

This is because most families encounter several unexpected events that influence their life cycle. Notice, for example, how common the following events are that influence the sequence of events in family life cycles.

- About 50% of American couples end their first marriage in divorce.
- About 20% of American people have more than one divorce.
- About 15% of couples do not have children.
- In how many families does one spouse die before they reach the typical age for retirement?
- How many children die before they reach the launching stage?
- How many children leave home or need alternative living arrangements before the usual "launching" age?
- After a spouse's death or a divorce, how many remain single?
- How many experience a remarriage?

- When there are "blended" families, how does it change the usual cycle?
- How many adult children return to live with their parents after they experience a divorce or their spouse dies? This is sometimes called the "boomerang" stage of family life.
- How many children remain single, but do not leave home when they reach 18, 21, 30, or 50?
- How many families have several children almost raised, and then have one or two additional children that are almost a separate family?
- What about single people? There are several ways they also are families. They are children, so they have parents and grandparents. Usually they also have brothers and sisters, and frequently they have nieces and nephews. They also often have aunts, uncles, and cousins, and some of them have children. What are the cycles in their family life?

These questions lead to several important insights about family life. First, they demonstrate there is great variability in the life cycles of families and individuals. Just as there are so many different types of families that we cannot talk about "the" American family or "the" English family or "the" Russian family, there are so many variations in family life that we cannot talk about "the" life cycle of individuals or of families.

A second idea is that even though there are great variations in the cycles of family life, there also are some aspects of these cycles that are fairly predictable. Courtship usually precedes weddings, and births (or adoptions) usually precede child rearing. One's own aging tends to come late in the cycle of family life, but coping with the aging of parents and grandparents comes earlier. Mid-life crises don't usually happen to people in their 20's or in their 80's. They tend to come when people are in their 40's and 50's.

There are, therefore, a number of rhythms and patterns in the ebb and flow of family life, and some of them are fairly predictable. The more we are aware of these patterns, the more we can help families prepare and cope with daily family life.

PATTERNS THAT ARE PREDICTABLE

Research has discovered a number of processes that are more predictable. I have found seven to discuss in the following pages.

Coping with aging and death.   One of the most predictable events in family life is that members of the family die. Families eventually find themselves coping with the process of preparing for death and trying to find ways to adjust to the feelings and changes that are created by death. In our contemporary society, most people do not die until they are over 70, so death usually is preceded by a period of aging. This period

Changing During the Life Course

JOURNAL OF THOUGHTS 10.1: YOUR TIME OF LIFE

1. Identify what phase of life you are in now. Are you in this phase "on-time" or off-time is some way?

333

2.   Where do you hope to be in ten years? Be specific.

usually involves illnesses, caregiving, decreased mental and physical abilities, and in some situations long periods of senility.

For most people, their first encounter with death is when the grandparents die. This is usually an important family process because parents find themselves helping their children learn how to cope with the kind of loss and change that occurs with the death of loved ones. At the same time the parents are helping their children cope with the death of their grandparents, they are coping with the aging and death of their parents. These changes inevitably alter the care patterns, visiting patterns, and patterns in the feelings of love and closeness.

Formation followed by maintenance. The formation period for a family begins when a couple starts to develop a serious relationship, gets engaged, or starts living together, and it usually continues for a period of time after most weddings.

During this stage of the family life cycle the couple is creating their rules of transformation and daily, monthly, and yearly routines and cycles. It also is when they are constructing unique patterns of problem solving and decision making, and ways of relating to friends and relatives. They also begin establishing their family themes, traditions, and rituals. It is a period when most couples spend a great deal of time getting to know each other and deciding how their family will be like the family she grew up in and different from it and how their family will be like the family he grew up in and different from it. It is a creative period because the new family is literally constructing the system it will be, its view of the world, and its way of relating to its environment.

The maintenance stage. Most families gradually move into a second stage that can be called the maintenance or management stage. The dynamics and processes of this next stage are different because the family system becomes relatively established and stable. The attention of the family shifts to different concerns such as child rearing, economic survival, ways of relating to changes in the environment, and ways to find fulfillment.

The difference between the formative stage and the maintenance stage is similar to the difference between building a ship and then sailing in the ship or building a building and then using the building. The formative stage gets the ship constructed enough that it will float and can operate. The main attention changes to use rather than constructing. Some changes in the ship will be made while it is being used, but many concerns that were important when the ship was being constructed can be forgotten, and many things about the nature of the ship can be assumed.

Birth leads to predictable patterns. The birth of an infant creates a complex set of predictable family events. It leads to some immediate changes in such things as routines, allocation of resources, the way time and energy are spent, and relationships between the members of the family. It also means that a different person is the youngest member of the family, and this changes relationships, privileges, and care giving.

It also creates a predictable series of long-term and gradual family changes that will occur as the infant matures. When the child gets old enough to go to school, the family will need to relate to school systems, friendship systems, and recreational systems differently. Later, when the child moves into adolescence, the child will introduce many new inputs into the family system such as new forms of music, recreation, ideas, anxieties, and aspirations. When children approach adulthood they tend to individuate and differentiate from the parental family, and eventually most children are launched from the family into families of their own.

As children become adults, the relationship between them and their parents changes to one of concerned fellow-adults. Later, when the children become middle-aged and the parents become aged the patterns of giving and receiving tend to reverse. The parent generation tends to be the receivers of attention, concern, care, and the younger middle-aged generation tends to become the givers.

Parting is inevitable.   Another predictable pattern is that weddings are followed by some type of marital separation. The traditional ideal is for marriage to last "til death do we part," but some type of parting is a predictable family process.

In earlier historical periods the vast majority of marriages ended with the death of one of the spouses. During the last century, however, an increasing number of mar-

SPOTLIGHT ON RESEARCH 10.1: HOW DO CHILDREN SPEND TIME?

Sandra Hoffreth and John Sandberg published a study in the *Journal of Marriage and the Family* (2001) that examined what children do with their time as they get older and families adapt to the age of the child. The data were collected from more than 2,500 families who completed time diaries for several weeks about their children's activities. In all, the report examines the lives of about 3,500 children.

Hoffreth and Sandberg found that children (ages 3–12 years old, average age about 7 years old) spend about 55% of their time eating, sleeping, or in personal care. Only about 15% of the time are they in a school setting. As they get older that ratio changes and they spend more time in school settings and associated activities. Less than 30% of a child's time is discretionary. These children spent about 15 hours a week playing and about 12 hours per week watching television (about one fourth of their free time). In contrast, children spend only about 9 hours a week in activities structured by adults. They spent very little time in learning activities initiated by their parents or caretakers. Only about 1 hour per week reading (anything!) and less than 2 hours per week studying. They spent less than 30 minutes per week doing anything that could be classified as housework responsibilities. And, they spent even less time than that in family conversations.

As children get older there are some changes of note. Kids 0 to 2 years spent more than 7 hours per week watching TV, 9 hours per week on average in daycare, and less than 25 minutes week outside doing anything. By the time a child is 8 years old, he/she is spending 5 hours on sports, 13 hours watching TV, 1 hour per week reading, 30 minutes in family conversation, 1 hour in church, and right at 2 hours per week studying (the survey was taken during the school year).

By the time the child is teenage, he/she has increased homework studying to a 'blazing' 20 minutes per day (dividing by 7 full days). They spend more than 1 hour per day in some type of organized sports activities and about 2 hours per day watching TV. Household conversation has dropped to less than 3 minutes per day.

Does this picture seem accurate to you? Reflect back to when you were living at home. Do these numbers seem to match? Do you believe that something is wrong with this picture? You as a parent, future parent, or grandparent can do something about this imbalance.

Your response:
If you have children, do you plan to (or do you now) limit the amount of TV viewing in your home? Explain your plan and reasoning.

riages have ended with divorce. The divorce rate, however, has leveled off since 1979, and the present pattern is that about 50% of "first" marriages that occur in our society end with a divorce and about 60% end with the death of one of the spouses.

Idealism to realism. Another predictable pattern in family life is that families tend to start out with considerable idealism, and this is gradually replaced with realism (Blood & Wolfe, 1960; Carter & McGoldrick, 1989). In many situations, the idealism is not replaced with realism, but with disenchantment, disillusionment, and despair. Most young couples have an idealistic view of the future of the family they are creating. They believe their love is unusually strong and deep, and they can communicate, relate, and share in unusually effective ways. As the years pass, the realities of a world that is, at best, complicated and unpredictable and often is cruel and unjust gradually weaken the idealism.

The empty-nest stage is getting longer. Several factors contribute to the empty-nest stage of family life becoming longer. Life expectancy has increased dramatically in the last century. Most people now live beyond the age of 75, and at the same time the number of children in each family has decreased. Since most people have their last child before their mid-thirties, they launch their last child when the parents are about 50. The result is that most people live more than 25 years after their children are launched.

Spending years single is typical. A final predictable pattern for American families is that most people are single for many years of their adult life. Many factors contribute to this pattern. One spouse usually dies before the other. Also, people tend to marry at later ages than at earlier times, and the higher divorce rate has increased the number of years people are single. This is especially the case for women because they do not remarry as frequently as divorced men.

When an individualistic perspective is used, it is common to assume that single adults are not in a "family."

However, from a family science perspective, being a single adult is a developmental stage most people experience in their family life cycle. Singles have parents, siblings, and grandparents; and many of them have children and grandchildren. Therefore, they are part of family life, and the family realm can be as important to them as it is to people who happen to be married.

Variability in Patterns of Change

Many factors create variability in family change. For example, some children leave home in their mid-teens. This pushes their families into the launching process earlier than most families. Other children never leave home, and this creates a different combination of change and stability.

Death is inevitable, but it is unpredictable. Families never know when they will need to cope with the processes of dying, bereaving, and finding ways to go on without loved ones. This adds unpredictability and variability to every family's life.

People also respond to the processes of aging differently, and this influences patterns of daily family life. For example, some people experience mid-life crises that dramatically change their lives, and this can influence the changes others may want to make or not make in their family.

The process of launching children changes the obligations and responsibilities of parents. There are many ways families can respond to these changes. Some families invest more or less energy in their careers, and others try new careers, move to new locations, or take up new educational pursuits.

The aging of parents and grandparents introduces variability and unpredictability in a family's daily life. When an aged parent needs emotional, financial, and physical assistance it can influence career options, the way a family's financial resources are used, the way the rooms of the house are used, and how people relate to each other.

Transitions

The concept of transitions was created when scholars realized that living systems usually do not have a constant rate of change. They tend to have periods of rapid change followed by periods of relative stability. The periods of rapid or dramatic change are called transitions and the periods of stability are called stages.

Most of the major transitions in families occur when there are changes in the membership in the family or in the way the family interacts with its environment. Many of these transitions are fairly predictable and normal, and they can be anticipated.. Some of them, however, are part of the unpredictable and variable parts of family life. Some examples of transitions that influence family life are: engagement, starting to live together, weddings, the birth of the first child, children starting to go to school, children moving into adolescence, children leaving home, death of a parent, retirement, death of a spouse, and one's own death.

Not all transitions in family life are routine. In Chapter Eleven, we will discuss events that are very unexpected and have a different texture to them in family life. For example, becoming unemployed or employed, the onset of a serious and chronic disease such as cancer or a heart ailment, the recovery from a serious illness, sudden fame or fortune, and sudden defamation or misfortune can create important transitions in family life, but they should not be thought of as routine changes.

Some changes are created by biological factors such as puberty, menopause, and senility. Some of them are created by experiences. For example, the process of experiencing pregnancy and birth creates many changes in the perspectives, insights, sensitivities, and concerns of the parents, and these experiential factors create part of the changes that occur in family transitions. The family emotional system changes over time, and changes often occur in the environment, and they also influence family transitions.

Some changes are created by a combination of factors. For example, the changes created by adolescence and the "mid-life crisis" are not caused by one event or process. They are created by the complex interaction of physiological, social, mental, economic, spatial, and emotional changes, and they create sizable transitions in the individuals and in the family life.

Social scientists have been studying developmental transitions since the beginning of the twentieth century. G. Stanley Hall, for example, published a book on the adolescent stage of development in 1904, and he gave the adolescent period a label that has been used ever since. He called it a period of "sturm und drang" (storm and stress).

Some transitions tend to be relatively easy and problem-free, yet others tend to be difficult. Also, some of them are easy for one family but difficult for another. For example, some families have a difficult time coping with children leaving home, but others find it an easy transition (Haley, 1987). Some families have a difficult time coping with retirement, but others find it easy. Some find the transition into parenthood easy, and others find it challenging. A small minority of parents find the transition into parenthood so difficult that they develop psychosis from it. Psychiatrists have developed a special name for the emotional illness that some get. It is called *post-partum psychosis*.

One important challenge for family scientists is to find ways to help families cope with transitions so they are growth producing and healthy periods rather than excessively difficult. Fortunately, in the late 1930s sociologists such as Leonard Cottrell (1942) began trying to identify the principles that are involved in making transitions easy and difficult, and scholars have tried to use these principles to identify strategies that families, therapists, and educators can use to promote family health. The principles Cottrell identified are fairly specific (not general), and they have since been revised and updated in light of subsequent research (Burr et al., 1979a). Three of these principles are now so widely understood and useful that they are included in this chapter.

ANTICIPATORY SOCIALIZATION

These ideas refer to the process of helping people learn what will be expected of them in new roles and situations. The term socialization refers to the process of gradually learning the norms, scripts, attitudes, values, and subtle rules a person needs to know to be able to function effectively in society. Infants are in an unsocialized condition, but gradually they go through the process of being socialized by parents, teachers, siblings and others who teach them how to act and feel.

Anticipatory socialization refers to learning that is done before people are in a role where they actually use what they have learned. An example is the book learning part of a driver-training program. It prepares future drivers for the written exam. They haven't yet started driving, but they are learning information they will need when they do.

Leonard Cottrell (1942) was the first scholar to develop the principle that anticipatory socialization helps people make transitions. Since then, other scholars such as Merton (1968, p. 316), Burr (1973), and Bronfenbrenner (1979) have refined it.

PRINCIPLE 10.1: ANTICIPATORY SOCIALIZATION

Families are better able to meet their goals and make successful transition into new stages of family life if they can anticipate and learn about the transition before it happens.

This principle helps us realize that timing is important in trying to help people learn what they need to do. There are moments of readiness or teachable moments when people are eager and motivated and other times when they are less interested in learning (Guerney & Guerney, 1981). When, for example, is the best time to teach someone to drive? When they are five, fifteen, or fifty? When is the best time to teach people about how to care for infants? When they are fifteen, fifty, or five months along in a pregnancy?

There are many ways family scientists can use this principle to improve the quality of family life. Some examples are to prepare educational materials that help people learn what will be expected of them in new family situations. These materials can be in many forms. They can be cartoons, booklets, and posters. They can be part of commercial advertisements, promotional materials, and fairy tales. They can be

Changing During the Life Course

JOURNAL OF THOUGHTS 10.2: EPIGENESIS

1. Describe the Epigenesis Principle in your own words.

343

2. What are you doing now that could have an effect on your life later on? (This assignment will only work if you are honest. Examine the good and bad.)

audio and videotapes, or articles for magazines or books. Some other ways of helping are to teach marriage preparation courses, parenting courses, work with industries in helping teach retirement preparation workshops, offer premarital counseling, and lead marriage and family enrichment workshops.

Another way to use this principle to improve the quality of family life is to influence social policies. For example, most hospitals now offer parenting workshops for expectant parents, but some do not. Letters and visits to the board of directors of hospitals that don't have these programs can help them realize the benefits of changing their policies.

Some of these strategies for trying to improve the quality of life can be used by people who are just beginning to study family science. For example, students taking an introductory course could develop class projects to find out what the resources are in their community. They can then use their resources to try to improve the community resources. These efforts will probably make the most difference when they are geared to groups who are least likely to have access to effective socializing materials. For example, there is considerable evidence that underprivileged and less well educated groups benefit more than those with more resources and education.

ROLE STRAIN

A second principle that helps people cope with transitions deals with role strain. Role strain refers to the felt difficulty people experience when they try to conform to the demands of a role. Some roles, such as caring for infants are so demanding that there can be abundant role strain. When the parents both try to work full time and they try to keep up all of the other activities they were used to before the pregnancy, it can create one type of strain, an over-load problem. To avoid this, couples need to learn that when they are expecting their first child, it usually helps to cut back on some of the roles they occupy. Frequently at least one parent and sometimes both parents need to adjust the amount of time they spend on their career, leisure time activities, educational pursuits, and the amount of time they spend in other activities.

The following principle that summarizes these ideas is called the Role Strain Principle:

PRINCIPLE 10.2: ROLE STRAIN PRINCIPLE

The greater the strain experienced in a role, the more difficult the transitions into the role and the easier the transitions out of it.

Many things can create role strain. For example, it can be introduced by ambiguity about what a person is supposed to do in a new situation, and by conflicting expectations about what should be done.

Part of the role strain principle tells us that strain helps certain transitions, the transitions out of roles. For example, adolescence is usually a period of considerable role strain. The expectations for adolescence are ambiguous, and the important people in an adolescent's life do not agree on many of the expectations. The parents, teens, friends, and educators, for example, usually have different opinions. This makes the transition into adolescence difficult, but it usually makes the transition out of it much easier.

In fact most people are glad to have the teenage years behind them, and they are thrilled when they and others finally view them as adults, a stage of life where the expectations are more clear and there is less strain. Since the adolescent stage of the family life cycle also tends to be difficult for parents and siblings, they too, usually, find the transition out of the teen years a welcome breath of fresh air.

The main issues in applying this principle are knowing what role strain is, knowing the kinds of things that cause it, and finding ways to minimize or prevent it. Good anticipatory socialization can help because it gives people clues about which roles are more and less demanding. It also, frequently, helps people learn that some roles are fairly incompatible with others. For example, it is helpful to know that roles such as dating, being engaged, and being married are fairly incompatible, and trying to do more than one of these at the same time can create more than a little strain.

William Goode (1960) identified a number of other strategies that can help minimize strain. One of them is to talk extensively with others to try to clarify the expectations and get a clear understanding of what is expected. This also helps create agreement with others about these expectations. Role theorists have a term for each of these two processes. They call them getting role clarity and role consensus.

Trying to get clarity and consensus is a natural process in many situations. For example, most engaged couples find it natural to talk for hours and hours, almost endlessly, about what they want and don't want when they are married and how they want to act and not act. Some couples, however, are not aware of the benefits of these conversations, and they would benefit from more of them.

Another of Goode's strategies for coping with role strain is to compartmentalize certain roles. When two roles, such as being an employee and lover, demand very different ways of acting, it is helpful to separate the situations and places where people are in these roles. Being an employee during working hours and a lover at other times helps the employee, employer, and lovers all minimize their strain. A different example is that the roles of caring for infants and having a career are fairly incompatible, so people usually separate them.

A third strategy is to periodically examine the role demands we have in our lives to determine if we are over-committed. Most of us go through short periods of time, such as during final examinations, when we have an overload, but it is an acceptable part of the ebb and flow of demands. However, sometimes we gradually take on one more obligation, and then another, and then another until we have inadvertently over-committed ourselves. In these situations, it is an effective strategy to reduce our obligations by eliminating some roles. Or, if we do not want to eliminate any of our roles, we can lower our "standards" in some roles.

TRANSITION PROCEDURES

The third principle about transitions deals with the procedures that are used in making a transition. The principle is called the Role Transitions Principle, and it is:

PRINCIPLE 10.3: ROLE TRANSITIONS PRINCIPLE

Families are better able to meet their goals during important transitions when the events that surround a transition are clear.

Imagine, for example, how difficult it would be if someone's wedding were spread out over several months. They wouldn't know for sure when they were finally married. At what point would they have made the important commitments to each other, and when should their friends start thinking of them as a married couple? This type of ambiguity in the transition procedures would make the transition into marriage much more difficult than it usually is. Anthropological research has found some cultures that spread out some aspects of weddings (Van Gennep, 1960), but they are careful to make each part clear and important.

It would be the same for retirement. What would it be like if a person weren't sure when during a three-month period they didn't need to come to work? It would be ridiculous! Yet many things we do with the transitions in our society are just as ridiculous.

It would be equally ridiculous to have a transition ceremony for every little transition in people's lives, but, apparently, in our contemporary society many families would be better off if more of their transitions were to be more clear.

MORPHOGENESIS AND MORPHOSTASIS

Morphogensis. Morphogenesis and morphostasis can be understood easily if they are divided into their two root words. First, let's examine morphogenesis: the morpho part of this word comes from the Greek term morpho and it refers to the form or shape of something. The genesis part comes from the Greek word genesis, which means beginning or creating, and in this word it also refers to changing or altering. Thus family morphogenesis refers to changing or altering the shape or form of a fam-

Chapter 10

ily life. It means more than just changing the number or the ages of the people in the family, as it includes other things like changes in family dynamics, traditions, routines, emotional responses, rules, rituals, and other processes.

PRINCIPLE 10.4: MORPHOGENESIS IN FAMILY SYSTEM

There is pressure in family systems to consider changing the way things are done.

The main idea that family researchers have developed about morphogenesis can be called the Morphogenesis Principle, and it is that:Some of the morphogenesis in families is routine and expected change and some of it is not. The difference is that routine changes are part of the typical life span or life cycle of individuals or families. For example, a member of a family may be paralyzed by an automobile accident. A family may win a large lottery prize, or someone in a family may go through a religious conversion. These and many other random and unforeseen events can create changes in the "form" of the families involved, but family scientists do not think of them as routine changes.

Morphostasis. The concept of morphostasis is the opposite of morphogenesis, and it is also easily understood when we break it into its two parts. Morpho refers to form, and stasis refers to static or stable. Thus, family morphostasis is the process of maintaining the status quo or avoiding change in a family life.

Family scientists also sometimes use the term homeostasis rather than morphostasis. These two words are synonymous and interchangeable. In this book the authors have chosen to use the word morphostasis rather than homeostasis.

The Morphostasis Principle was one of the first principles to be identified after scholars began thinking with a family process point of view (Jackson, 1957). The idea in this principle is that:

PRINCIPLE 10.5: MORPHOSTASIS IN FAMILY SYSTEMS

When one part of a family system tries to change, one of the reactions by families is to try and preserve the status quo or the ways things have always been.

When these ideas were being developed, the scholars who were creating them paid most of their attention to morphostasis, and they ignored morphogenesis

348

(Jackson, 1963). This meant that during the 1950s and 1960s, family scholars who were developing these ideas assumed that family life was fairly stable and unchanging, and the primary tendency in them is to resist innovation and development.

The current view in the field is that, on the one hand, there are always pressures, events, and processes that tend to create change in family life. And, at the same time, there are always pressures, events, and processes that tend to create stability and resist change. The two processes oppose each other and are incompatible, but both are inherent and unavoidable, and apparently they are natural and inevitable parts of family life.

WHY DOES MORPHOSTASIS OCCUR?

There are many reasons morphostasis is an inevitable and fundamental part of family systems. Three of these reasons are:

1. Rules that are created in the early stages of a relationship become the first part of a complicated web or set of rules. Later on, if there are attempts to change the first rules it has implications for many parts of the web. One result of this pattern is that it creates some tendency to resist change.
2. A great deal of what happens in families is unconscious; or, using the iceberg analogy, it is beneath the surface and fairly invisible. Also, people have enough of a desire to control their lives (Rollins and Thomas, 1979) that they like some degree of stability, security, and predictability. These tendencies lead to some resistance to change.
3. Family processes deal with many of the most fundamental and deeply experienced emotional processes that humans experience. For example, they deal with mating, reproduction, personal territory, intimacy, and belonging. People are highly motivated to arrange their life so these deeply experienced affective experiences are comfortable. One example of this is the unbelievable contortions humans, and many lower forms of life, go through to find a mate and settle down. When people get these parts of their life organized so the inner and core affective conditions are comfortable, they have very strong, affectively motivated reasons to resist attempts to change things. This is one reason divorce and death are resisted so much, and why they are such tremendously disruptive experiences when they can't be avoided. They force us to reorganize some of the most fundamental parts of our lives.

PRACTICAL IMPLICATIONS OF KNOWING ABOUT MORPHOGENESIS AND MORPHOSTASIS

Ambivalence. When we understand the twin processes of morphogenesis and morphostasis in family life, it gives us ideas that have several implications. One implication is that it helps us be aware that families always experience ambivalence when they encounter significant change. Ambivalence is feeling two opposite affective states or desires at the same time. Even when families encounter desirable changes like weddings, births, graduations, children going out on their own, career opportunities, and other new challenges and opportunities, there is always ambivalence in the family about them.

The ambivalence is frequently uneven. This means that sometimes one side of the feelings for or against something are stronger than the opposing feelings. Usually, when a change helps people attain important goals the dominant feelings are in favor of the change. When a change interferes with important goals or is threatening in other ways, the dominant feelings are against the change.

Sometimes perceptions determine the nature of the feelings, but perceptions are sometimes deceptive. Remembering the iceberg analogy, when a change has implications for the hidden parts of family life, people may not be aware of all of the pressures and processes. For example, a younger sibling may be relieved when an older sibling leaves home. They get a new bedroom. There's less hassle about the bathroom. No more getting picked on, etc. The feelings of loss and emptiness may be very real and may have an effect on the child, but the child may not be aware of what is happening.

Early intervention. Another implication of these two ideas is that, since systems tend to become increasingly rigid as time passes, generally speaking, the earlier in the life of an individual or family system we try to influence the system, the greater the impact we will usually have. The biblical admonition to "train up a child in the way he should go: and when he is old, he will not depart from it" (Proverbs 22:6) is a good example of this idea.

In family science, there are many ways this can be applied. For example, we can make more difference in the way a couple relates by helping them early in their marriage rather than later. We can have more impact on people's lives if we influence them early in their life than if we influence them later (Bronfenbrenner, 1979).

When we try to apply these insights, we also need to be aware of the readiness of individuals and families for change (Guerney & Guerney, 1981). People are ready at certain times and not ready at others. For example, we would probably have little impact on a person's life by trying to teach them something about careers when they are three. They need to be more ready than most three year olds usually are.

It has become widely believed in our society that the first years of a child's life are the most important, and the principle of morphostasis is consistent with this idea. Family scientists, therefore, ought to do what they can to help parents find the resources they need to be able to exert the influence and care during this period that most parents want to have and children need.

Time interventions close to transitions. Family scientists have discovered that periods of transition are a good time to try to influence family life (Klonsky & Bengston, 1996). Often it is the most effective to try to create a change just before a transition or just after it. Some of the reasons transitions are a good time to try to make changes are because the morphogenetic processes are more powerful at transition points and systems are in a period of flux. After the transition the family system tends to move into a new "stage" and the morphostatic processes take over and systems tend to resist change and promote stability.

An example of this idea is that just prior to the birth of the first child in a family is a good time for family scientists to help couples prepare to care for infants. The parents are thinking about the birth, anticipating it, and they are highly motivated by the emotions that surround birth and procreation. This is, therefore, a teachable moment or time of readiness for new ideas, skills, and ways of doing things. Attempts to help people learn how to cope with infants are not as effective before a couple is pregnant.

Another example is that it is not very effective to try to teach parents of infants how to deal with the transition into the teenage years. However, when the oldest child in a family is about 12 the parents are much more receptive to ideas about how to cope with teenagers.

However, this idea does not always work. Many other processes are always at work simultaneously in family systems, and we need to consider as much of the total system as possible. This is sometimes called having a holistic attitude or orientation. For example, if we just paid attention to the morphostasis and morphogenesis principles, we would conclude that the best time to help young couples prepare for marriage is just before the marriage. Experience in trying to help engaged couples, however, has revealed that the period just prior to a wedding is not a very good time to try to influence couples. Research about the effects of educational and counseling programs has revealed that they have very little impact when they are in that transition (Druckman, 1979). Apparently what is happening is that the period just prior to weddings is such an intensely emotional time that couples are not receptive to new ideas. They are apparently so concerned about the relationship and the preparation for the wedding that intervention programs have little impact.

Studies have found that premarital programs that have a follow-up phase about six months after the wedding are much more helpful than programs that just work with couples before marriage (Druckman, 1979; Bader et al., 1980). What is apparently happening is that after couples have had time to settle into their marital relationship, they move into a period when they are more ready to learn than they are just prior to the wedding.

Epigenesis.   Remember the Epigenesis Principle from Chapter 2. This principle has three main ideas in it. One idea is that what is done during earlier stages of a life cycle sometimes limits future opportunities, and it can make later challenges more difficult. A second idea is that what is done during earlier stages of a life cycle also can expand future opportunities, and this can make later challenges easier to cope with. The third idea is that what is done during earlier stages of a life cycle tends to create habits or tendencies in family systems and in individuals' behavior, and these tendencies are continued later even though the families or individuals have the capacity to do things differently. What this means is that such things as rituals, patterns, traditions, routines, themes, and mannerisms tend to be continued once they are established.

There are also many situations that illustrate this principle. One is that what couples do in the formative stages of their family life cycle can influence their options later. For example, assume a couple is beginning to get serious and they develop a pattern of talking openly and honestly about their feelings. In the process of developing this pattern, they create a complex set of rules about how they are going to interact in their relationship—in their system. The rules are "understandings" about how they are going to act in relation to each other. Many of these rules are established without ever talking about them. They may develop rules such as agreeing they will try to be willing to take the time to listen to the other one when there is an indication they have a strong emotion. They'll try to be "understanding," and they'll try to avoid being demeaning or critical. They also will probably come to an "understanding" about such things as how hard they ought to try and what kinds of things, such as being "really tired," can interfere without it being a problem. In this example, we have only identified a half dozen of the "understandings" a couple could develop in this area, but if space were to allow, it would be possible to identify hundreds of these subtle rules about how a couple communicates about feelings.

The rules that are developed in the early stages of a relationship become the framework that is used to develop more elaborate and complicated rules and understandings. They also influence what can be done in the future. If a couple creates a pattern of being open and candid with their feelings, their system will then demand of them certain behaviors, and they will get certain things out of their system. The rules of openness demand that they take the time to listen to each other carefully and that they are patient and understanding whenever the other one wants to talk about feelings. They will get out of their system a certain degree of understanding, sense of belonging, closeness, and bondedness.

Some of these basic affective states are desires for territory, belonging, leaders and followers, a sense of meaning and purpose, maintaining the species by reproducing ourselves, sexual arousal, and being connected to each other in ways that are at least minimally secure.

Most of these emotional processes are so deeply experienced that we are not very conscious of them. We don't have vocabularies to describe them well, and by-and-large they are imperceptible. The result is that they result in very vague emotional feelings like anger, attraction, love, and desires. This means that we don't have very good access to these affective experiences to know how to deal with them consciously or deliberately, yet they are so powerful that they exert tremendous effect on our lives.

JOURNAL OF THOUGHTS 10.3: TRANSITIONS

1. What type of transitions are the most difficult for you? Why?

2. What can make transitions easier? Take the information from your chapter and make it work here.

3.   When do "normal" transitions and phases of life become "not-so-normal." How do you react when things do not turn out for you as you thought they should or could have?

Changing During the Life Course

The point of all of this is that when people establish the "rules" they are going to have in their family they are dealing with many of the most fundamental emotional aspects that we humans experience, and when we get our "system" established, we find it a deeply disruptive emotional experience if we have to go back and renegotiate or change fundamental parts of it.

The intensity of the affective aspects of these processes can be somewhat appreciated if we think about all of the elaborate human rituals, songs, dances, tokens, celebrations, covenants, and legal apparatus that are connected to the resolution of these.

Most of the discussion of this principle has focused on how it applies to family life, but it also applies to developmental processes in individuals. What this means is that what a person does in response to developmental changes and processes has important implications for what that person can and will tend to do later in their life.

There are many examples of this process in individuals. If students do not apply themselves academically, they gradually eliminate future opportunities that demand educational excellence. If a person becomes proficient with a musical instrument, that person has choices that a person without the proficiency does not have. When people learn early in life how to express themselves orally and in writing, these skills open up many avenues that would otherwise be closed to them. When people learn social skills, or when they do not develop social skills, these characteristics influence what they can and cannot do the rest of their lives.

This principle is a useful idea, but there are many aspects of it that we do not yet understand, and more research needs to be done about it. For example, some of the "rules" that are created early in relationships seem to change easily at later times, but some are very resistant to change. We don't yet know very much about which operate which way and why. These are some of the unknowns that future analysis, theorizing, and research can help answer.

SUMMARY

This chapter discussed ways human development and routine family processes influence what happens in families. Some are predictable. Families can anticipate them and prepare for them. Most families tend to be similar in these predictable processes. There also are many family processes that are not predictable. These unpredictable processes create great variability in family development and individual development.

The chapter also discussed ways families can manage transitions so they are as manageable and growth-producing as possible. The processes of morphogenesis, morphostasis, and epigenesis were also discussed and illustrated, and several strategies for using these concepts were given.

One of the main ideas in the chapter is that those of us who want to understand families should always be sensitive to processes of change. We should never ignore them, even when we're concentrating on other parts of family processes or other things that are known in the field.

Another implication of this is that the developmental ideas should be integrated with the ideas about the family realm, generational dimensions, and affect to form an increasingly comprehensive and helpful set of ideas.

Changing During the Life Course

1. Name several "predictable" patterns of family life. Why do we pay attention to these?

2. Explain the idea that we move from idealism to realism as we get older. Think of a good example of this in your life.

3. Explain the concept of "anticipatory socialization."

4. What is the difference between morphostasis and morphogenesis?

5. How can the epigenesis principle be applied using the information from this chapter?

6. What is role strain? How can you tell if a role you are in is stressful?

KEY TERMS

Anticipatory socialization
Change in families
Predicitable patterns
Transitions
Role strain
Morphorgenesis
Morphostasis
Ambivalence

CHAPTER
ELEVEN

Coping With Turbulence, Gains, and Losses

Coping With Turbulence, Gains, and Losses

Main Points:

1. There are many "stressor events" that can create stress in family life.

2. Some of the stressor events are more serious than others. Also, some of them come from the environment, and others come from inside the family.

3. There are developmental processes and predictable patterns in the way family stress is managed. Recent research has identified five different ways families respond to stress.

4. Research about families has begun to identify coping strategies that families can use to deal effectively with stressful situations.

5. Some Level I coping strategies seem to be helpful and several can be less effective in certain stressful situations.

6. Recent research has begun to identify coping strategies that deal with Level II and Level III changes in family processes.

7. Some coping strategies are helpful with certain types of stressor events (such as death or economic loss) but not helpful with other stressors.

Coping With Turbulence, Gains, and Loses

Success in family life comes not from avoiding stressful events and problems, but in coping with them effectively. Author Unknown

INTRODUCTION

Challenges such as death in a family, loss of a home, or a broken arm can create stress in individuals and also in family processes. In some situations the stress can be severe, disabling, and enormously difficult. In other situations, the stress is more temporary, fleeting, and easy to cope with. Sometimes, the behavior of professionals increases the family stress.

Most families find themselves coping with stressful situations many times and many different ways, and it is not uncommon for a number of them to occur at the same time. This chapter describes the various types of stressor events that families experience, and it describes the effects they have on family processes. It also summarizes what is known about enabling and disabling strategies that families tend to use.

TYPES OF STRESSOR EVENTS

> *In our view family stress is often greatest at transition points from one stage to another of the family developmental process, and symptoms are most likely to appear when there is an interruption or dislocation in the unfolding family life cycle.* (Carter & McGoldrick, 1989, p. 4–5)

A stressor event is something that happens to a family that cannot be managed effectively with the family's usual ways of doing things. Some stressor events tend to cause more disruption in family processes than others. Holmes and Rahe (1967) developed a method of ranking the relative magnitude of various stressor events, and their ranking is shown below. The method they used was to ask 394 people to rate the seriousness of various changes people encounter. They gave marriage an arbitrary value, and asked them to compare other changes with this number. Their instructions said:

The Holmes and Rahe table is helpful because it demonstrates there are a large number of stressor events families encounter, and they occur in many different parts of life. Here are some of the stressors events listed by Homes and Rahe. In the Journal of Thoughts Exercise, you task is to examine the following events some of which come from the Holmes and Rahe research. Choose which ones you think would be the most dramatic for your family. Which ones would create the most disruption in your family?

STRESSOR EVENTS ORIGINATING OUTSIDE THE FAMILY REALM

War separation or reunion.
Social discrimination.
Economic depression.
Natural disasters: floods, tornadoes, hurricanes, etc.
Home being robbed or ransacked.
Banks going bankrupt and losing savings.
Family member in an airplane crash.
Political revolution.
Member of family being sued or arrested.

STRESSOR EVENTS ORIGINATING INSIDE THE FAMILY REALM

Alcoholism of a family member.
Senility of a family member.
A family member becoming mentally ill.
Serious illnesses: Cancer, heart attack, stroke, etc.
Rape of a member of the family.
Family member in trouble with the law.
Increased tasks and time commitments.
Automobile accidents.
Child running away.
Family member contracting AIDS.
Problems with schools.
Desertion or return of a deserter.
Unwanted pregnancy.
Inability to bear children.

Coping With Turbulence, Gains, and Loses

Adolescent in family prematurely pregnant.
Family member committing suicide.
An affair or emotional triangle.
Strained family relationships.
Infidelity.
Nonsupport.
Physical abuse of a family member.
Family member being sexually abused.
Prolonged or serious depression.
Child being born illegitimately.
Relative coming to live with family.
House burning.

When stressor events come one at a time, it is relatively easy for families to cope with them. However, it is common for several stressor events to happen at the same time, and for new ones to occur while the family is still dealing with previous stressor events. When this happens, it increases the difficulty families have in coping effectively with the new inputs. McCubbin and Patterson (1982) used the term *stress pile up* to refer to the stress that families experience from several changes occurring simultaneously, or several occurring in a short period of time.

FAMILY STRESS AS A PROCESS

Systems theory has a number of concepts that help us understand how families are different when they are experiencing stress. To understand what happens when stressor events occur, it is helpful to review what happens in a system when families are not in stressful situations.

When things are "normal" a family system is in a process of transforming inputs into outputs with relative ease. It transforms inputs such as energy, time, space, and behavior into love, attention, discipline, growth, development, satisfaction, bonds, heritage, closeness, learning, and security. To carry out these transformation processes, each family develops a large number of rules of transformation that govern the hourly, daily, and weekly routines and cycles of life. Some of the rules are explicit, but most of them are implicit "understandings" about how to do things. Each family is continually monitoring to see if the results are within the agreed-upon standards or limits in attaining the family goals.

Development and other changes create morphogenesis in a family, but during "normal" periods the morphogenetic tendencies are moderated by morphostatic tendencies. The result is a dynamic balancing of change and order, innovation and constancy, and creativity and predictability. There also is a continual balancing and rebalancing of the needs people have for togetherness and separateness, and the system is always responding to generational, emotional, affective, economic, social, and ecological factors outside and inside the family.

Even during those rare times when family life settles down to what can be considered "normal" family life, the family interactions are an evolving and dynamic flow of energy, resources, activity, tension, agreements, diversity, consensus, love, anger, new information, and old and new traditions. Additionally, there is a changing composition of age, gender, and involvement. As families evolve through time they develop what systems theorists call a *requisite variety* of rules of transformation. This means they develop enough rules about how things should be done that they are able to transform the inputs into outputs that meet minimal standards in attaining goals.

Stress occurs when the families realize that that some of the events and results do not meet acceptable standards. For example, if a new infant is born and the family has the "requisite variety" of rules to cope with the new input, there isn't stress. If the new infant is born with a serious handicap, this event can threaten the ability to create some desirable outputs—such as to have healthy, normal children, and that creates stress.

All of these kinds of events cause some kind of change in family life, but stressor events that the family does not know how to handle with its available rules, traditions, and patterns of interaction create changes that are stressful.

For example, if a family has not had any experience dealing with the juvenile courts, and the family is sitting in front of the house when a police car drives up they don't experience much stress. However, if the officer gets out, comes toward the family, and informs the family he is there to arrest the 17-year-old daughter, they may not have the "requisite variety" of rules to know how to deal with the situation, and stress begins. If the officer informs the daughter that because of a ticket she did not pay there

Coping With Turbulence, Gains, and Loses

---

1. Which type of stressor events do you think are the most problematic for you? Why?

   I think stressor events that originate within the family would be the most problematic. I think these would be more stressful because the problems are directly related to the family and are more likely to involve other family members. I think both stressor events originating inside and outside of the family can affect other family members, but stressor events that take place within the family are more likely to have an affect on the relationships family members have with eachother. The stressor events that originate outside of the family tend to be uncontrollable. While there is no doubt that stressor events of any kind can dramatically effect a person, I feel that stressor events inside the family would be more traumatic for me. I think this because my family & I would be more directly affected.

2. Tell about a serious stressor event your family faced when you were growing up. If you do not want to tell about this, think of a friend or neighbor.

When I was growing up I didn't really experience any of the stressor events listed. My mom did get divorced from my biological dad when I was two. It affected me a little because I would ask my mom about where he was. After a while I stopped asking about things and didn't really think about the separation. I think it would have been more of a stressor event for me if I was a little older + understood more of what was going on. I kinda knew what was happening, but my attachment to my dad wasn't as strong because I was not around him very much before my parents separation. That factor made it easier for me to transition.

is a warrant for her arrest and he needs to handcuff her and have her come with him to the police station, this type of situation is probably an "unusual" event for them and is, therefore, a stressor event. The parents may follow the police car to the station, help the child post bail and go home, but the family is now a bit different than it was before. For most, this would not be a life changing stressor event, but the immediate stress of this situation will remain as they develop new "understandings" or requisite variety of rules and can resume the normal routines of life.

PATTERNS IN FAMILY STRESS

When a stressor event occurs in a family, a number of processes can evolve. If the family is able to cope quickly, the normal family processes will not be as disrupted, and the family will be able to resume its normal routines and traditions. However, if the stressor event is serious enough that the family is not able to adjust quickly, other patterns will emerge.

There are two kinds of patterns that can emerge when a stressor event is so severe that the old ways of solving things do not work: an acute phase in which energy is directed toward minimizing the impact of the stress, and a reorganization phase in which the new reality is faced and accepted (McCubbin & Dahl, 1985, p. 154).

The acute stage of family stress is usually a short period of time. During this time families try to examine the breadth and width of the problem, they try to get routines back to "normal," they may attempt breaking the situation into manageable parts, getting their emotions under control, and trying to get information about the problem. During the reorganization stage they are creating new rules, changing the ways they

367

..

relate, gradually coming to terms with their emotions, getting help from others if they need it, trying to be adaptable, and learning how to accept the new realities.

When family scientists first began to study family stress in the 1930s and 1940s, they assumed that all families went through the "roller-coaster" pattern of adjustment that was first described by Koos (1946). After the stress occurs a family moves into a period of disorganization during the acute stage. During this period of time, some of the normal transformation processes are disrupted as the family's attention is diverted to dealing with the stress. If the family is able to make adjustments that cope effectively with the stressor event, they move into a period of recovery.

During the reorganization phase families rearrange their rules and transformation processes so they gradually recover. In some situations they are eventually better off than they were before the stressor event. For example, it may be stressful to move, but if the economic condition of the family improves after the move, the "normal" level of organization of the family may be higher. In other situations, a family may never recover fully from a stressor event, and the new "normal" level may be lower than before the crisis. This often occurs with problems such as a child in a family running away, conflict that can't be resolved, loss of trust in a relationship, alcoholism and other forms of substance abuse, and economic losses.

Recent research that suggests the Koos' roller-coaster pattern is an accurate description of the developmental pattern for some but not all families. Burr et al. (1994) interviewed families who had experienced six different types of stress, and they found the roller-coaster pattern was the response pattern only about half of the time. They found five different developmental patterns. About 18% of these families experienced a pattern they called increased effectiveness. In these families their family life became better as a result of the stressful situation, and the families didn't experience a period of disorganization. In 10% of the families the response pattern was no change; the family life didn't improve or get worse. About 5% of the families experienced decreased effectiveness, and 11% had a mixed pattern where they initially were better off and then experienced the roller-coaster pattern. This research helps us realize there are several different developmental patterns in the way families respond to stress.

There is a paradox in these insights. We usually don't think about stressful situations being desirable. We assume they bring pain, discomfort, anxiety, frustration, and anguish. Therefore, we usually assume it is better if we can avoid problems. While it is true that life would be simpler and less painful, it also is apparently true that when we back off and take a long-term view of life, we realize that stressful situations also can have beneficial aspects. And, ironically, when we look at the total life span and its experiences, we realize that some stress and problems are actually desirable.

One reason it is often "desirable" to encounter difficulties and stress is that sometimes when we experience pain, frustration, disappointment, tragedies, and other adversities we are able to experience the deepest and most satisfying joy, happiness, and sense of accomplishment and fulfillment. The joy that comes from being needed and from nursing loved ones who are ill, for example; the challenge of caring for a handicapped child can bring bonds of closeness, learning about the richness of sacrificing, abilities to be patient and loving, and insights about the subtle beauties of the human spirit that can be deeply rewarding.

COPING STRATEGIES

One of the goals of the scientists who have studied family stress has been to identify the coping strategies families find helpful in dealing with stressful situations. This research began in the 1930s (Angell, 1936), and there are now a large number of studies that have discovered many helpful strategies (McCubbin et al., 1980; Boss, 1987).

Coping strategies are processes, behaviors, or patterns of behaviors that families go through to adapt to stress (McCubbin & Dahl, 1985). According to Pearlin and Schooler (1982), having a large repertoire of coping strategies is more important than using one or two strategies well. They stated that:

> *It is apparent from the foregoing analyses that the kinds of responses and resources people are able to bring to bear in coping with life-strains make a difference to their emotional well-being. And it is equally apparent that there is no single coping mechanism so out-standingly effective that its possession alone would insure our ability to fend off the stressful consequences of strains. The magical wand does not appear in our results, and this suggests that having a particular weapon in one's arsenal is less important than having a variety of weapons.* (Pearlin & Schooler, 1982, p. 127)

LEVEL I STRATEGIES THAT ARE GENERALLY ENABLING OR DISABLING

Research has been conducted on a large number of stressor events, and there are several strategies that seem to be helpful in dealing with all of them and in all of the developmental stages of family stress. These strategies all deal with Level I processes in families. Burr et al. (1994) have suggested that the best way to think about these family coping strategies is to group them according to the seven different aspects.

It is helpful to understand that researchers have discovered these coping strategies focus on a wide range of stressor events. These include severe economic depression (Angell, 1936; Cavan & Ranck, 1938; Komorovsky, 1940, etc.) the trauma of fathers being drafted for military service, and also the adjustments that are necessary when they return after being gone for a long period of time (Hill, 1949), alcoholism (Jackson, 1956; Steinglass et al., 1987), divorce (Goode, 1956), famines

(Sorokin, 1941), having a mentally challenged child (Tizard & Grad, 1961), disasters such as floods and tornados (Young, 1954), and mental illness (Vogel & Bell, 1967). This is only a partial list: the research continues to grow in volume every day.

Cognitive strategies.   These strategies are things families can do intellectually or mentally to help them cope with stress. Many researchers have found that having an optimistic or positive attitude when faced with problems is an effective coping strategy (Caplan, 1964; McCubbin, Balling, Possin, Frierdich, & Bryne, 2002). Practical methods of keeping a positive attitude include focusing on the positive aspects of life, visualizing a good outcome, and finding ways to help feel in control of the situation.

Part of the reason this strategy is helpful is because the attitude families have about stressful situations tends to become a self-fulfilling prophecy. Recall the *Perception as Reality Principle* from Chapter Two. This principle says simply: If people define situations as real, they are real in their consequences.

Therefore, when the members of a family develop a positive attitude and believe they can cope effectively, they tend to cope effectively. When they believe a situation is too difficult to cope with, it tends to actually make it more difficult than it would be if they had different beliefs.

When people have confidence in their ability to cope with a situation they tend to have different "striving behaviors" than when they believe they are defeated. They invest more energy and try harder. They tend to focus on solutions rather than the overwhelming aspects of the problem situation, and this makes them more effective in finding and implementing solutions. Also, these attitudes often are contagious, and others often work harder and more effectively when a positive attitude prevails.

This principle does not mean that families should be unrealistic in their attitudes, and it doesn't mean that merely having a positive attitude will do everything that needs to be done to cope with stressor events. A positive attitude can simultaneously exist with realism, a good knowledge of the realities of situations, and efforts toward solving problems. What this idea means is that the "definition of the situation" tends to have a predictable influence on how seriously stressor events influence families and on how families tend to cope.

Another of the cognitive strategies is getting accurate information. Kaplan et al. (1973) found in their research about how families cope with serious illnesses such as leukemia that it helps families if they get accurate information as soon as possible. It seems as though this would be an obvious thing to do, but research about how families actually operate in stressful situations indicates a large number of families do not do this well.

Of the families studied, 87% failed to resolve successfully even the initial task of coping—that is, the tasks associated with confirmation of the diagnosis. Parents' reactions vary but fall into certain recognizable classes. Their most common reaction is to deny the reality of the diagnosis in as many ways as possible. Such parents avoid those who refer to the illness as leukemia. They themselves use euphemisms (for

Coping With Turbulence, Gains, and Loses

example, virus, anemia, blood disease) in speaking of the child's illness. They may even be fearful that the child will hear the news from someone outside the family (Kaplan et al., 1973).

In addition, the Kaplan research team found that it is helpful if all of the family members who are mature enough to understand are informed about the nature of the problem and the seriousness of it. All of the family having accurate and prompt information allows the family to properly mourn if necessary, to face up to future consequences, to make plans, and to take realistic action (Kaplan et al., 1973).

Without knowledge about details of the stressor event and how it might affect the family, none of these things can be done. Without information at the first, it is difficult to engage in short term or long term coping strategies such as finding ways to acquire social and emotional support and construct a realistic but positive definition of the situation. In addition, people who do not receive information promptly tend to become anxious and angered when a stressful situation is occurring. Often they concentrate on the worst possible alternatives, invent unrealistic expectations and explanations, and jump to false conclusions. Thus, the lack of information tends usually to make situations worse than they should be.

Another aspect of cognitive strategies is that when stressor events are precipitated by events outside the family, families seem to be able to deal with them more easily and effectively (Angell, 1936; Hill, 1949, etc.). This finding has several implications for the acute stage of coping. One implication is to try to externalize blame if possible. Another is to realize that, when it is not possible to attribute the blame outside the family, it is an important issue for the family that needs to be dealt with carefully. If someone in the family is blamed for the stressor event, the blaming itself tends to be another stressor event that can create a number of emotional, interpersonal, and perceptual reactions.

Communication strategies. There are a number of communication-oriented strategies that families seem to find helpful. Just having someone to "listen" and "try to understand" can be enormously helpful. Trying to be honest and open in communication also tends to be helpful in most families. Two other communication strategies that tend to be helpful are to be empathetic and be sensitive to non-verbal messages (McCubbin & Figley, 1983).

Emotional strategies. Research about family stress documents that stressor events tend to create strong emotional reactions. For example, when disasters strike, people become frantic in their attempts to locate members of their family. When couples discover they are not able to bear children it usually takes years to adjust to the deeply felt emotional reactions (Snowden & Snowden, 1984).

Another aspect of managing emotions is that with some stressor events, such as chronic illnesses, families find themselves dealing with the painful emotions over and over again. They get their feelings resolved at one stage of the illness, but as the illness moves to a new stage or new experiences occur, the emotional reactions re-surface, and they need to deal again and again with feelings such as helplessness, loss, and "why does this happen?"

According to Caplan (1964) and McCubbin et al. (2002), the management of emotions involves two fairly different processes: (1) being aware of the emotions and fatigue, and (2) finding constructive ways to release or come to terms with the emotions.

The Differentiation/Fusion principle described in Chapter Eight helps us realize that when emotions become intense they tend to "take over." When emotions intensify, they can incapacitate a family, and interfere with the process of coping with the stressful event. Families who are effective at coping with stress gradually learn that when emotions become intense, the attempts to "be sensible" and "reasonable" and "get things done" need temporarily to be set aside while the emotional reactions are dealt with.

To ignore the emotions, pretend they don't exist, or tell people they "shouldn't feel that way" doesn't eliminate them. It just forces the emotions into the part of the family "iceberg" that is below the surface, where family members are not aware of what is going on. Usually what happens in these situations is the emotions find a way to surface in other ways. Some examples of other ways emotions can surface are: People get angry at minor incidents, they lose their temper often, they develop physical illnesses such as having an upset stomach or always being tired or depressed, they turn to excesses with alcohol or sex, etc. Therefore, emotions that are involved in a stressful experience need to be dealt with so they do not make coping more difficult. This can be facilitated by using the family as a collective support group, hugging, talking with others, being close, crying, reassuring, listening, getting feelings out, and being around loved ones.

Changing relationships.   The first generalization that was developed in the research about family stress is the idea that being flexible, pliable, or willing to change is helpful. Usually family scientists use the term adaptability to describe this. One of the first studies was by Robert Angell (1936), and this idea was the main conclusion his book contributed to the field. Since then, this idea has been found again and again to be an important coping strategy (Caplan, 1964; McCubbin et al., 1988; Boss, 1987, etc.).

Adaptability is in essence the ability to be flexible and try something new. Families with this ability tend to be more accepting of change and therefore "roll with the punches" so to speak. Families that are relatively adaptable are also more willing to try other coping strategies at all levels of change. In addition, this willingness to try more coping strategies will end up helping the family be more proficient at the use of a wider variety of coping strategies, which increases their requisite variety.

The various parts of family life tend to be intertwined. Therefore, changes in one part of the family tend to influence other parts. Kaplan et al., (1973) recognized this interdependence and suggested that it is helpful if the individuals in families can

JOURNAL OF THOUGHTS 11.2: RESOURCES

1. What do you think is the most important resource a person could have in times of stress and crisis? Why?

The most important resource a person could have are coping strategies. These help people behave in affective ways, while coping with the stress at the same time. If there is no coping strategy there will be chaos in the persons life & behaviors. They wouldn't be able to separate the crisis from the rest of their daily functions. Coping strategies could be therapeutic or just having someone to talk to about their problems. This makes the crisis easier to deal with. People should not ignore emotions or pretend they don't exist. Adaptability is also very crucial in getting through hard times & making changes accordingly.

2. List the resources you have that you could use to respond to a crisis if one happened today (a Level II or III crisis)

If a crisis happened today, I would have some family & friends to talk to. There are always services at Purdues Student Wellness Center to talk about stressor events and concerns. If I had a crisis, I would talk to my family & professional if needed. If I really needed to change my fundamental beliefs I would try to make adjustments to fit what needed to be changed. I also think religion would be helpful to give me strength & clarity about my life. I think believing that things will get better really helps people get through tough times b/c it gives them something positive to think about.

cope and mourn together when serious stressor events occur. A family can offer its individual members the potential of mutual support and access to its collective coping experience. According to Hill (1958), when helping an individual cope or handle stress, the individual should be treated as a family member not as an independent individual. Thus, again, the idea that the family realm has more impact than most people realize keeps emerging. Here again, the emotional, generational, and other ties to the family are so great that they are dealt with the most effectively when there is a network of family members who are involved.

Thus, families who can emotionally lean on each other have an advantage when dealing with life's problems. As McCubbin et al. (2002) observed, maintaining family togetherness, even by taking the time to do little things with the children and plan family outings, is an effective coping strategy for dealing with family stress.

Spiritual strategies. Many families find it helpful to turn to spiritual sources for strength, meaning, and assistance when they are experiencing family stress. These strategies include such things as praying, trying to have more faith or seek help from one's God and becoming more involved in religious activities.

Strategies with the environment. Families can do many things with their environment to help them cope with stress. Support can come from family members, friends, work, clubs, police, churches, etc. In addition to varying in source, social support also can vary in the type of support it is. It can be emotional, financial, physical, mental, etc.

Many studies indicate that social support makes individuals and families less vulnerable when they experience such stressor events as losing a job or participating in a difficult line of work (Cobb, 1982; Gore, 1978; Maynard et al., 1980); raising a chronically ill child (Nevin, 1979); recovering from a natural disaster (Erickson et al., 1976); or adjusting to war-induced separations (McCubbin et al., 1976; McCubbin & Dahl, 1985, p. 156).

Cobb (1982) stated that social support was an exchange of information between the family and environment that provided families with: (1) emotional support, leading the recipients to believe they are cared for and loved, (2) self esteem, leading them to believe they are valued, and (3) network support which gives them a sense of belonging.

Bronfenbrenner's (1979) review of the research in this area added an important new insight to the role of supportiveness inside families and in the amount of support families receive from the community and friends. When individuals and families are not coping with stressful events, it is growth producing to have considerable independence and autonomy and to have relatively little overt help, assistance, or support. However, when things are not going well, it then is helpful to have more supportiveness inside the family and between the family and the community. Another way of saying Bronfenbrenner's idea is that high supportiveness tends to be enabling when dealing with serious stressor events, but it can actually be disabling when things are going well.

Individual development. There is some research that suggests it can be helpful to focus on some aspects of individual development. Some of these strategies are such things as trying to promote self-sufficiency (without overdoing it), working out to keep physically fit, and being sure to keep up one's obligations to other organizations such as one's employment.

Disabling strategies. Research has identified a number of ways of responding to stressor events that seem to usually have disabling or destructive effects. One of these is to react with violence. A number of research studies have found people tend to be more violent when experiencing stressful situations such as undesirable behavior by a child, unemployment, unhappiness in their marriage or in their employment, or illnesses (Christoffersen, 2000; Gelles, 1974; Gil, 1970; Lyoyd & Taluc, 1999; Steinmetz, 1979). The violence, however, tends to make the situations worse. It destroys positive emotional feelings toward the violent individuals and creates a number of negative emotions such as mistrust, anger, confusion, shame, and hate.

Other strategies that usually are disabling are denial, avoidance, rejection, increased use of alcohol, hostility, producing garbled and dishonest communication about the problem, preventing communication, prohibiting and interrupting individual and collective grieving within the family, and weakening family relationships precisely when they most need to be strengthened (Kaplan et al., 1973, p. 67; McCubbin et al., 1980). These strategies usually aggravate the original problem and create other problems such as less ability to plan solutions for the original problem (Kaplan, 1973).

COPING STRATEGIES AT HIGHER LEVELS OF ABSTRACTION

Chapter 5 described three different "levels" of abstraction in family life. Level I refers to the observable processes of daily interaction. Level II refers to meta-level processes or the rules about the rules, and Level III refers to the family paradigms, or the abstract beliefs and assumptions that make up a family's philosophy of life or "world-view."

These three levels are helpful in understanding how stressor events influence families and how families try to cope with stress because families seem to do different things when they are focusing on Level I processes than when they are forced to deal with Level II processes or their paradigmatic beliefs and assumptions.

According to Robert Burr's (1989) theory of family stress, families tend to focus on Level I processes when they start into the recovery stage of family stress. If the Level I changes are enough, families don't bother to disrupt the more complicated and fundamental parts of Level II processes. However, if their Level I attempts to cope

Coping With Turbulence, Gains, and Loses

SPOTLIGHT ON RESEARCH 11.1: INTERGENERATIONAL TRANSMISSION OF DIVORCE

Feng, Giarrusso, Bengtson, and Frye (1999) published an article that shows how there is an effect of the parent's marriage on their children's marital quality. The research about divorce shows that if your parents divorce there is a dramatic increase in the chance that you will also (Amato, 1996; Bumpass, Martin, & Sweet, 1991; Glenn & Kramer, 1987). The effects of getting divorced on your children's marital quality seems to hold more true for women than men. However, how this happens has been something of a mystery to researchers. Researchers have wondered if it was associated with life course factors, education levels, family support and help, communication and other inner family processes, or individual ideologies and paradigms. The argument is that children adopt the ideologies of their parents, know the same friends, have similar upbringing, and share the same neighborhoods. For example, we know that economic well-being is passed from one generation to the next. So, also, could the propensity to divorce.

These authors found that the intergenerational transmission of divorce was much stronger from parents to daughters and not as strong for sons. They also found that there were several conditions that contributed to the divorce of both parents and children. That is, some events had large effects on the chances of getting a divorce. For example, events such as schooling, lower levels of socio-economic orientation, and most important how young the people got married were all factors. In other words, while divorce itself was an important consideration, more important was whether the child and parents had similar life course contexts influencing their relationships. Children whose parents got married earlier both got divorced and sent a message to their children about getting married earlier. The patterns seem to transmitted, not just the one event of getting divorced.

These authors indicated that some parents are poor role models for a variety of interpersonal behaviors, decision making skills, and for skills that exemplify relationship connection. This study offers hope. Many young people believe that if their parents get a divorce, there is little they do about the higher chance they will also get one. On the contrary, this research suggests that what the parents pass on (or don't pass on) are certain skills that help us avoid trouble. Those skills can be learned and patterns from the past can be broken. It is often difficult, but can be done.

Your response:
Children of divorce are more likely to divorce themselves. In your own words, why do you think this is?

are not effective, they eventually find it necessary to deal with Level II phenomena such as their meta-rules, their way of governing the family, the hierarchies of power, etc. If families are able to deal effectively with their stressful situations by dealing with these Level II aspects, they do not usually question or revise their family paradigms. However, if their attempts to cope by dealing with Level II processes don't cope effectively with the stress, they eventually find themselves re-examining their basic assumptions and philosophy of life.

Level II coping. When families are able to deal effectively with stressor events by using Level I processes, they return to a "normal" level of functioning. When this happens, life can go on in a normal way, and attention is again returned to other things such as the job, career, arts, sports, leisure, service, etc.

Many times, however, the Level I coping strategies aren't successful, and when this is the case, families gradually find themselves in a deeper and deeper crisis. In these situations, merely rearranging rules or changing the superficial or obvious aspects of the family is not enough. The family needs to make more fundamental changes.

Several examples of this process help illustrate what is involved with Level II crises. If a child has broken a serious family rule, that event will usually be defined as a "Level I" crisis and try to use Level I strategies to cope. They will do such things as use more severe disciplinary methods such as grounding the child more, restricting privileges, withholding resources, changing rules, etc. If these methods do not solve the problem, the parents may need to reevaluate their whole approach toward discipline, and this is a Level II process. For example, they may need to realize they have been using methods of discipline that are appropriate for a young child, but their child is old enough that they need to use a set of more "adult" methods of relating to the child.

Another example is what happens in some marriages when one spouse wants to change the relationship. For example, a couple may have grown up in more traditional families where the males were dominant and females submissive, but one spouse gradually decides she or he does not like that type of relationship. This type of change is usually a stressor event, and merely changing Level I rules may not be enough. For example, he may believe that "letting" her have her own checking account, "letting" her get a job, or "letting" her take classes at the university may not be enough. The couple may need to rearrange fundamental aspects of their relationship. For example, they may need to change the idea that the husband is supposed to "let" the wife do things, and move to an equalitarian relationship where neither of them is responsible for what the other does. Changes such as these are more complicated, abstract, and fundamental than Level I changes because they deal with the "rules about the rules."

Another example of the difference between Level I and Level II coping is the way a family might respond to a child starting to use illegal drugs. A Level I strategy that deals with family boundaries would be to restrict the child's friends. This would change the family boundaries so they are less open. However, the change would just be in one area of the family boundaries, so it would only be a Level I change. However,

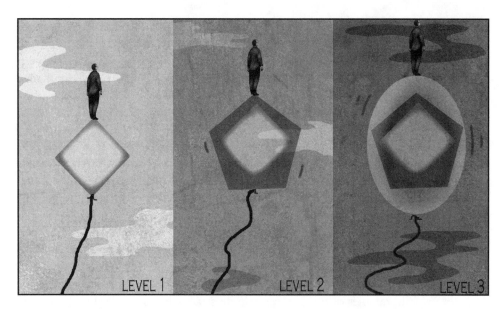

if this did not work, the family may decide the family boundaries in general are too open, and they may decide to become more closed overall. This would be a Level II change because it would change a more fundamental aspect of the family processes.

Many families use Level II methods, but most of them probably are not aware of the differences in abstraction involved. It is likely that most families would need to study these concepts in a family science course or get professional help to understand these differences. Some of the coping strategies that are involved in second order or Level II change are getting professional help, making implicit rules explicit, reviewing basic methods of coping, discussing the rules about how rules are made and changed in the family, and discussing the methods that are used in decision making.

Pauline Boss (1975, 1988, 1998) introduced another concept into the field that deals with Level II coping strategies. The concept is boundary ambiguity. This occurs when families are uncertain in their perception of who is in or out of the family or who is performing what roles and tasks within the family. Her initial research was with military families and families who experience Alzheimer's disease. Military families find this problem especially severe when the father is listed as missing-in-action (MIA). The problem also occurs with families experiencing divorce, joint custody, desertion, and some chronic illnesses.

When families, or professionals working with families, understand this concept, they can use it to help families cope because they can try to get the ambiguity within tolerable limits. Some strategies for helping families deal with their boundary ambiguity are to talk about who is in and out of the family, whether family members will be in or out for an identifiable period of time, and what the boundaries inside the family ought to be. Other strategies are to avoid keeping a physically absent family member psychologically present when it is disruptive for the family.

===

Level III coping. When families are able to deal effectively with stressor events by using Level I or Level II processes, they return to a "normal" state. However, in some situations, families are not able to manage the new events with these strategies. When this occurs, the family gradually slips into a deeper and more serious crisis situation.

When this happens, the very fabric of the family is in trouble, and the paradigmatic assumptions are called into question. The family's basic philosophy and orientations to life are examined, and these basic beliefs may evolve, change, be discarded, or reconstructed.

Examples of this would be changes in the way a family relates to its environment, changes in beliefs about who the family can "count on" when the chips are down, changes in beliefs about God and the role of the spiritual part of life, changes in beliefs about whether people are inherently good or bad, and differentiation from kin.

The following illustrates the differences that are involved in a Level III crisis. If a family that did not believe in drug use found themselves in a situation where a teenage boy was adopting a life style that they did not understand, this could be a serious stressor event. The first strategies this family would tend to use involve trying to create Level I changes. There are many different specifics that this or other families could do to create Level I change. For example, the parents could talk to the son about his life and why he was making the choices he was. If these particular Level I methods do not work, the family might try other Level I changes such as making him come in earlier, grounding him, and taking away resources such as his access to money, etc. There is no limit to the specific Level I changes that families can try.

If the Level I methods take care of the stress then there is no need to try additional coping strategies. However, if they do not work, the family would eventually resort to more fundamental changes, Level II changes. They may try to change their basic parenting methods, try to get professional assistance to make other changes, change where the child lives, or change the basic structure of the family.

If these Level II methods do not work, the family will tend eventually to question some of their basic beliefs. For example, they may adopt a more fatalistic view of life and conclude that things will happen as they will and they have less control over their world than they thought they had. They may rearrange their priorities in life and become more or less involved in trying to change their community values and structure. They may reevaluate their beliefs about the choice their children make try to understand him or her more fully.

COPING STRATEGIES THAT ARE RELEVANT FOR SPECIFIC SITUATIONS

Some stressor events are relatively different from other stressor events, and some of the strategies that are helpful in one context are not helpful in others. We have only begun to discover what it is that is unique about different types of stressors, but a few ideas have been developed. This section of the chapter reviews some of the strategies that are helpful in coping with specific types of stressful processes.

Coping with death. Death is a very important part of family life. As Freedman has observed:

> *Death is the single most important event in family life. From an individual point of view it marks the end; from a family point of view it is often a beginning that initiates processes in the family that can continue for generations.* (Freedman, 1988, p. 168)

With most stressor events, it is helpful if families to try to eliminate the stress process as quickly as possible. For example, if someone has lost their job, the speed with which a new job is found correlates with the stress levels. If families acquire a new member, lose a member, have an accident, have an illness, etc., the family tends to have less disruption, and the crisis is coped with best if it is resolved quickly.

Death, however, is an exception to this general rule. When a member of a family dies it creates such a wide range of emotional reactions, and the emotions are so deep and fundamental, that it takes a long period of time to work through them. As Walsh and McGoldrick (1988) observed, "the process of mourning is likely to take at least 1 to 2 years, with each new season, holiday, and anniversary re-evoking the loss" (p. 311).

One way family scientists think about this principle is to talk about the "angle of recovery" in the bottom of the roller-coaster diagram. A number of research studies have found that, with most stressor events, the smaller the angle of recovery the better for the family (Hill, 1949; Waller & Hill, 1951, p. 468). With death, however, a larger angle is more effective because it allows the family time to experience the mourning and bereavement that is necessary.

Another activity that is helpful in coping with death is to assemble family members to provide a time when they can work through unresolved concerns and begin the process of reorganizing family processes.

Interpersonal and occupational stressors. Different resources are helpful in situations where the main concerns are emotional than when occupational and economic stress occurs. Pearlin and Schooler (1982, p. 134) found that with relatively impersonal stressor events, such as those stemming from economic or occupational experiences, the most effective forms of coping involved the manipulation of goals and values in a way which increases the emotional distance of the individual from the problem. On the other hand, problems arising from the relatively close interpersonal relations in the family realm are best handled by coping mechanisms in which the individual remains committed to, and engaged with, the relevant others. In other words,

JOURNAL OF THOUGHTS 11.3: WHAT CAN YOU DO?

1. Think about the types of crisis events you probably will face in the future (next 10 years, or so). What can you do prepare? Why is it important to think about preparing?

In the next ten years I will have more commitments with work and family. I will have the responsibility of a career and raising a family at the same time. Hopefully I won't have to deal with crisises, but sometimes it is inevitable, my parents will be aging, and I may have to deal with their illnesses + the changes in their roles. I think the best way to prepare for a crisis is to realize that they are out of your control + what is done is done. It is however important to have coping strategies. The strategies are needed to get people through the tough times + help them adjust.

2. What kinds of crisis can you not really prepare for?

I think most stressor events that occur outside of the family are difficult to prepare for.

3. Is it better to face a crisis that you have anticipated or one that is a surprise? Why?

ACTIVITY 11.1 - ANALYZE A FAMILY CRISIS

Find a family crisis by first finding an example to use. You may use an example from a film (*Accidental Tourist, The River, Hoop Dreams, Places in the Heart*, to name a few), novel, or actual family event from your family or one you know.

Part I. Describe the crisis the family is experiencing in detail. What are the primary incidences that we need to understand?

Part II. What type of stressor events are these? (Internal to the family? External? Chronic or short term, etc.).

Part III. What resources could they have brought to bare on the situation?

Part IV. What new resources did they seek out? If they didn't seek out new resources, what resources could they have sought out?

Part V. What was the result? How did the situation end?

when dealing with stress in the family, it is better to keep close relationships and not to avoid the individuals, the relationships, or the stress.

Because people can move in and out of the business world relatively easily, it is relatively easy and helpful in the public realms to make changes that will distance stressful situations. However, because the family realm is unique in that there is a certain permanence to family relationships, it is more difficult and even unhealthy to avoid or distance self from most problems inside the family realm.

SUMMARY

There are a large number of events that create stress in families, and some stressor events are more serious than others. Also, some of them come from the environment, and others come from inside the family. The process of family stress has phases and there seem to be five different patterns in the way families respond to stress: a roller-coaster pattern where some families experience disorganization followed by reorganization, a descending pattern where some families become disorganized and stay there, an ascending pattern, where some families get better off in a stressful situation and stay there, a no change pattern and a mixed pattern where some families are better off and then have the roller-coaster experience. Research about families has begun to identify coping strategies that families can use to deal effectively with stressful situations and seven different types of coping strategies were discussed. During the recovery stage of family stress, families use Level I, Level II, and Level III coping strategies.

Chapter 11

STUDY QUESTIONS:

1. Name four types of stressor events.

2. Name three stressful events that can originate outside the family.

3. What are the primary elements of the stress process?

4. Give an example of a Level II stressor event and then tell how a family could generate a coping strategy to match.

5. Why would the suicide of a family member be so devastating? Use the information in this chapter to explain your answer.

KEY TERMS

Stressor events
Coping strategies
Levels of coping

Bibliography

Bibliography

Alexander, J. F. (1973). Defensive and supportive communication in family systems. *Journal of Marriage and the Family, 35*, 613-617.

Allport, G. (1937). *Personality: a psychological interpretation.* New York: H. Holt and Company.

Amato, P. R. (1996). Explaining the intergenerational transmission of divorce. *Journal of Marriage and the Family, 58*, 628-640.

Anderson, S. A., & Fleming, W. M. (1986). Late adolescents' identity formation: Individuation from the family of origin. *Adolescence, 21*, 785-796.

Angell, R.C. (1936). *The family encounters the depression.* New York: Scribner.

Aries, E. (1982). Verbal and nonverbal behavior in single-sex and mixed-sex groups are traditional sex roles changing. *Psychological Reports, 51*, 127.

Aries, E. (1996). *Men and women in interaction: Reconsidering the differences.* New York, NY, US: Oxford University Press.

Bader, E., Microys, G., Sinclair, C., Willet, E., & Conway, B. (1980). Do marriage preparation programs really work?: A Canadian experiment. *Journal of Marriage and Family Therapy, 6*, 171-179.

Ball, F. L., Cowan, J. P., & Cowan, C. P. (1995). Who's got the power? Gender differences in partners' perceptions of influence during marital problem-solving discussions. *Family Process, 34*, 303-321.

Barnes, M., & Buss, D. (1985). Sex difference in the interpersonal behavior of married couples. *Journal of Personality & Social Psychology, 48*, 657-661.

Bartle-Haring, S., & Sabatelli, R. (1998). An intergenerational examination of patterns of individual and family adjustments. *Journal of Marriage and the Family, 60*, 903-911.

Bartle, S. E., & Sabatelli, R.M. (1989). Family system dynamics, identity development, and adolescent alcohol use: Implications for family treatment. *Family Relations, 38*, 158-265.

Baydar, N., & Brooks-Gunn, J. (1998). Profiles of grandmothers who help care for their grandchildren in the United States: The family as a context for health and well-being [Special Issue]. *Family Relations: Interdisciplinary Journal of Applied Family Studies, 47*, 385-393.

Bavelas, W.R., & Segal, L. (1982). Family system theory: Background and implications. *Journal of Communication, 32*, 99-107.

Baxter, L.A., & Wilmont, W. (1985). Taboo topics in close relationships. *Journal of Social and Personal Relationships, 2*, 253-269.

Beavers, W. R. (1982). Healthy, midrange and severely dysfunctional families. In F. Walsh (Ed.), *Normal Family Processes.* (pp. 45-66.). New York: Guildford.

Beavers, W.R. (1985). *Successful Marriage.* New York: Norton.

Beck, A. (1988). Anxiety and depression: An information processing perspective. *Anxiety Research, 1*, 23-36.

Bell, R. A., Daly, J. A., & Gonzalez, M.C. (1987). Affinity-Maintenance in marriage and its relationship to women's marital satisfaction. *Journal of Marriage and the Family, 49*, 445-454.

Bennett, L. A., Wolin, S.J., Reiss, D., & Teitelbaum, M.A. (1987). Couples at risk for transmission of alcoholism: Protective influences. *Family Process, 26*, 111-129.

Berger, P., Kellner, & Hansfried (1973). Marriage and the construction of reality. In Glazer-Malbin, Nona & Waehrer, Helen Youngelson (Eds.), *Woman in A Man-Made World: A Socioeconomic Handbook* (pp. 22-58). New York: Rand McNally & Company.

Beutler, I. F., Burr, W. R., Bahr, K. S., & Herrin, D. A. (1989). The family realm: Theoretical contribution for understanding its uniqueness. *Journal of Marriage and the Family, 51*, 805-830.

Bischoping, K. (1993). Gender differences in conversation topics, 1922-1990. *Sex Roles, 28*, 1-18.

Blood, R. O., & Wolfe, D. M. (1960). *Husbands and Wives.* New York: Free Press.

Bibliography

Blum, J., & Mehrabian, A. (1999). Personality and temperament correlates of marital satisfaction. *Journal of Personality, 67*, 93-125.

Bograd, R. & Spilka, B. (1996). Self-disclosure and marital satisfaction in mid-life and late-life remarriages. *International Journal of Aging & Human Development, 42*, 161-172.

Booth, A., Carver, K., & Granger, D. A. (2000). Biosocial perspectives on the family. *Journal of Marriage and the Family, 62*, 1018-1034.

Borceaux, F. (2001). Cambridge studies in advanced mathematics. Cambridge, MA: Cambridge University Press.

Boss, P. (1975). *Psychological father absence and presence: A theoretical formulation for an investigation in to family systems interaction.* Unpublished doctoral dissertation, University of Wisconsin.

Boss, P. (1987). Family stress. In M.B. Sussman & S. K. Steinmetz (Eds.), *Handbook of Marriage and the Family,* 22-42.

Boss, P. (1988). *Family Stress Management.* Newbury Park, CA: Sage.

Boss, P. (1998). *Ambiguous Loss.* Cambridge, MA: Harvard University Press.

Bossard, J.S., & Boll, E.S. (1950). *Ritual in family living.* Philadelphia: University of Pennsylvania Press.

Boszormenyi-Nagy, I., & Sparks, G.M. (1973). *Invisible loyalties: Reciprocity in intergenerational therapy.* New York: Gardner.

Botwin M. D., Buss, D. M., & Shackelford, T. K. (1997). Personality and mate preferences: five factors in mate selection and marital satisfaction. *Journal of Personality, 65*, 107-36.

Bouchard, G., Lussier, Y., & Sabourin, S. (1999). Personality and marital adjustment: utility of the five-factor model of personality. *Journal of Marriage and the Family, 61*, 651-660.

Bowen, M. (1976). Theory in the practice of psychotherapy. In P. Guerin (Ed.), *Family Therapy.* New York: Gardner.

Boyce, W. R., Jenson, E. W., James, S. A., & Peacock, J. L. (1983). The family routines inventory: Theoretical origins. *Social Science Medicine, 17*, 193-200.

Broderick, C. B. (1988). *Marriage and the Family.* Englewood Cliffs, NJ: Prentice-Hall.

Broderick, C. B. (1993). *Understanding family process: Basics of family systems theory.* Newbury Park, CA: Sage.

Brody, N., & Ehrlichman, H. (1998). *Personality psychology: The science of individuality.* Upper Saddle River, New Jersey: Prentice-Hall.

Bronfenbrenner, U. (1979). *The ecology of human development.* Cambridge, MA: Harvard University Press.

Bumpass, L.L., Martin, T. C., & Sweet, J.A. (1991). The impact of family background and early marital factors on marital disruption. *Journal of Family Issues,* 22-42

Burgess, A. W., et al. (1978). *Sexual assault of children and adolescents.* Lexington, MA: D. C. Heath.

Burr, et al. (1994). *Reexamining family stress: New theory and research.* Thousand Oaks, CA, US: Sage.

Burr, R. G. (1989). Reframing family stress theory. Unpublished master's thesis, Brigham Young University, UT. Later published as Chapter 2 in W.R. Burr & S. Klein(1994). *Managing Family Stress* (pp. 8-28). Newbury Park, CA: Sage.

Burr, W. T. (1973). *Theory construction and the sociology of the family.* New York: Wiley.

Burr, W. R., Leigh, G. K., Day, R. D., & Constantine, J. (1979). Symbolic interaction and the family. In W. R. Burr, R. Hill, F. I. Nye & I. L. Reiss (Eds.), *Contemporary theories about the family* (Vol. II, pp. 42-111). New York: Free Press.

Camden, C. T., & Kennedy, C. W. (1986). Manager communicative style and nurse morale. *Human Communication Research, 12*, 551-563.

Caplan, G. (1964). *Principles of preventive psychiatry.* New York: Basic Books.

Carter, B., & McGoldrick, M. (Eds.). (1989). *The changing family life cycle: A framework for family therapy (2nd ed.).* New York: Allyn and Bacon.

Bibliography

Cashdan, E. (1995). Hormones, sex, and status in women. *Hormones & Behavior, 29,* 354-366.

Cashdan, E. A. (1985). Natural fertility, birth spacing, and the "first demographic transition." *American Anthropologist, 87,* 650-656.

Caughlin, J. P., & Vangelisti, A. L. (1999). Desire for change in one's partner as a predictor of the demand/withdraw pattern of marital communication. *Communication Monographs, 66,* 66-89.

Cavan, R. S., & Ranck, K. H. (1938). *The family and the depression.* Chicago: University of Chicago Press.

Cherlin, A. J. (1999). *Public and private families: An introduction (2nd ed.).* New York: McGraw-Hill.

Christoffersen, M. N. (2000). Growing up with unemployment: a study of parental unemployment and children's risk of abuse and neglect based on national longitudinal 1973 birth cohorts in Denmark. England: Sage Publications.

Chun, Y., & MacDermid, S. (1997). Perceptions of family differentiation, individuation, and self-esteem among Korean adolescents. *Journal of Marriage & the Family, 59,* 451-462.

Cobb, S. (1982). Social support and health through the life course. In H. I. McCubbin, A. E. Cauble, & J. M. Patterson (Eds.) *Family stress, coping and social support* (pp. 351-372). Thousand Oaks, CA: Sage.

Coleman, J. S. (1988). Social capital in the creation of human capital. *American Journal of Sociology, 94 (suppl):* S95-S120.

Coleman, J. S. (1990). *Foundations of social theory.* Cambridge, Mass: Belknap Press of Harvard University Press.

Condry, J., & Condry, S. (1976). *Sex differences: A study of the eye of the beholder. Child Development, 47,* 812-819.

Constantine, L. L. (1986). *Family paradigms.* New York: Guilford Press.

Cottrell, L. S., Jr. (1942). The adjustment of the individual to his age and sex roles. *American Sociological Review, 7,* 617-620.

Crocker, C. (1973). *Shaughnessy.* New York: Basic Books.

Cronen, V., Pearce, W., & Harris, L. (1979). The logic of the coordinated management of meaning: A rule-based approach to the first course in inter-personal communication. *Communication Education, 23,* 22-38.

Curran, D. (1983). *Traits of a healthy family.* Minneapolis, MN: Winston Press.

Daly, K. (1996). *Families in time: Keeping Pace in a hurried culture.* Newbury Park, CA: Sage.

Davis, J. A., & Smith, T. W. (1996). General social surveys, 1972-1996. *Cumulative Codebook.* Chicago: National Opinion Research Center.

Day, R.D., Gavazzi, S., & Acock, A. (2000). Compelling family process. In Thornton, A. (Ed.) The well-being of children and families. Ann Arbor MI: University of Michigan Press.

D'Antonia, M. (1998, December). The 5 minutes that changed their worlds. *Redbook,* 1998, 132-137.

Dickson-Markman, F., & Markman, H. J. (1988). The effects of others on marriage: Do they help or hurt? In P. Noller & M. A. Fitzpatrick (Eds.), *Perspectives on Marital Interaction* (pp.33-63). Philadelphia, PA: Multilingual Matters.

Doty, W. G. (1986). *Mythography: The study of myths and rituals,* University, AL: University of Alabama Press.

Druckman, J. M. (1979). *Effectiveness of five types of pre-marital preparations programs.* Grand Rapids, MI: Education for Marriage.

Duck, S. (1997). *Handbook of personal relationships: theory, research, and interventions.* Chichester, New York: John Wiley & Sons.

Duncan, G.J., Hill, M. S., & Hoffman, S. D. (1988). Welfare dependence within and across generations. *Science, 239,* 467-471.

Duvall, E. (1955). *Family Development.* New York: Lippincott.

Ehrlich, F. (2000). Dialogue, couple therapy, and the unconscious. *Contemporary Psychoanalysis, 36*, 483-503.

Elkin, M. (1984). *Families under the influence: Changing alcoholic patterns*, New York: Norton.

Erickson, P. E., Drabek, T. E., Key, W. H., & Crowe, J. L. (1976). Families in disaster: Patterns of Recovery. *Mass Emergencies, 1*, 203-216.

Etziono, A. (Ed.). (1998). *The essential communitarian reader*. Lanham, MD: Rowan & Littlefield.

Etzioni, A. (Ed.) (1995). *New communitarian thinking: persons, virtues, institutions, and communities*. Charlottesville: University Press of Virginia.

Etziono, A. (1993). *The spirit of community: The reinvention of American Society*. New York: Simon & Schuster.

Eysenck, H.J. (1952). *The scientific study of personality*. New: Praeger.

Fagot, B., & Leinbach, M. (1987). Socialization of sex roles within the family. In Carter, D. (Ed). *Current conceptions of sex roles and sex typing. Theory and research*. (pp. 111-144). New York, NY: Praeger Publishers.

Falbo, T., & Peplau, L. A. (1980). Power strategies in intimate relationships. *Journal of Personality and Social Psychology, 38*, 618-628.

Farley, J. (1979). Family separation-individuation tolerance: A developmental conceptualization of the nuclear family. *Journal of Marital and Family Therapy, 5*, 61-67.

Feng, D., Giarrusso, R., Bengston, V., & Frye, N. (1999). Intergenerational transmission of marital quality and marital instability. *Journal of Marriage and the Family, 61*, 451-464.

Fleming, A. S., Ruble, D., Krieger, H., Wong, P. Y. (1997). Hormonal and experiential correlates of maternal responsiveness during pregnancy and the puerperium in human mothers. *Hormones and Behavior, 31*, 145-58.

Flynn, M., & England, B. (1995). Children stress and family environment. *Current Anthropology, 36*, 854-866.

Ford, F. R. (1983). Rules: The invisible family. *Family Process 22*, 135-145.

Framo, J. L. (1970). Symptoms from a family transactional viewpoint. In N. W. Ackerman, J. Lieb, & J. K. Pearce (Eds.), *Family therapy in transition* (pp.202-244). Boston: Little & Brown.

Freedman, J. (1988). Families in death. In C. Falicov (Ed.) Family transitions: Continuity and change over the life cycle (pp.166-190). New York: Guilford Press.

Friedman, E. H. (1985). *Generation to generation*. New York: NY: Guilford Press.

Galston, W. (1998). A liberal-democratic case for the two-parent family. In A. Etzioni (Ed), *The essential communitarian* reader (pp.145-156). Lanham, MD: Rowan & Littlefield.

Galvin, K., & Brommel, B. (1991). *Family communication: Cohesion and change (3rd ed.)*. Glenview, IL: Scott & Foresman.

Gavazzi, S. M. (1993). The relation between family differentiation levels in families with adolescents and the severity of presenting problems. *Family Relations, 42*, 463-468.

Gavazzi, S. M. (1994). Advances in assessing the relationship between family differentiation and problematic functioning in adolescents. *Family Therapy, 21*, 249-259.

Gavazzi, S. M., Anderson, S. A., & Savatelli, R. M. (1993). Family differentiation, peer differentiation and adolescent adjustment in a clinical sample. *Journal of Adolescent Research, 8*, 205-225.

Gavazzi, S. M., & Sabatelli, R. M. (1990). Family system dynamics, the individuation process and psychosocial and adolescent adjustment in a clinical sample. *Journal of Adolescent Research, 8*, 205-225.

Geist, R., & Gilbert, G. (1996). Correlates of expressed and felt emotion during marital conflict: Satisfaction, personality, process, and outcome. *Personality & Individual Differences, 21*, 49-60.

Gelles, R. J. (1974). *The violent home: A study of physical aggression between husbands and wives*. Beverly Hills, CA: Sage.

Gil, D. G. (1970). *Violence against children: Physical child abuse in the United States.* Cambridge, MA: Harvard University Press.

Gillis, J. (1996). *A world of their own making: myth, ritual, and the quest for family values.* New York: Basic Books.

Glenn, N. D. & Kramer, K. B. (1987). The marriages and divorces of the children of divorce. *Journal of Marriage and the Family, 49,* 811-825.

Goldberg, S. (1990) Attachment in infants at risk: Theory, research, and practice. *Infants and Young Children, 2,* 11-20.

Goldstein, A. (1999, December 20). The victims: Never again. *Time, 154,* 52-57.

Gontang, R. & Erickson, M. T. (1996). The Relationship Between Millon's Personality Types and Family System Functioning. *American Journal of Family Therapy, 24,* 215-226.

Goode, W. J. (1956). *After divorce.* Glencoe, IL: The Free Press.

Goode, W. J. (1960). A theory of role strain. *American Sociological Review, 35,* 483-496.

Goodrich, T. J., Rampage, C., Ellman, B., & Halstead, K. (1988). *Feminist family therapy: A casebook.* New York: Norton and Co.

Gore, S. (1978). The effect of social support in moderating the health consequences of unemployment. *Journal of Health and Social Behavior, 19,* 157-165.

Gottman, J. M. (1994). *What predicts divorce?: The relationship between marital processes and marital outcomes.* Hillsdale, NJ: Lawrence Erlbaum Associates.

Gottman, J. M. (1999). *The seven principle for making marriage work.* New York: Crown Publishers, Inc.

Gottman, J., Coan, J., Carrere, S., & Swanson, C. (1998). Predicting marital happiness and stability from newlywed interactions. *Journal of Marriage and the Family, 60,* 5-22.

Granger, D. A., Weisz, J. R., & Kauneckis, D. (1994). Neuroendocrine reactivity, internalizing behavior problems, and control-related cognitions in clinic-referred children and adolescents. *Journal of Abnormal Psychology, 103,* 267-76.

Green, R. J., & Werner, P. D. (1996). Intrusiveness and closeness-caregiving: rethinking the concept of family "enmeshment." *Family Process, 35,* 115-136.

Greenberg, G. S. (1977). The family interactional perspective: A study and examination of the work of Don D. Jackson. *Family Process, 16,* 385-412.

Guerney, B., & Guerney, L. (1981). Family life education as intervention. *Family Relations, 30,* 591-598.

Haley, J. (1963). *Strategies of psychotherapy.* New York: Grune & Stratton.

Haley, J. (1976). *Problem solving therapy.* San Francisco: Jossey-Bass.

Haley, J. (1987). *Reflections on therapy and other essays,* Washington DC: The Family Therapy Institute.

Hall, A. D., & Fagen, R. E. (1956). Definition of system. *General Systems Yearbook, 1,* 18-28.

Hansen, J. E., & Schuldt, W. J. (1982). Physical distance, sex, and intimacy in self disclosure. *Psychological Reports, 51,* 3-6.

Harris, K. M. (1997). *Teen mothers and the revolving welfare door.* Philadelphia: Temple University Press.

Hess, R. D., & Handel, G. (1959). *Family worlds.* Chicago, University of Chicago Press.

Hill, R. (1949). *Families under stress.* New York: Harper Brothers.

Hill, R. (1958). Sociology and marriage and family behavior, 1945-56: A trend report. *Current Sociology, 7,* 1-98.

Hill, J. E., Hawkins, A. J., Ferris, M., & Weitzman, M. (2001). Finding an extra day a week: The positive influence of perceived job flexibility on work and family life balance. *Family Relations, 50,* 49-58.

Hill, R. L., & Hansen, D. A. (1960). The identification of conceptual frameworks utilized in family study. *Marriage and Family Living, 22,* 299-311.

Bibliography

Hobbes, T. (1947). *Leviathan*. New York: Macmillan. (Original work published 1651).

Hoffreth, S. L., & Sandberg, J. F. (2001). How American children spend their time. *Journal of Marriage and Family, 63*, 295-308.

Holmes, T. H., & Rahe, R. R. (1967). The social readjustment rating scale. *Journal of Psychosomatic Research, 11*, 213-218.

Imber-Black, E., & Roberts, J. (1992). *Rituals for our time*. New York: Harper Perennial.

Jackson, D. D. (1957). The question of family homeostasis. *Psychiatric Quarterly Supplement, 31*, 79-90.

Jackson, D. D. (1963). Suggestion for the technical handling of paranoid patients, *Psychiatry, 26*, 306-307.

Jackson, D. D. (1965a). Family rules: Marital quid pro quo. *Archives of General Psychiatry, 12*, 589-594.

Jackson, D. D., & Yaom, I. (1965b). Conjoint family therapy as an aid to intensive psychotherapy. In A. Burton (Ed.), *Modern psychotherapeutic practice: Innovations in technique* (pp. 81-97). Palo Alto, CA: Science and Behavior Books.

Jackson, J. K. (1956). The adjustments of the family to alcoholism. *Marriage and Family Living, 18*, 361-369.

Jacob, T. (1987). Family interaction and psychopathology: Historical overview. In T. Jacob, (Ed.) *Family interaction and psychopathology: Theories, methods, and findings* (pp. 242-283). New York: Plenum Press.

James, D. & Clarke, S. (1993). Women, men, and interruptions: A critical review. In D. Tannen, (Ed.) (1993). *Gender and conversational interaction. Oxford studies in sociolinguistics* (pp.35-95). New York: Oxford Press.

Jerome, R., & Haederle, M. (1999, December 20). Raising Arizona. *People Weekly, 52*, 56-61.

John, O.P. (1990). The "big five" taxonomy: Dimensions of personality in the natural language and in questionnaires. In L.A. Pervin (Ed.), *Handbook of personality: Theory and research* (pp.66-100). New York: Guilford.

Johnson, M.P., & Ferraro, K.J. (2000). Research on domestic violence in the 1990s: Making distinctions. *Journal of Marriage and the Family, 62*, 948-963.

Kalil, A. (2002) Cohabitation and child development. *Just living together: Implications of cohabitation on families, children, and social policy*. Mahwah, NJ: Lawrence Erlbaum Associates.

Kalmuss, D., & Straus, M. (1982). Wife's marital dependency and wife abuse. *Journal of Marriage and the Family. 44*, 277-287.

Kantor, D., & Lehr, W. (1975). *Inside the family*, San Francisco: Jossey-Bass.

Kaplan, D. M., Smith, A., Grobstien, R., & Fischman, S. E. (1973). Family mediation of stress. *Social Work, 18*, 60-69.

Keirsey, D. (1998). *Please Understand Me*. New York: Prometheus Nemesis Press.

Kennedy, C. & Camden, C. (1993). Interruptions and nonverbal gender differences. *Journal of Nonverbal Behavior, 8*, 44-52.

Kerr, M. (1981). Family systems theory and therapy. In A. S. Gurman & D.P. Kriskern (Eds.), *Handbook of family therapy* (pp. 212-244). New York: Brunner/Mazel.

Kerr, M. E., & Bowen, M. (1988). *Family evaluation*. New York: Norton.

Kirchler, E. (1989). Everyday life experiences at home: An interaction diary approach to assess marital relationships. *Journal of Family Psychology, 2*, 311-336.

Klein, D. M., & Hill, R. (1979). Determinants of family problem-solving effectiveness. In Burr, W. R., Hill, R., Nye, F. I. & Reiss, I. L. (Eds.), *Contemporary theories about the family* (Vol. 1 pp. 301-333). New York: Free Press.

Klein, D. M., & White, J. M. (1996). *Family theories: An introduction*. Thousand Oaks, CA: Sage.

Klonsky, J., & Bengston, V.L., (1996). Pulling together, drifting apart: A longitudinal case study of a four-generation family. *Journal of Aging Studies, 10*, 255-279.

Bibliography

Koos, E. (1946). *Families in trouble*. New York: King's Crown Press.

Komorovsky, M. (1940). *The unemployed man and his family*. New York: Dryden Press.

Krauss, R., & Fussell, S. (1996). *Social psychological models of interpersonal communication. In Higgins, E. & Kruglanski, A. (Eds.). Social Psychology: Handbook of basic principles.* (pp. 44-82). New York: The Guilford Press.

Laing, R. D. (1972). *The politics of the family*. New York: Vintage Books.

Laird, J. (1988). Women and ritual in family therapy. In Imber-Black, E., & Roberts, J. (Eds). *Rituals in families and family therapy*. New York: W.W. Norton & Co, Inc.

Larmer, B. (1996, February 10). The barrel children. *Newsweek, 127*, 45-46.

Lidz, T. (1963). *The family and human adaptation*. New York: International Universities Press.

Lloyd, S. & Taluc, N. (1999). The effects of male violence on female employment. *Violence Against Women, 5*, 244-256.

Mackey, R. A., & O'Brien, B. (1995). *A lasting marriage: men and women growing together*. Westport, CT: Praeger.

Marsiglio, W., Amato, P., Day, R. D., & Lamb, M. E. (2000). Scholarship on fatherhood in the 1990's and beyond. *Journal of Marriage and the Family, 62*, 1173-1191.

Maynard, P., Maynard, N., McCubbin, H.I., & Shao, D. (1980). Family life and the police profession: Coping patterns wives employ in managing job stress and the family environment. *Family Relations, 41*, 237-244.

Mazur, A., & Michalek, J. (1998). Marriage, divorce, and male testosterone. *Social Forces, 77*, 315-330.

Mazur, A., & Booth, A. (1998). Testosterone and dominance in men. *Behavioral & Brain Sciences, 21*, 353-397.

McCrae, R.R.., & Costa, P.T. (1991). Adding Leibe und Arbeit: The full five-factor model and well-being. *Personality and Social Psychology Bulletin, 17*, 227-232.

McCubbin, M., Balling, K., Possin, P., Frierdich, S., & Bryne, B. (2002). Family resiliency in childhood cancer. *Family Relations, 51*, 103-111.

McCubbin, H.I., Cuable, J. C., Comeay, J., Patterson, J., & Needle, R. (1980). Family stress and coping: A decade review. *Journal of Marriage and the Family, 42*, 855-871.

McCubbin, H.I., & Dahl, B. (1985). *Marriage and Family*. New York: Wiley.

McCubbin, H.I., Dahl, B., Lester, G., Benson, D., & Robertson, M. (1976). Coping repertoires of adapting to prolonged war-induced separations. *Journal of Marriage and Family, 38*, 461-471.

McCubbin, H. I., & Figley, C. (1983). *Stress and the family: Vol. 1. Coping with normative transitions*. New York: Brunner & Mazel.

McCubbin, H.I., & Patterson, J. (1982). Family adaptation to crises. In H. I. McCubbin (Ed.), *Family stress, coping and social support* (pp. 49-96). Springfield, IL: Charles C Thomas.

McCubbin, H. I., Thompson, A. I., Pirner, P. A., & McCubbin, M. A. (1988). *Family types and strengths: A life cycle and ecological perspective*. Edina, MN: Burgess International Group Inc.

McLanahan, S., & Bumpass, L. (1988). Intergenerational consequences of family disruption. *American Journal of Sociology, 94*, 130-152.

McGoldrick, M., Gerson, R., & Schellenberger, S. (1999). *Genograms in family assessment*. New York: Norton.

Meredith, W. H. (1985). The importance of family traditions. *Wellness Perspective, 2*, 17-19.

Meredith, W., Abbott, D., & Adams, S. (1986). Family violence: Its relation to marital and parental satisfaction and family strengths. *Journal of Family Violence. 4*, 75-88.

Meredith, W. H., Abbott, D. A., Lamanna, M. A., & Sanders, G. (1989). Rituals and family strengths: A three-generation study. *Family Perspectives, 23*, 75-84.

Merton, R. K. (1968). *Social theory and social structure*. Glencoe, IL: Free Press.

Miller, S., Nunnally, D., & Wackman, S. (1988). *Alive and aware: improving communication in relationships*. Minneapolis: Interpersonal Communication Programs.

Milner, J. S., & Wimberly, R. C. (1980). Prediction and explanation of child abuse. *Journal of Clinical Psychology, 36*, 875-884.

Minuchin, S. (1974). *Families and family therapy*. Cambridge, MA: Harvard University Press.

Minuchin, S. (1981). *Family kaleidoscope*. Cambridge, MA: Harvard University Press.

Minuchin, S. (1996). *Mastering family therapy: journeys of growth and transformation*. New York: John Wiley & Sons.

Minuchin, S., & Nichols, M. (1993). *Family healing: Tales of hope and renewal from family therapy*. New York: Free Press.

Monroe, P. A., Bokemeier, J. L., Kotchen, J. M., & Mckean, H. (1985). Spousal response consistency in decision-making research. *Journal of Marriage and the Family, 47*, 733-738.

Nevin, R. (1979). Parental coping in raising children who have spina bifida cystica. *Dissertation Abstracts International, 39*, 791-2057.

Nichols, M. P., & Shwartz, R. C. (1995). *Family therapy: Concepts and methods* (3rd ed.). Needham Heights, MA: Allyn & Bacon.

Niska, K., Snyder, M., & Lia-Hoagberg, B. (1998). Family ritual facilitates adaptation to parenthood. *Public Health Nursing, 15*, 12-22.

Noller, P., & Feeney, J. (1998). Communication in early marriage: Responses to conflict, nonverbal, accuracy, and conversational patterns. In Bradbury, T. (Ed.), *The developmental course of marital dysfunction* (pp.11-43). New York: Cambridge University Press.

Noller, P., & Fitzpatrick, M. (1990). Marital communication in the eighties. *Journal of Marriage and the Family, 52*, 832-843.

Noller, P., & Fitzpatrick, M.A. (1993). *Communication in family relationships*. Englewood Cliffs, New Jersey.

Noller, P (1984). Clergy marriages: A study of a uniting church sample. *Australian Journal of Sex, Marriage and Family, 5*, 187-197.

Norman, W.T. (1963). Toward an adequate taxonomy of personality attributes: Replicated factor structure in peer nomination personality ratings. *Journal of Abnormal and Social Psychology, 66*, 574-204.

Oakley, D. (1985). Premarital childbearing decision making. *Family Relations: Journal of Applied Family & Child Studies, 34*, 225-266.

Okun, B., & Rapport, L.J. (1980). *Working with families*. Belmont, CA: Wadsworth.

Olson, D. H., & DeFrain, J. (1994). *Marriage and the family: Diversity and strengths*. Mountain View, CA: Mayfield Publishing Company.

Olson, D. H., & McCubbin, H. I. (1982). The circumplex model of marital and family systems VI: Applications to family stress and crisis intervention. In McCubbin, H. I., Cauble, A. C., & Patterson, J. M. (Eds.), *Family stress, coping and social support* (pp.132-150). Springfield, IL: Charles C. Thomas.

Pagelow, M. D. (1984). *Family violence*. New York: Praeger Special Studies.

Palazzoli, M. S. (1974). *Self-starvation: From the intrapsychic to the transpersonal approach to anorexia nervosa*. London: Chaucer.

Palazolli, M. S., Boscolo, L., Cecchin, G., & Prata, G. (1978). *Paradox and counterparadox*. New York: Jason, Aronson.

Palazolli, M. S., Cirillo, S., Selvini, M., & Sorrentino, A. M. (1989). *Family games*. New York: Norton.

Papero, D. V. (1983). Family systems theory and therapy. In Wolman, B.B. & Stricker, G. (Eds.), *Handbook of family and marital therapy* (pp. 144-190). New York: Plenum.

Parke, R., Kim, M., Flyr, M., McDowell, D., Simpkins, S., Killian, C., & Wild, M. (2001). *Managing marital conflict: Links with children's peer relationships*. In Grych, J. & Fincham, F. (Eds.), *Interpersonal conflict and child development: Theory, research, and applications* (pp. 207-257). New York: Cambridge University Press.

Pearlin, L., & Schooler, C. (1982). The structure of coping. *Journal of Health and Social Behavior, 19*, 2-21.

Pines, A. M. (1998). A prospective study of personality and gender differences in romantic attraction. *Personality & Individual Differences, 25,* 147-157.

Pleck, E.H. (2000). *Celebrating the family.* Cambridge, MA: Harvard Press.

Polmin, R. (1994). *Genetics and experience: The interplay between nature and nuture.* Thousand Oaks, CA: Sage.

Quinn, W. H., Newfield, N. A., & Protinsky, H. O. (1985). Rites of passage in families with adolescents. *Journal of Family Processes, 24,* 101-111.

Reiss, D. (1981). *The family's constructive of reality.* Cambridge, MA: Harvard University Press.

Reiss, D. (1995). Genetic influence on family systems: Implications for development. *Journal of Marriage and the Family, 57,* 543-560.

Reiss, D. (1995). Genetic questions for environmental studies: differential parenting and psychopathology in adolescence. *Archives of General Psychiatry, 52,* 925-936.

Reiss, I. L., & Lee, G. R. (1988). *Family systems in America* (4th ed.). New York: Holt, Rinehart and Winston.

Roberts, J. (1988). Setting the frame: Definition functions, and typology of rituals. In E. Imber-Black, Roberts, J. & Whiting, R.A. (Eds.), *Rituals in families and family therapy* (pp. 3-46). New York: Norton.

Rollins, B. C., & Thomas, D. L. (1979). Parental support, power, and control techniques in the socialization of children. In Burr, W. R., Hill, R., Nye, F. I., & Reiss, I. L. (Eds.), *Contemporary theories about the family* (Vol. 1, pp.34-89). New York: Macmillan.

Rosenfeld, L., & Bowen, G. (1991). Marital disclosure and marital satisfaction: Direct-effect versus interaction-effect models. *Western Journal of Speech Communication,* 55, 112-133.

Rowe, D.C. (1994). *The limits of family influence: Genes, experience, and behavior.* New York: Guilford Press.

Sabatelli, R. M., & Anderson, S. A. (1991). Family systems dynamics, peer relationships and adolescents' psychological adjustments. *Family Relations, 40,* 363-369.

Sabatelli, R. M., & Cecil-Pigo, E. F. (1985). Relational interdependence and commitment in marriage. *Journal of Marriage and the Family, 47,* 931-938.

Sabatelli, R. M., & Shahan, C. L. (1992). Exchange and resources theories. In Boss, P., Doherty, W., LaRossa, R., Schumm, W. & Steinmetz, S. (Eds.), *Sourcebook of Family Theories and Methods: A Contextual Approach* (pp. 385-411). New York: Plenum.

Satir, V. (1967). *Conjoint family therapy; a guide to theory and technique.* Palo Alto, California, Science and Behavior Books.

Satir, V. (1972). *Peoplemaking.* Palo Alto, CA: Science and Behavior Books.

Sauer, R. J. (1982). Family enmeshment. *Family Therapy: The Bulletin of Synergy, 9,* 298-304.

Scanzoni, J. (1988). Joint decision making in the sexually based primary relationship. In Brinberg, D. & Jaccard, J. (Eds.) *Dyadic decision making* (pp.143-165). New York: Springer-Verlag.

Schvaneveldt, J. D., & Lee, T. R. (1983). The emergence and practice of ritual in the American family. *Family Perspectives, 17,* 137-143.

Seccombe, K. (2000). Families in poverty in the 1990s: Trends, causes, consequences, and lessons learned. *Journal of Marriage and the Family, 62,* 1094-1113.

Seccombe, K. (1999). *So you think I drive a Cadillac?: Welfare recipients' perspectives on the system and its reform.* Boston, Mass: Allyn and Bacon.

Shaffer, D. R. (1989). *Developmental psychology.* Pacific Grove, CA: Brooks & Cole.

Sieburg, E. (1985). *Family Communication: An Integrated Systems Approach.* New York: Gardner Press.

Smith, J. (1999). The amazing triumph of a teenage mom. *Redbook, 195,* 166.

Snowden, R., & Snowden, E. (1984). *The gift of a child.* London: George Allen and Unwin.

Sorokin, P. A. (1941). *Social and cultural dynamics* (Vols. 1-4). New York: American Books.

Sprey, J. (1979). Conflict theory and the study of marriage and the family.

Sprey, J. (2000). Theorizing in family studies: Discovering process. *Journal of Marriage and the Family, 62*, 18-31.

Steinglass, P., Bennettt, L. A., Wolin, S. J., & Reiss, D. (1987). *The alcoholic family*. New York: Basic Books.

Steinmetz, S. K. (1979). Disciplinary techniques and their relationship to aggressiveness, dependency and conscience. In Burr, W. R., Hill, R., Nye, F. I., & Reiss, I. L. (Eds.), *Contemporary theories about the family* (Vol. 1, pp. 222-252). New York: Free Press.

Stenberg, S. (2000). Inheritance of welfare recipiency: An intergenerational study of social assistance recipiency in postwar Sweden. *Journal of Marriage and the Family, 62*, 228-239

Strauss, M.A., Gelles, R.J., & Steinmetz, S.K. (1988). *Behind Closed doors: Violence in the American family*. Newbury Park, CA: Sage.

Swinford, S. P., Demaris, A., Cernkovich S. A., & Giordano, P. C. (2000). Harsh physical discipline in childhood and violence in later romantic involvements: The mediating role of problem behaviors. *Journal of Marriage and the Family, 62*, 508-519.

Tannen, D. (1986). That's not what I meant!: How conversational style makes or breaks your relations with others. New York: Morrow.

Tannen, D. (1990). *You just don't understand: Women and men in conversation*. New York: Morrow.

Thompson, L., & Walker, A. J. (1989). Gender in families: Women and men in marriage, work, and parenthood. *Journal of Marriage and the Family, 51*, 845-871.

Tizard, J., & Grad, J. C. (1961). *The mentally handicapped and their families: A social survey*. New York: Oxford University Press.

Tolstoy, L. (1993). *Anna Karenina*. In Kent, L. J. & Berberova, N. (Eds.), New York: Random House. (Original work published 1878)

Troll, L., & Bengston, V. L. (1979). Generations in the family. In Burr, W. R., Hill, R., Nye, F.I. & Reiss, I.L. (Eds.). *Contemporary theories about the family* (Vol. 1, pp. 333-355). New York: Free Press.

Turner, R. A., Altemus, M., Enos, T., Cooper, B., & Mcguinness, T. (1999). Preliminary research on plasma oxytocin in normal cycling women: Investigating emotion and interpersonal distress. *Psychiatry, 62*, 97-113.

Turner, V. (1967). *The forest of symbols: Aspects of Ndembu ritual*. Ithaca, NY: Cornell University Press.

Udry, J.R., Morris, N., & Kovennock, J. (1995). Androgen effects on women's gendered behavior. *Journal of Biosocial Science, 27*, 359-369.

United States Congress House. Committee on Science. Subcommittee on Energy and Environment (2001). The human genome project: hearing before the Subcommittee on Energy and Environment on the Committee on Science, House of Representatives, One hundred sixth congress, second session. Washington: U.S. G.P.O.

University of California, San Francisco, Department of Energy (2001, September). Human Genome Project. Retrieved September, 2001, from the Department of Energy Website: www.jgi.doe.gov

U.S. Bureau of Justice Statistics (1994). *Supplementary homicide report, 1992*. [Computer file]. Ann Arbor, Mich.: Inter-University Consortium for Political and Social Research.

Uvans-Moberg, K., Widstrom, A., Nissen, E., & Bjorvell, H. (1990). Personality traits in women 4 days postpartum and their correlation with plasma levels of oxytocin and prolactin. *Journal of Psychosomatic Obstetrics and Gynecology, 11*, 261-273.

Van der Hart, O. (1983). *Rituals in psychotherapy: Transitions and continuity*. New York: Irvington.

Vangelisti, A. (1994). Family secrets: Forms, functions and correlates. *Journal of Social & Personal Relationships, 11*, 113-135.

Vangelisti, A. & Caughlin, J. (1997). Revealing family secrets: The influence of topic, function, and relationships. *Journal of Social & Personal Relationships, 14*, 222-243.

Bibliography

Van Gennep, A. (1960). *The rites of passage*. Chicago: University of Chicago Press.

Vogel, E. F., & Bell, N. W. (1967). The emotionally disturbed child as the family scapegoat. In G. Handel (Ed.), *The psychosocial interior of the family; a sourcebook for the study of whole families* (pp.145-166). Chicago: Adeline Publishing Co.

Waite, L., & Gallagher, M. (2000). *The case for marriage: why people are happier, healthier, and better off financially*. New York: Doubleday.

Waller, W., & Hill, R. (1951). *The family: a dynamic interpretation*. New York: Dryden.

Walsh, F., & McGoldrick, M. (1988). Loss and the family life cycle. In C. Falicov (Ed.), *Family transitions*. New York: Guilford.

Watzalwick, J., Beavin, H., & Jackson, D. (1967). Pragmatics of human communication; a study of interactional patters, pathologies, and paradoxes. New York: Norton.

Waring, E., & Chelune, G. J., (1983). Marital intimacy and self-disclosure. *Journal of Clinical Psychology, 39*, 183.

Watzlawick, P., Weakland, J. H., & Fisch, R. (1974). *Change: Principles of problem formation and problem resolution*. New York: Norton.

Wedekind, C., Seebeck, T., Bettens, F., & Paepke, A.J. (1995). MHC-dependent mate preferences in humans. *Proceeding of the Royal Society of London, 260*, 245-249.

Whiting, R. A. (1988). Guidelines to designing therapeutic rituals. In E. Imber-Black, Roberts, J. R., & Whiting, R. A. (Eds.), *Rituals in families and family therapy*. New York: Norton.

Wise, G. W. (1986). Family routines, rituals, and traditions: Grist for the family mill and buffers against stress. In S. Van Zant (Ed.), *Family strengths 7: Vital Connections* (pp.45-66). Lincoln, NE: Center for Family Strengths.

Wolin, S., Bennett, L. A., Noonan, D., & Teitelbaum, M. (1980). Disrupted family rituals: A factor in the intergenerational transmission of alcoholism. *Journal of Studies on Alcohol, 41*, 199-214.

Wolin, S. & Bennett, L. A. (1984). Family rituals. *Family Process, 23*, 401-420.

Wynne, L. C. (1984). The epigenesis of relational systems: A model for understanding family development. *Family Process, 23*, 297-318.

Yerby, J., & Buerkel-Rothfuss, N. L. (1982). *Communication patterns, contradictions, and family functions*. Paper presented at the Speech Communication Association Convention.

Young, M. (1954). The role of the extended family in disaster. *Human Relations, 7*, 383-391

Index

Index

Index

Index

Index

Index

mate selection, 85,105
maximizing self interest, 70
meeting family goals using rituals and
    routines, 299
membership changes, 300
metaphor, 291
metarules, 204, 205
mid-life crisis, 341
military families, 19, 380
moderate ritualization, 305
money, 6,14
mores, 179
morphogenesis, 53, 290, 347-349
morphostasis, 53, 347-349
mothers, 42
multiple interactions, 182
murder, 21

N

negative emotion, 209
negativity, 259
neuroticism, 83, 100
non sequitur, 225, 239
non-abusive behaviors, 122

O

obligations, 143
Occam's Razor, 40
off-time transitions, 58
open families, 158, 159
openness, 99
oppression, 14
order, 305
ordinary, 291
over-monitored, 263
overritualization, 307
oxytocin, 80

P

paradigm, 167
paradigmatic beliefs, 158
parental alliance, 119, 120

parenting strategy, 256
parting is inevitable, 336
patriarchal, 20
patterns of interaction, 51, 179
permeable, 115
personality, 79, 86, 95-97, 101, 105, 106
    characteristics, 105
    definition of, 95
    introversion, 95, 105, 106
    mate selection, 96
    traits, 81, 83
philosophy of life, 141
Piaget, Jean, 51
pituitary, 79
please understand me, 100
poverty, 6, 32, 119, 122
power and gender, 90
predictability, 305
    in family life, 331
    patterns, 332
premarital counseling, 22
privacy, 121
private family life, 6
Protean family, 32
psychology, 32
psychotic, 119

Q

qualitative researchers, 49

R

random families, 158, 160
rational choice, 58
rearing children, 26
reductionism, 41
    approach, 42
    view, 49
reinforcing, 231
relationship difficulty, 106
religious ideology, 19

Index